Praise for *Landing Your Perfect Nursing Job*

"I truly enjoyed the book and found it to be the most comprehensive A-Z reference for novice *and* experienced nurses seeking new positions. Every concept and possible scenario is addressed and covered, providing readers with an ultimate guide for conducting their job search, preparing for interviews, and eventually landing their ideal job."

–Denise J. Scholz, BSN, RN
San Francisco Bay Area, California

"This is a powerful book! At a time when nurses are struggling to find jobs, Thomas brings all the right advice to the table. She spells everything out in great detail, not just what to do, but why and how. Nothing is left to chance. There's something here for nurses in any stage of their career. I plan to recommend it to all my nursing clients."

–Susan Speetzen, MS
Career Consultant
Fairview Health Services
St. Paul, Minnesota

"Lisa Mauri Thomas uses her knowledge of human behavior to help nurses introspect before and during job search and career development. The book is a procedure manual for nurses who are interested in landing the perfect nursing job. It provides solutions to some of the struggles new nurses and seasoned nurses encounter during career development. This book is a must-have for all nurses."

–Beverley Powell Morgan, MSN, RN
Immunization Coordinator
Delray Beach Health Department, Florida

"This book is for nurses in any stage of their career who are looking to land a perfect job. Find out how to use networking skills, polish off your resume, and achieve success in that interview. *Landing Your Perfect Nursing Job* is an easy read with great insight on setting realistic goals for your successful career in nursing."

–Julie Jones, MS, RN
Chair of the Global Technology & Innovation Taskforce of STTI
VSN Foundation President
Co-Leader for Vermont Nursing Informatics

"In *Landing Your Perfect Nursing Job*, Lisa Mauri Thomas provides all generations with an enlightening and logical guide to assist in transforming and transporting nurses to their destination career. From supportive self-discovery to networking and reframing the nursing world as they know it, Thomas sets the course for nurses to advance through life-expanding career choices. She thoughtfully provokes nurses to dispose of career-seeking myths and focus on positive attributes that exemplify personal expertise and marketability for successful career planning."

–Jennifer L. Embree, DNP, RN, NE-BC, CCNS
Visiting Assistant Professor
Indiana University School of Nursing-IUPUI

"Thomas presents a well-organized, informative, and specific guide, with easy-to-understand concepts and worksheets to supplement the text. This fresh approach of viewing a job search as a career development process is applicable to all stages of a nurse's career, from a graduate nurse's first position through the experienced nurse with advanced degrees transitioning into new areas of responsibilities."

–Tamara Lynn Wardell, MSN, RN
PhD candidate, Duquesne University School of Nursing

"Lisa Mauri Thomas, while not losing sight of the art and science of the profession, guides novice and expert nurses through the journey of finding their place in the profession. This step-by-step guide offers explanation while incorporating a workable and reasonable timeline in securing the ideal situation. This publication is a must-have not only for the new graduate, but for the veteran nurse still trying to find her way."

–Christy M. Fain, MSN/Ed, RN
Nurse Educator

"This book is a great resource for nurses beginning, advancing, or just wanting to improve their professional status in nursing. Thomas provides the tools for nurses to demonstrate their professional skills both on paper and in person. The realistic approach to searching for and landing that perfect job makes this a must-read to become a front runner in the job market today. Coupling the roadmap to success with self-reflection exercises is a win-win for any nurse wanting to exemplify the professionalism of nursing leaders guiding us into the future of nursing."

–Glenda M. Feild, MS, RN
PhD Student
University of Tennessee

"Whether a new grad seeking that first job or a seasoned professional looking for a change, this book is essential for your toolbox. Thomas has it all: self-exploration, networking, even a little homework as some of the many elements that come together to help you reach your goal."

–Pamela J. Miller
Retired LPN

Landing Your Perfect Nursing Job

Lisa Mauri Thomas, MS

Sigma Theta Tau International
Honor Society of Nursing®

The Honor Society of Nursing, Sigma Theta Tau International (STTI), is a nonprofit organization whose mission is to support the learning, knowledge, and professional development of nurses committed to making a difference in health worldwide. Founded in 1922, STTI has 130,000 members in 90 countries. Members include practicing nurses, instructors, researchers, policymakers, entrepreneurs, and others. STTI's 486 chapters are located throughout Australia, Botswana, Brazil, Canada, Colombia, England, Ghana, Hong Kong, Japan, Kenya, Malawi, Mexico, the Netherlands, Pakistan, Singapore, South Africa, South Korea, Swaziland, Sweden, Taiwan, Tanzania, the United States, and Wales. More information about STTI can be found online at www.nursingsociety.org.

Sigma Theta Tau International
550 West North Street
Indianapolis, IN, USA 46202

To order additional books, buy in bulk, or order for corporate use, contact Nursing Knowledge International at 888.NKI.4YOU (888.654.4968/US and Canada) or +1.317.634.8171 (outside US and Canada).

To request a review copy for course adoption, e-mail solutions@nursingknowledge.org or call 888. NKI.4YOU (888.654.4968/US and Canada) or +1.317.634.8171 (outside US and Canada).

To request author information or for speaker or other media requests, contact Rachael McLaughlin of the Honor Society of Nursing, Sigma Theta Tau International, at 888.634.7575 (US and Canada) or +1.317.634.8171 (outside US and Canada).

ISBN: 9781937554712
EPUB ISBN: 9781937554729
PDF ISBN: 9781937554736
MOBI ISBN: 9781937554743

Library of Congress Cataloging-in-Publication Data

Thomas, Lisa Mauri.
Landing your perfect nursing job / Lisa Mauri Thomas.
p. ; cm.
ISBN 978-1-937554-71-2 (print : alk. paper) -- ISBN 978-1-937554-72-9 (epub) -- ISBN 978-1-937554-73-6 (PDF) -- ISBN 978-1-937554-74-3 (mobi)
I. Sigma Theta Tau International. II. Title.
[DNLM: 1. Nursing. 2. Career Choice. 3. Nursing Staff. 4. Vocational Guidance. WY 16.1]

610.73--dc23

2012039591

First Printing, 2012

Publisher: Renee Wilmeth
Acquisitions Editor: Emily Hatch
Development and Project Editor: Deb Buehler
Cover Designer: Aleata Howard
Interior Design/Page Layout: Rebecca Batchelor

Principal Book Editor: Carla Hall
Editorial Coordinator: Paula Jeffers
Indexer: Johnna Van Hoose Dinse
Copy Editor: Clifford Shubs
Proofreader: Jane Palmer

Dedication

This book is dedicated to everyone who cheered me on throughout this project; you know who you are. Support systems are so important in achieving our dreams and so should be cherished.

Acknowledgements

It is with dearest thanks to the following people who were especially helpful in bringing this book to life: Marlo Dworsky, BSN, RN; Susan Speetzen; Stacy Siebert, MA; Charleana (Coleman) Harris; Carla Pogliano; Janet Izzo, RN; Tricia Thomas, PhD, RN; Sonya Jahn, BSN, RN; Christina Wichelman, RN; and so many other wonderful nurses who shared their stories and tips along the way. Special thanks to the wonderful team at the Honor Society of Nursing, Sigma Theta Tau International (STTI), without whom this project would not have been possible, including Emily Hatch, acquiring book editor; editors Deb Buehler and Cliff Shubs; Carla Hall, principal book editor; and the STTI board of directors.

My parents and brother were regular sources of encouragement. Last but not least, it is with love and appreciation that I thank James and Aidan for all the long hours of writing they cheerfully endured along the way.

About the Author

Lisa Mauri Thomas, MS, is a job search strategist and resume writer with nearly 20 years experience helping job seekers and career advancers find success in their quest for meaning in the workplace within various roles, including human resources director, recruiter, career center director, director of institutional effectiveness, college faculty member, and more. She is currently dean of education at a career college in Minneapolis, overseeing an array of programs, including two in health care. From 2007-2011, Thomas was the managing partner of Change Your Job, Change Your Life, LLC, where she consulted with job seekers across the globe in many industries, including nursing and related health care specialties. An energetic and purposeful speaker and writer, she has presented job search and resume writing strategies at numerous workshops and conferences over the years, including the Twin Cities Healthcare Professional Network, the 2011 Minnesota Student Nurses' Association Convention, and the Minnesota Workforce Centers. Furthermore, she has served as an expert contributing author at www.nursetogether.com.

Thomas holds a BA in sociology and an MS in applied psychology: vocational counseling, both from St. Cloud State University. In 2008-2009, she served as state chair of the Minnesota ACE Network, an organization that supports women leaders in higher education, and was an active, contributing member of the board for 5 years, during which time she earned the first-ever Sustainability Award.

To learn more about Lisa Mauri Thomas, please connect with her on LinkedIn: www.linkedin.com/in/lisamaurithomas.

Table of Contents

1 **Painting a Workable Job Search Picture 1**

Self-Assessment: Current Beliefs About Job Searching 2

Quiz Results 3

Avoid Myths, Find Truth 13

Living an Advancement Lifestyle Versus Going Through the Job Search Motions 13

The Differences Between Human Resources and Recruiting 15

Apply Online but Don't Stop There 17

Silence From Companies Is a Form of Highly Useable Feedback 18

Quality Over Quantity. 20

Assessing What Works and What Doesn't Work 21

2 **Networking Starts With Talking 25**

Conscious Awareness 28

Strengths and Weaknesses 31

Taking Responsibility 36

Celebrate Your Strengths 38

Be Purposeful 40

3 **Laying the Foundation for a Successful Search 43**

Knowing How Your Skills Fit Into the Market 44

Keywords When Networking. 45

Keywords Within Professional Development Opportunities 47

Keywords Within Job Postings 49

Keywords on Resumes 51

Keywords in Interviews 51

Don't Guess—Find Out 52

Company Insiders Are Your New Best Friends. 54

Developing Confidence 55

Networking Events for Nurses 59

4 The Heart of Resumes and Cover Letters. 61

Follow-up Starts Sooner Than Later 62
Paving the Way 63
The Anatomy of a Successful Resume 67
Name and Contact Information 69
Title Bar 70
Professional Profile 71
Customizable Skills Area 72
Education and Certifications 74
Clinical Rotations 74
Preceptorships 75
Clinical Nursing Experience (Work History) 75
Non-nursing Experience (If Applicable) 80
Volunteerism 80
Publications 81
Honors and Awards. 81
Where to Learn More 81
Best Resume Format Ever 83
Speak the Language of Your Audience 85
Customizing Your Resume for Specific Roles. 85
Resume Critique Worksheet 89
Crafting a Cover Letter That Commands Attention . . . 89

5 Confronting Negativity and Turning It Around 93

Clear Away What's Holding You Down. 94
Forming Your Plan to Get Ahead 100
Ready, Willing, and Able 109
Raising the Bar 114

6 Your Short- and Long-Term Goals 119

Doing Versus Dreaming—
Letting Go. 119
Strategize Constructively 126
Calendar Exercise to Stay on Track and Timely 130

7 Fine-Tuning Your Approach for Job Search and Career Success . . . 137

Consistency . . . 138

Trusting Your Gut . . . 141

Doing and Looking Your Best . . . 142

Handling Pressure . . . 142

Budgeting Your Time . . . 143

(Not) Taking Things Personally . . . 144

Being Fair and Ethical . . . 144

Graciousness . . . 145

Etiquette . . . 150

Nursing and Workplace Etiquette . . . 151

Advancement/Promotion Etiquette . . . 152

Meeting Etiquette . . . 153

Management Etiquette . . . 154

Company Party Etiquette . . . 155

First Week on the Job Etiquette . . . 156

Being Unique . . . 157

8 Interviewing: The Floor Is Yours . . . 163

Being Genuine . . . 164

The Larger Picture . . . 167

It's Not Bragging if It's True . . . 169

Ready, Willing, and Able . . . 171

Negotiating Offers . . . 175

9 Be the Best Nurse Candidate Ever . . . 183

You Were Interviewed Twice This Week Already . . . 184

Swimming Successfully in the Recruiters' Pool . . . 186

Optimism or Law of Attraction . . . 189

Visibility Plus . . . 190

Mission . . . 191

Vision . . . 191

Values . . . 192

Job Search Activity . . . 192

10 Effectively Marketing the Nurse in You 197

Basic Marketing and Promotional Approaches. 198

E-mail blast 198

Direct Mail Postcards 200

Cold Calling 200

Create a Video Introduction or Video Resume. 201

Business Cards 202

Maximizing Your Marketing 202

Education 203

Experience 204

Attitude 205

Giving Back 206

11 The Nursing Culture and Impacts Upon the Job Search 209

Defining the Nursing Culture. 210

Fit In 214

Stand Out 216

Networking for Long-Term Benefit 221

Conclusion 223

Appendix

A Nurse Resume Critique Checklist. 229

B Interview Resources. 237

C Sample Job Search Calendars 243

D Tools That Work for You 251

E Best Resume Ever Template 255

Index. 257

Introduction

Nursing is both an art and a science—a noble calling. To give selflessly to those most vulnerable takes a special brand of courage, optimism, and practical-mindedness. The mere decision to become a nurse requires deep introspection, self-awareness of weaknesses, personal sacrifice, and a strong sense of perseverance in the face of daily challenges. Once the decision is made, each day becomes a bold step into the unknown as one explores the very heart of life and death. That is the world of nursing. As a profession, it knows both praise and controversy as nurses navigate overlapping and conflicting roles and responsibilities, unions, credentialing issues, and the ever-present threat of a fatal mistake, all while demonstrating quick thinking and compassion for everyone present and promoting evidence-based outcomes.

Nursing, like all career fields, has its share of economic ups and downs, and there comes a time for nurses to weather the storm, make waves, and journey through advancement. Job searching is one part of the larger umbrella of career development. One can easily argue that job searching is a form of career development, though career development need not necessarily involve job searching.

Traditional career development models focus on either time-oriented processes, characteristics in context, or a combination of both. This book takes a combined view that time-oriented processes form the basis for one's career path, but that characteristics in context provide the scope and depth to how your career develops over time. In other words, there is an underlying presumption that your age correlates closely to the stage you are in your career (beginning, climbing, peaking, declining, or retiring); however, characteristics such as education, continued training, experience, personality, personal issues, and the size of your wallet can directly and significantly impact the trajectory of your career over time. Whether you are a new nurse fresh out of school at any age, a mid-career nurse looking to make changes, or a veteran nurse looking to transition toward retirement while keeping a foot in the field, this book is for you.

If you are a nurse interested in improving your job searching skills, it is helpful to recall what assistance you received along the way to support your endeavors: when, where, how much, and by whom. Were you required to take a specific course in college that helped to ensure your preparedness, or were you simply directed to the career services office? Were your professors clearly knowledgeable and skilled in the realities of job search, or were you left with far more questions than answers? Was it assumed that with a nursing degree in hand you would naturally land a great nursing job on your own? If you received assistance along the way, that's great! If not or if you need a refresher, read on to gain wisdom and confidence as you approach short-term job searching and long-term career development from a far more strategic vantage point.

New nurses may have a challenging time landing their first role for two reasons: depressed economic circumstances and/or a preconceived view of what their role should be that doesn't bear out in interview opportunities. In other words, a new nurse may find that interview opportunities do not result after many applications are made, or that initial salary offered is lower than expected. Setbacks can lead a new nurse to worry about what may appear to be a lousy return on their initial investment. This book is geared to help any job-seeking nurse understand how to navigate such murky waters. At some point, whether right out of college or later on in one's career, job searching will seem far more difficult than it should be as the economic pendulum continues to swing back and forth. Take heart! This book has practical and timely answers to such concerns.

Experienced nurses should always be on the lookout for opportunities for professional growth and development, which include additional skills training, robust connections developed and leveraged through networking, and regular interviewing for both internal and external opportunities for advancement. Job-searching skills should be developed and maintained for the long term and not just for short-term moments of desperation. Too many nurses take exactly that view; they search for a job only when they truly need it, versus strengthening those skills even when they don't. Every nurse who has suddenly experienced job loss, an injury or illness, or an awful new supervisor can attest to the need to plan ahead, to always have a Plan B.

Veteran nurses exploring semiretirement options (or those taking a planned "time out") need to learn how to navigate less-than-traditional waters. The good news is that the range of options is generally far wider than perceived by the individual nurse who has spent a career assured by "certain truths" about career development, which seem to turn on their ear when seeking out an entirely new way to look at "work." In other words, climbing the proverbial ladder or earning another degree is likely no longer the aim, but rather, applying well-developed nursing expertise and a lifetime of experience working effectively with people to solve heath care problems in new and novel arenas. Imagine nursing in another country or out in international waters, caring for the most vulnerable children in remote corners of the world, serving on an international health care panel, contributing research skills to better understand and educate others about an emerging health care trend, or developing new ways to promote dignity and quality of life within elderly populations. There's no limit to the possibilities!

This book assumes that as a nurse, you have been largely responsible for your own job search needs and that you have received little professional guidance along the way. Internet searches on nursing program curriculum and career development courses for nurses bear this out. A review of the nursing curriculum at more than 30 nursing schools shows not one full course devoted to job searching approaches and techniques, and it can be unclear to what extent career preparation and job search material is embedded within other courses. When career development is noted, it is usually in the context of adding technical skills or affirming specific competencies versus the actual understanding and application of solid job search strategies. A basic entry-level resume template for new nurses that does little to convey impact, may or may not have been included. Beyond the schools, professional nursing societies and organizations have emerged as the frontrunners in identifying challenges for nurses navigating the employment landscape. As such, they have devoted time, space, and resources to easing those challenges for their members.

Know this: You are a skilled nurse. You have invested energy and intelligence toward your career preparation and advancement. But perhaps you sense something is missing, or you are encountering roadblocks to career success. You may not be sure how to break through these barriers and fully realize your goals and dreams.

This strategic guide is dedicated to nurses and those who love them. Jump into this step-by-step guide and realize that your understanding of the job search process increases with every page. Appreciate the a-ha! moments and active self-coaching reflections in every chapter. Grab a pen and start jotting your fresh, new ideas in the margins. A new, crystal clear job search and career development strategy plan will emerge before your eyes.

This book takes you on a journey to expand your professional world through self-discovery and strategic intent that come to fruition in a plan already well underway by the final chapter. Everyone has heard about the power of networking, and no matter whether the very idea invigorates you or scares you, Chapters 2 and 3 will have you taking the world by storm. Thinking it's just a matter of dusting off your resume? Resumes are not tackled until Chapter 4; in other words, there's plenty to do before then. And how do you handle the time between realizing the need to search for a new opportunity and finding the right fit? The middle chapters were written just for you. Nervous about being in "the hot seat" during interviews? Chapter 8 will serve as your road map for tackling the selection process with confidence. Not sure how to market yourself in a way that commands attention? The final chapters will give you the edge you need to communicate your true impact to the world at large.

Note of caution: This book also confronts your fears and illuminates realities of the nursing job market that you might not have expected. It will positively challenge your current beliefs and expand your comfort zone. You have nothing to lose and everything to gain. Let's get started!

1

It is more important to know
where you are going
than to get there quickly.

–Mabel Newcomber

Painting a Workable Job Search Picture

When you were little, you probably dreamed about what you wanted to be when you grew up. Whether or not you chose "nurse" from a tender age, chances are good you never dreamed about HOW you would get that job, other than perhaps going to school for it. Kids never dream about job search activities; they don't envision long and tedious application forms or having to "sell themselves" as a valuable commodity in the job market. So it is no wonder that such realities come as harsh truths when they grow up, graduate from college, and wonder where the jobs are.

Self-Assessment: Current Beliefs About Job Searching

If you watched your parents struggle to find work, you had some idea of what it took to find a job; you may well have developed a very bad feeling about it. Recognize that what you have observed of other people's successes or failures around job searches will directly (if subconsciously) impact your approach to such tasks. If you saw others struggle, you may have planned in some way to help ensure you would not face similar trials and tribulations.

On the other hand, if your loved ones always held jobs for long periods of time, you may have no idea how that happens. Rather, you assumed it would magically happen for you, too. If those lucky people spoke up about what to expect in most cases, they did you a service. Otherwise, they either figured you'd learn on your own, someone else would teach you, or the magic would happen for you some other way. Either way, whether you watched others struggle or they "got lucky," neither group is in a great position to give you solid job search advice.

No matter what early understandings you had about job searches and career development, it is helpful to reflect back and determine which of these past scenarios influenced your current thinking. Good, bad, or ugly, understanding these forces will help you to recognize limiting contributors or buried strengths to your own successes.

Everyone comes to the job search arena with preconceived notions about what it will look like, what you will or won't encounter, and your prospects for success within a reasonable time frame. What are those preconceived ideas, exactly? They may be so ingrained in your thinking that you don't even realize they are in play. Only when we tease them out into the open can you start to constructively see them for what they are and analyze their effectiveness toward your goals.

Take the following quiz. Mark each statement as being true or false. Doing so will help you learn which beliefs you hold and how they express themselves in the approaches you have been taking. Your responses will also help to fine-tune your overall strategy around job searching and career development. You may have noticed there are no selections of "maybe" or "sometimes." This is intentional, as there is no straddling the fence or skirting the edges of such direct statements. Respond honestly from the heart and not from popular sentiment that you may have gleaned from casual conversation or the media.

Beliefs About Searching for a Job	TRUE	FALSE
Finding a new job is easy.	_____	_____
Finding a new job can take several months.	_____	_____
A generic resume sent out for 100 job openings is bound to end in success.	_____	_____
Job search success is more about *what* you know than *who* you know.	_____	_____
Networking is for business people, not nurses.	_____	_____
For a great resume, find a nice-looking resume template and fill it in.	_____	_____
Cover letters are necessary.	_____	_____
Job fairs are a valuable use of time and energy.	_____	_____
A bad experience in the past will follow me to another setting.	_____	_____
Being a great nurse should be enough to land a great new job.	_____	_____

Now let us look at what your responses say about your approach to job searches and career development. As the following text shows, there is more than meets the eye when pondering the above statements. As you go forward in this book, you will delve deeply into these themes. You will analyze what these statements mean and how to read between the lines in order to evaluate the power of assumption that can exist within them.

Quiz Results

Finding a new job is easy. You were more likely to perceive this statement as true if you have found easy successes in the past. Perhaps the last opportunity fell into your lap, or the economy was booming and skilled nursing jobs were in short supply due to a higher number of openings. It could also be that you have seen what looked like easy successes for other nurses, and your assumption was that easy success should be true for you, too. If you perceived the statement about *ease* to be false, you likely based your response on your own difficulties in landing new roles, or you heard the "horror stories" of others. For example, perhaps you heard of people who were talented and qualified for any number of jobs, but after sending out hundreds of resumes and cover letters, they have not gotten a single bite—never mind job offers, these folks didn't even get interviews.

LAND THAT JOB!

- How quickly have you been able to land new roles in the past?
- Did it happen through applying for open positions or by making the most of your connections?
- Do you know anyone who has had a horrible job search experience?
- Have you had a horrible search experience?
- Are you staying in a current position you dislike because you have not been able to land a new one?
- What experiences around the ease of job search have influenced your beliefs?

Finding a new job can take several months. While similar to the first item, this statement focuses on the perceived amount of time it takes to land a new role from the point when you started looking. While the statement does not indicate the time frame as either positive or negative, take a moment and reflect upon whether you felt positively or negatively about the statement. This correlates to whether you find the idea of a job search taking several months acceptable or not.

If you find the premise acceptable, that is a healthy attitude and suggests you are approaching your job search or professional objective from a position of strength. You have time on your side and are interested in finding the best fit for you. However, if you find the idea negative, beware! It suggests you are unrealistic about the time a job search or objective takes. It might also mean you cannot afford a process that takes several months because of your financial situation, or you find your current situation distressing and unpleasant.

Anytime you approach a project from a point of frustration or desperation, you are operating from a weakened position, which can directly and negatively impact the likelihood of success. At this point, start jotting down what has brought such a scenario about. By recognizing what these variables, constraints, or challenges are, you can begin to adjust your outlook and approach.

LAND THAT JOB!

Job seeking can be discouraging. Plan ahead. What strategies will you use to support yourself in staying engaged in the search?

How will a job search help you meet your long-term goals? Make a list of the ways in which job seeking can strengthen your career development goals. Keep this list handy so when the going gets rough, you have written reminders of your personal vision.

A generic resume sent out for 100 job openings is bound to end in success. This statement is loaded with potential assumptions, so your response is pretty interesting either way. Let's break down the three different variables in play here. First, think about your gut reaction to the word *generic* and why you responded to the word as you did. A generic resume is general, all-inclusive, and "big picture" in scope. It tends to list what you have done in the past, whether or not those roles were in health care. It is "multipurpose," and the hope is that any recruiter or nursing supervisor will find what they are looking for in it and give you a call. The second striking part of the statement is the number *100*, which is a *quantity*, and it is the value judgment you placed on that quantity that is important. You probably don't know exactly how many resumes you sent, but you believe that by sending out a lot of them, you are bound to hit your target. This way of thinking emphasizes quantity over quality. Third, the focus is on *job openings*. Estimates vary, but most employment experts agree that a large number of openings go unposted, and the ones that are posted are likely earmarked for a specific individual. Other postings go unfilled due to hiring freezes and internal restructuring. For those postings that are legitimately open, your competition is fierce because they are "out there" in the public eye, drawing attention to themselves for anyone to pursue. In other words, by chasing posted ads, you drastically limit your range of opportunity. When you consider all three elements, you may need to rethink how likely "bound to end in success" really is.

LAND THAT JOB!

How have you identified openings for which you have applied? Did you rely on posted advertisements, word of mouth, informational interviews, or a combination of these strategies?

If you answered the above question with only one approach, what skills, contacts, or resources will you need to use other strategies on this list? Keep reading to learn more about effectively expanding your approach.

Job search success is more about what *you know than* who *you know*. If you answered true for this statement, you likely hold the historical premise in nursing that a nursing degree virtually guarantees you a job. But job search success and career development are predicated on many variables, not just your education. You have direct or indirect control over some of them, but it is how you network with other professionals that can align the other variables in your favor. By realizing this, you can move variables from the "cannot control" category into areas where you have greater influence. Job search and career development outcomes are directly and positively impacted when your activities focus on developing *essential contacts* or *strategic allies* versus chasing posted job leads.

This aspect of career development is often overlooked or underestimated. Your comfort level in this area is directly related to your gut-level reaction to words such as networking, outreach, informational interviews, or "meet and greets." If you are naturally outgoing, you may be comfortable with most networking activities. It is not just about being an extrovert, but rather your willingness to be the first person to approach someone new. If you wait to be approached by someone new, networking activities may feel rather foreign to you. Take heart. You'll see as you read this book that there's a cure for *networkphobia*!

LAND THAT JOB!

Whom would you like to know better in your workplace? By identifying people in leadership positions whom you would like to know, you can be intentional about relationship building. Think about what you'd like for them to know about you as well, remembering that you are always making an impression.

Networking is for business people, not nurses. This statement supposes that the act of networking is role-based and has little to do with the nursing profession. As you saw in the previous assessment item, when networking is viewed as the way to develop strategic allies, your specific field becomes moot. In other words, it is the act of finding those in a position to help you reach your objective—to help you move from point A to point B—that will make the difference toward reaching your goals. If you responded to the statement as true, you either a) haven't seen networking as building alliances and/or b) you are uncomfortable with the idea and are hoping that the statement is true. It is not.

There is a business side to all industries, and health care is no exception! Businesses are concerned with growth and development, staying competitive, and gaining market share. Businesses make money. Even nonprofit organizations are very business-minded. All organizations need to allocate available resources wisely, cut costs where feasible, and analyze the strengths of and threats to their market. All businesses aim to succeed, to thrive.

When you network with nurses and other health care professionals, you get to demonstrate not just your nursing expertise but your business acumen as well. You get to show off the fact that you "get it," that you understand the business of health care and support the need to get things done as efficiently and effectively as possible.

LAND THAT JOB!

Consider your work experience both in and out of nursing. What expertise do you have to offer? Think about, write down, and practice messages you would like others to hear when you are networking.

In what ways have you supported measures undertaken by previous employers to improve efficiencies, reduce unnecessary costs, or create greater service value for patients? Practice describing your work in these terms with family and friends, so that in a networking setting you will be able to describe your roles, responsibilities, and experiences with confidence and ease.

For a great resume, find a nice-looking resume template and just fill it in. It is not uncommon for nursing job seekers to assume that a great resume has more to do with how it looks than anything else. Rest assured, there are a lot of really bad nursing resumes out there, and you can use this fact to your advantage. But how do you make sure your resume looks better than the competition?

Complicating matters is that today's automated applicant tracking systems do not "play well" with templates. Here's something all job seekers need to realize: Many templates available online for free, general use were created prior to the explosive rise of online application systems. These templates make use of graphics, tables, and columns to achieve a crisp, clean look. However, such elements don't work well within online application systems. Such systems are created to "read" your resume and organize its content into a database. The database "houses" your information for proper storage until a recruiter or hiring manager is ready to retrieve it. What does this mean in plain English? If an online system cannot "read" your resume, it won't easily be able to store it. If it cannot be stored well, those looking for great candidates won't find you.

The good news is that automated applicant tracking systems have recently become far more savvy and dynamic, which has mitigated such problems. Current systems solve the problem of one document needing to impress two sets of "eyes," computer and human, and only doing justice to one or the other.

While a resume does need to be effectively formatted so it's visually appealing, the content and substance are what counts. Your resume needs to have IMPACT. A resume is a marketing tool, and you can choose how you structure it, what you include, and what you leave out. A resume serves as a bridge between your professional past, present, and future. It highlights your technical and universal strengths and downplays any receding tasks or skill sets. Technical skills are those that are specific to nursing a patient. Universal skills are those that are important to all careers, such as communication ability and time management.

Ultimately, you have two benchmarks by which to evaluate your resume's content and impact: It must resonate strongly with a prospective employer's needs, and it must be true for you.

Look at your current resume with a critical eye. What are the strongest

LAND THAT JOB!

pieces of your resume in terms of content and impact? Weakest? Ask someone you trust to take the same critical look and identify what's missing, needed, or ineffective.

Have you ever served on a search committee for an open position? Volunteering to provide assistance when openings occur on your team is an excellent way to see effective and ineffective resumes.

Cover letters are necessary. If you consider this statement to be true, you likely recognize one or more truisms about cover letters. These truisms include: If your resume is impressive, your cover letter will also be expected to impress; if you and another candidate's resumes are similar, the cover letter can serve as a tie breaker; and cover letters require more customization than your resume.

If you feel the statement is false, it is likely because you're not using cover letters; you've relied more on applications than resumes, or you've heard (and believe) that cover letters are unnecessary. It is easy to conclude that cover letters are more trouble than they are worth, which is why so many job seekers use a standard cover letter that is so generic, only the date is customized.

What is a cover letter intended to accomplish? It serves to introduce your resume when you are not there to do so in person. It is a professional document that harkens back to social graces used to make a formal introduction to others. It conveys concern about the problem at hand (the need for a qualified nurse to fill an important role) and clearly states that you wish to solve the problem (starting with the interview). Above all, it should show that you stand above the rest in terms of nursing skills, business acumen, compassion, communication skills, and more.

LAND THAT JOB!

- To what extent have your letters combined a strong sense of professional contribution and social grace? Consider writing three or four interchangeable paragraphs. Use these writing prompts to get started:
- My experience and expertise are a perfect fit for the opening of ... *(fill in the title for which you are applying)* because I am ... *(use strong descriptors—examples might include well organized, attentive to details, a strong communicator with patients and doctors ... remember to make these personal to your own experience.)*
- Over the course of my career, I have ... *(describe in detail some of the expertise you've gleaned across your work experience.)*
- My most recent experience has included ... *(this could be on-the-job training, professional development, and increasing leadership roles.)*

Job fairs are a valuable use of time and energy. Your thoughts on this statement are in direct relation to your philosophy and experience with job fairs. For a job fair to be a valuable use of time and energy, certain conditions need to be met: They need to exist in your area, they need to be well-attended by employers, and you have to know how to effectively "work the room." If just one of these conditions is not met, you will not have a good experience. It is important to consider the idea, however, that if the first two conditions were met, but you did not have a good experience, the problem likely lies with the third condition, you. The good news is that the third condition is within your control.

How do you find such events in your area? They are marketed online, in newspapers, on flyers at community centers and churches—you name it. Start by conducting a web search using keywords such as "job fair" and "nursing" along with the city you live in or the ones closest to you. Most are free but not all are accessible; in some cases they are affiliated with a local college and intended for students and alumni. Some are industry specific and are available only to members of a particular organization. Look also for "open house" events sponsored by local health care systems and professional organizations. There are even job fairs held online.

LAND THAT JOB!

Before attending a job fair, do your homework. Many job fairs offer online links to companies that will be present. Visit company websites to research position openings, learn about the company's mission and vision and gather information you may use to formulate effective questions when visiting a company booth. Identify companies for which you would like to work, regardless of whether they have an opening at the moment. Job fairs provide an opportunity to meet hiring personnel and showcase your skills, experience, and expertise. Career fairs can be challenging, with more candidates than openings. Plan your time and strategy before attending, so that you meet companies for which you are best aligned.

Working a job fair or career event effectively is easy when you know what to bring and what to say. Bring materials such as resumes printed on nice paper and, even more importantly, personal cards, which resemble business cards but contain your contact information and the type of positions you are seeking. Wear your best suit along with your best smile and handshake. Prior to each event, visualize yourself as though you were on stage in a role, because you will be putting up your best performance for each employer. Navigate the room with a keen eye. Look for organizations of interest. Monitor traffic flow and move in as soon as you see a break in traffic around your favorite employers' tables. Bring a notepad and pen and jot down answers to your questions, and safely house all business cards you collect. Give them your resume and card, a last genuine smile and firm handshake, and promise to follow up with them soon. Then do so.

LAND THAT JOB!

When is the last time you attended a job fair or similar career event?

What did you accomplish, and how did your comfort level enhance or detract from your objectives?

Who sponsors such events for nurses and health care professionals in your area?

A bad experience in the past will follow me to another setting. This is an easy one if you have not had any bad experiences. You know if you've had them: getting fired or laid off; a poor grade point average in school; an abusive supervisor; a major mistake; drug or alcohol problems; inability to work well with others, regardless of whose "fault" it was; any history that won't pass a background check; or any on-the-job performance or conduct issues.

Bad experiences can be real, perceived, or both. Whatever your situation might be, categorize them as public facts, privately documented, or shameful perception. A criminal history can be part of the public record and largely inescapable, which presents unique challenges. A poor performance review is a company document that cannot be shared with others unless you share it or the information is requested by subpoena. Such issues do have practical solutions. If the bad experience is more of a perception, a label, or anything you feel ashamed about, recognize that the largest challenge lies in how YOU handle it going forward.

It is important to keep what you label as a bad experience in perspective. You may not have liked a job, or you had a difficult supervisor, or you didn't feel confident in your work or comfortable in your environment, but these don't necessarily qualify as "bad experiences," nor are they inordinately difficult to get beyond.

LAND THAT JOB!

Are there any bad experiences that you feel are holding you back, professionally?

What are they, and how is it that they negatively impact you?

Have you been holding a grudge or keeping bad feelings alive as a way to feel "right" about whatever happened? Are you free of such experiences? If so, that's great! If not, seek career counseling or coaching support so that you will be prepared to respond positively to challenging questions.

Being a great nurse should be enough to land a great new job. This statement combines several of the assumptions questioned earlier with the addition of a few more. This statement is loaded with expectation, even entitlement. Of course you want a great job and believe you deserve one—you do! However, wanting and believing do not automatically translate into reality; such is the stuff of fairy tales.

The qualifier in this statement is the word "great," which is used in two contexts. First is the presumption that everyone holds the same idea of what makes a great nurse. Beware of disconnects here. Don't mistake hard work, adequate skills, or having a degree as synonymous with great—they aren't, at least not on their own. In the second context, think about what a "great job" looks like to you and why the particular elements you identify are important to you. Is it money? Power and control? Flexible schedule? Less stressful environment? Wonderfully fast-paced? Better patients?

"Great" may be interpreted as the desire to earn a higher salary and better benefits, climb the ranks, make room for other interests in your life, travel, contribute to the greater good, de-stress, ramp up, or change your scenery. Understanding what exactly would be "great" to achieve will help narrow and define your approach to getting it.

LAND THAT JOB!

Describe for yourself your ideal job. Be specific: What will this job pay? What type of people will you be working with? What will your hours be? What kind of challenges will prove exciting or intriguing to you? What does the setting look like? How much autonomy, flexibility, and responsibility do you desire? Explore your ideal job ideas with people you trust. Ask them to consider with you, things you might have left out of your vision.

Avoid Myths, Find Truth

There are five common myths or traps that many job seekers fall into, simply because they are so common. In fact, some myths are so prevalent, they show up in and are propagated through routine advice given by "resume experts." However, you can avoid these myths and traps once you know how to spot and interpret them for what they are. Instead of highlighting myths here, the focus is upon recognizing differences and polarities in the ways you might have viewed these ideas up until now. The following ideas or constructs should serve as guiding principles as you progress on your job search or career development path.

Living an Advancement Lifestyle Versus Going Through the Job Search Motions

There's a real difference between passively or actively looking for a new job and truly furthering your career. Either approach is fine depending on your more immediate versus long-term goals. In other words, you need to think critically about what you need most: Are you feeling desperate for a new job, or do you want to craft a progressing career path that will help satisfy who you are at heart?

If you are feeling desperate about your job search, sit back and breathe. Desperation will never help you think clearly, act strategically, or progress from a position of strength. You need to clarify your plans and reformulate your approach. Start by determining why you feel desperate. Have a bad boss? Drowning under too much pressure on the job? Need more money to improve your personal circumstances? These are truly difficult situations, without a doubt. Reading this book is an excellent first step to place yourself in a greater position of strength as you move forward.

An advancement lifestyle, by contrast, is a set of ideals you believe in, paired with activities you engage in regularly that are geared toward propelling you forward in your career. Identify what is important to you, including compensation, rank, or recognition. For example, you may wish to continue to climb the health care system ladder and improve your income year after year. Or you may value your flexibility, autonomy, or the ability to travel the world far more than career glory or a large staff, and you need only enough income to live simply yet comfortably. Both are pictures of career success; it's all in how you perceive, define, and craft it. This is how your ideals are structured.

The activities you engage in will lend substance to your ideals and will make them tangible by virtue of being actionable. Activities should be productive and add measurable value. They also help us to feel that we are doing something, getting something done, or getting somewhere even if the pace is a bit slower than we'd like. Activities are about gaining traction, sowing the ground for the seeds of our ideals to take root and flourish. Such activities may not bear fruit overnight but truly pave the way for long-term success.

Advancement lifestyle activities include:

- Networking regularly through nursing societies, professional health care organizations, special events hosted by your employer, and local networking groups that bring together multiple segments of the local community (nursing students can often join at a discount)
- Presenting yourself professionally in all aspects of your life, both on and off the clock. Being mindful how you dress, groom yourself, and interact with others in public and on social media sites.
- Identifying industry and organizational professionals and connecting with them to form partnerships
- Observing and analyzing health care needs and opportunities along with your nursing skills and background, positioning yourself for opportunities for career advancement. Broadening your understanding of the health care industry or specializing in an area of acute need by continuing your education through another degree, certificates, or CEUs
- Volunteering, aiding a cause, or showcasing a hobby in ways that both serve the community and get you noticed for your talents and generosity
- Doing all of the above in a consistent, positive, and professional manner, every day

It is the "every day" aspect that separates a typical job search from an advancement lifestyle. By developing ways to do something each day that move you forward or at least strengthen your foundation, your activities become as natural as breathing until you are scarcely aware that you're doing them. To understand how ingrained such habits have become already, note which activities you already engage in and how frequently or consistently. Keep a daily career advancement journal to track your progress.

The Differences Between Human Resources and Recruiting

These two entities are similar yet different, and each plays a role in your job search and career development processes. Human resources (HR) is the larger umbrella in any health care system under which various sub-units may be organized and managed. Recruiting is one of those sub-units and may be organized in-house or managed through third-party vendors. The smaller the organization, the more "hats" the HR personnel will wear, or the "HR hat" itself will be one of many worn by the owner. Larger organizations will have more diverse yet specialized HR roles in play. At any size, an organization may decide to outsource its recruiting function, in part or in full.

Third-party health care recruiters are independent contractors whose clients are health care organizations. Unless you are paying a recruiter to locate a new position for you (and such arrangements do exist), *they do not work for you*. Their focus is on filling open positions for their client, which may or may not include you. It is a small but important distinction: They are not paid to promote your interests or to find you a job. Recruiters often have a poor reputation among job seekers who wrongfully assume otherwise.

Interact with third-party recruiters as though they were in-house recruiters with a direct line to the hiring manager, charge nurse, or medical director. Be professional and polite at all times. Find out what it takes to get to the top of their candidate pool—this is the list of candidates whose qualifications are most likely to make the recruiter look good. Recruiters survive on repeat company business, and they will not promote job seekers who jeopardize their income.

When companies outsource their recruiting efforts, they are able to focus inwardly on their own current employee base. Their organizational structure is able to achieve internal goals around cost containment of compensation and benefit expenses, succession planning, training and development, and employee performance issues.

Knowing the distinction between HR and recruiting is important, because it helps you know whom you should seek out to best support your goals. For example, in large health care systems that use third-party recruiters, HR departments may not be structured to handle your application materials. They may or may not forward your materials to the recruiters contracted to provide that service, nor can they confirm the receipt of your materials or share with you the status of your application. They might not even be involved in scheduling interviews. That means your focus needs to be on establishing rapport with the third-party recruiters that support them.

By contrast, if you are currently employed in a large health care system, those internal HR professionals who specialize in organizational effectiveness, succession planning, training and development, or human capital development are the ones you want to meet. Help them get to know your talents and strengths well. They often will work in tandem with your supervisor, so make sure they are in your corner, too. When your boss, his or her boss, and HR all think well of you, your chances for a promotion or positive transfer increase, especially if you have 1 to 3 years' experience in your current role. This is also true if you are looking more for flexibility and autonomy than "climbing the ladder," because you can learn which opportunities are more in line with your needs. They can also help you specialize in ways that few others can, which strengthens your negotiating position.

Strategies for connecting with the HR department:

- Ask your supervisor to introduce you to the HR professionals in your organization.
- Stay connected in positive ways; too often HR professionals know best those who are underperforming. Building a relationship will help you be recognized as someone with the potential to be groomed for a new position.
- Share your vision for your future; talk with HR personnel about how you might grow in the organization. Make it known that you would like to be considered for succession opportunities.
- Update your internal resume. Once you have completed a certification program, be sure your HR professional is aware that you have new training and skills.

Apply Online but Don't Stop There

One common job search myth is that you can simply apply online, and you will get called for interviews. Results of this approach tend to be very poor. There are several reasons why.

First, the automated applicant tracking systems put in place to connect job seekers to employers can be cumbersome to use on both sides, quirky at best, and fraught with technical glitches and bugs. This reason alone accounts for why many applications aren't even seen by recruiters and hiring managers. These application systems often require customization that the HR crew doesn't want to make because of time, cost, confidentiality concerns (if others do it), or lack of in-house IT expertise to fully adapt and test the systems to the current workflow. If you've ever heard anyone complain that they have "applied online for hundreds of jobs and never got a single response," the very systems designed to ease the process are often at fault, and the players on either side don't even realize it. In other words, what works in theory doesn't work so well in practice.

Recruiters and hiring managers don't know I exist!

To combat this problem, send your materials to them by mail or e-mail (mail is preferable, but e-mail can be used if it is unclear who the recruiter actually works for or where they are located), but make it clear you also applied online as directed. This can prompt them to look for you in the system if your materials capture their interest.

Second, despite the fact that many automated applicant tracking systems work poorly, recruitment workflows are often set up so that job seekers are forced to enter through the online "door" to express their interest in the company. Recruiters often cannot do anything with you unless your application comes through the system, because it is your online application that triggers the next steps in the electronic recruiting workflow. In other words, without your online application in the system, recruiters have no access to click a button that rates your application against the qualifications of the position, and if they cannot rate your application, they cannot click the button that moves you to the interview phase.

Submitting applications online is such a pain!

To combat this problem, network with recruiters and hiring managers within the health care systems that excite you and spend your time applying for positions you really want. Those who know you and want to bring you into the organization will work with you to navigate their automated systems.

Third, applying online is a rather cold and impersonal approach to job search. Most job seekers use a multipurpose, multiuse, generic resume and cover letter for every application in an effort to speed up the number of applications they can make online in the shortest time. But in trying to "speak" to everyone, they connect with no one. This is not to say that generic resumes don't get lucky from time to time; however, that is wholly dependent upon the number and quality of competing candidate resumes recruiters have to choose from that will make or break any generic resume's chance of success.

I send the same resume and cover letter for every posting.

To combat this particular problem, focus on quality over quantity, and customize your materials for each position and organization. Instead of addressing your materials to "HR" or "to whom it may concern," take a few minutes to find a name of someone in HR, on the recruiting team, or the actual hiring manager to which to "speak" directly. Using someone's name is more likely to get their attention and even impress them if it hadn't been made readily available to most candidates for the position.

Silence From Companies Is a Form of Highly Useable Feedback

If the primary form of feedback you have received in your job search has been silence, use that information to your advantage. Even deafening silence gives you several clues about exactly what is wrong and what needs to be fixed for better results going forward. Silence from organizations points to four likely problems: 1) They don't know you have applied, 2) they posted the position because they have to; they have already identified the candidate they want, 3) your resume doesn't provide the substance or impact they are looking for, or 4) the quality of your materials is poor.

The first problem could relate to the automated applicant tracking system issues identified in the previous section of this book—the system failed to choose you as a relevant candidate. It could be that your materials are sitting in limbo in a pile of papers on someone's desk due to a hiring freeze or a company restructuring. Another possibility is that the posting you applied to is outdated yet still circulating out there on the web. To avoid this particular silence-inducing problem, focus on your networking and outreach efforts. In other words, get to know the players first and use your application materials as a follow-up activity versus a first point of contact.

The second scenario is not uncommon. There is no legal requirement for employers to post a position unless in a union environment. However, the organization may have a policy to post all openings as a good-faith attempt at transparency, to show a position did not open within 6 months of the same position being eliminated, and to show it does not discriminate or endorse favoritism.

The third possibility speaks again to the need to customize your materials so that they truly focus on the company in question and convey that you could be an excellent fit for the position. If you find yourself groaning or rolling your eyes at the mere thought (as it does mean more effort on your part), realize that at least one of your competitors for that cool, interesting position WILL adapt their materials and close the deal, especially in non-unionized environments. No matter what health care environment you target, you still need to make a strong case for why and how you meet or exceed the qualifications in question. Don't allow prospective employers to assume what you can or cannot do on the job; spell it out for them, because if they assume anything, chances are their assumptions may be the opposite of what you intended.

The fourth possibility gets personal. While no one wants to believe they have terrible materials, it happens more often than you think. And for those who suspect their materials are less than desirable, instead of improving them, they simply hope someone will consider them good enough. Do you fall into this category? If you have applied for multiple jobs and received no response, you have to consider the possibility that the problem lies with your materials. For example, you may have a very short work history, or your materials are poorly formatted or are not transmitting well for proper viewing, usage, or storage. This doesn't make you a bad person; it means you need help with your resume, as you might not know where or how to begin overhauling it on your own. Ultimately, deafening silence from companies in response to your application materials means one thing above all else: Stop what you are doing.

I'm doing everything "right" but nothing works!

To combat this problem, you must first recognize and admit that what you are doing is not working. This is the point where you need to shift gears and focus on a different set of activities to get you from where you are to where you want to be in the short or long term. Face facts: If what you are doing results in silence, you are not doing the right things.

Quality Over Quantity

This entire first chapter has at times hinted at and other times shouted the need for quality over quantity throughout the job search process. This concept applies equally to your overarching career development activities.

The idea of quality over quantity is an interesting one for nurses to contemplate. The emphasis on quantity in nursing is immediately felt when looking at nursing caseloads, patient beds to cover, the amount of documentation required by the end of one's shift, hours worked per shift, expedient care, etc. Quality is emphasized when looking at mortality indicator improvements, nursing school curriculum, holistic community benefits, differences of care across populations, and more. All health care organizations strive to achieve balance between the two, yet nurses are often caught on the fine line in the middle. "Hands-on" nursing is seen as a quality indicator among patients, whereas thorough, immediate documentation is a key quality indicator for administrators, because there are numerous interdisciplinary team members for every one patient who all need up-to-date status information and feedback through the care cycle. As a professional group, nurses often feel forced to choose between the two as though they cannot coexist together, as mutually incompatible ideals. However, with the emergence of evidence-based practice models, nurses can see firsthand what does and doesn't work and adapt their nursing strategies accordingly with stronger organizational support.

That said, if you routinely find yourself in a position to favor quantity over quality on the job, real or perceived, that is very likely to spill over into your job search and career development approaches. So try your hand at taking more of an evidence-based practice model with your job search.

Assessing What Works and What Doesn't Work

On the next page is an exercise to assist you in this process of determining all that you do toward your job search and career development and then rating the effectiveness of each in terms of actual outcomes or results produced. The first two lines are examples to guide your assessment. Add more lines in a notebook if needed.

Throughout this first chapter, you have begun to paint a workable picture of what your job search and career development efforts can look like. Now that your focus has become clearer, it is time to turn thoughts into action.

Activity	Desired result	Actual result
Apply online for 10 jobs	Get 3+ interviews	Silence
Go to local nursing conference	Earn CEUs	Met 4 new hospital administrators

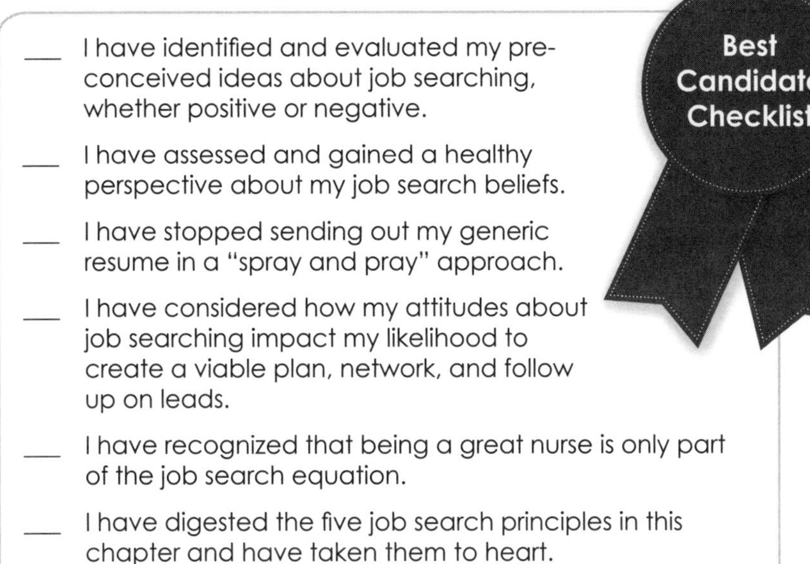

Best Candidate Checklist

___ I have identified and evaluated my preconceived ideas about job searching, whether positive or negative.

___ I have assessed and gained a healthy perspective about my job search beliefs.

___ I have stopped sending out my generic resume in a "spray and pray" approach.

___ I have considered how my attitudes about job searching impact my likelihood to create a viable plan, network, and follow up on leads.

___ I have recognized that being a great nurse is only part of the job search equation.

___ I have digested the five job search principles in this chapter and have taken them to heart.

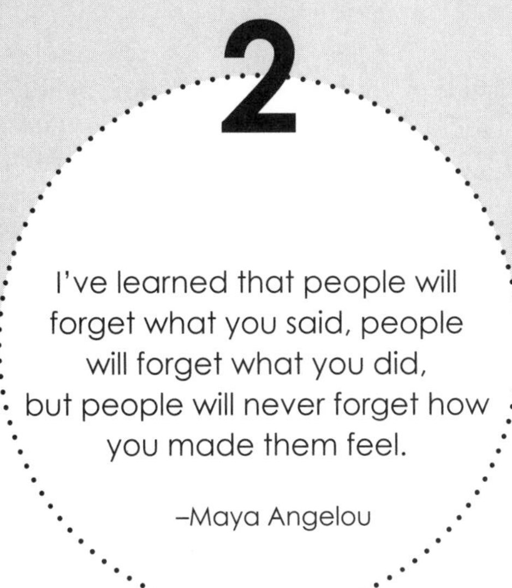

2
I've learned that people will
forget what you said, people
will forget what you did,
but people will never forget how
you made them feel.
–Maya Angelou

Networking Starts With Talking

Everybody talks to themselves, either as inner dialogue or out loud when no one else is around. How you talk to yourself influences how you talk to others. This concept of self-talk is important and directly applicable to how you approach and reflect upon your job search and career development activities. Therefore, it is essential to assess what you frequently say to yourself about yourself, how, and why. This initial exploration will help you to better understand the ease or difficulty you may find when talking to and networking with others.

To get a better handle on this concept and how it applies to you, grab a pen and paper or jot your ideas in the margins of this book. Take time to reflect on the following questions:

> What do you say to yourself about what you want in life, for your career?
>
> What are the most common topics or themes that run through your mind about yourself? Is the tone of those ideas more positive or more negative in nature?
>
> Are your thoughts elevated by feelings of excitement or diminished by a sense of desperation?
>
> Do the ideas and tone mirror what others say about you, or are those things at odds with how others perceive you?
>
> How do you view yourself as a professional nurse?
>
> What do you claim as strengths or weaknesses?
>
> How does that compare or contrast with such assessments from others, including your coworkers, supervisors, professors, and patients?

You project whatever it is that you hold within you, wherever and however you go, positively or negatively. This applies to all environments or situations you seek out or find yourself in. The point is this: If you think about yourself in professional and positive terms, you bring that into your job search and career development activities. This is true with unprofessional or negative ideas as well. Wherever you go, there you are.

LAND THAT JOB!

What do you like about yourself? List at least five items right off the top of your head. Then list five things that you don't like. Whatever comes to mind quickly is very telling, as is whether you are able to come up with positives or negatives quicker. Looking at your lists, what do you see that can serve to enhance or support your career? What are the detractors, and how could they impair or derail your efforts if you let them?

This activity is worth its weight in gold. Although you might experience discomfort with some of the questions or insights gained, you now recognize these aspects of yourself. That is where the true value of this exercise lives and breathes. Self-awareness is a glorious thing and an essential component to success in both career and life.

It is important to acknowledge whether you believe this exercise doesn't apply to you or if you feel cynical about the activity of self-reflection. If this is you, figure out why. Otherwise, it forms a barrier to your forward progress. Remember, wherever you go, there you are. You will bring your barriers with you; there is no skirting around them or leaving them behind. Perhaps you have heard the phrase about leaving your baggage at the door. That adage is used to describe issues that translate directly into unprofessional, inappropriate, or unethical behaviors on the job.

While you are unlikely to actively demonstrate unwanted behaviors in your nursing role, how you internalize such baggage comes with you from patient to patient. You may keep a "poker face" in place or "play a role" when working in an attempt to hide or disguise your internal reality. Those who do this don't fool anyone for long. In fact, you can probably think of at least one person who tries to do so without success. Are you that person? If so, now is the time to go back and revisit the questions above. The good news is that you are very likely able to push through any discomfort that might arise. By pushing through discomfort, you expand your comfort zone. When you expand your comfort zone, well, that's when the magic really starts to happen!

You can expand your comfort zone by journeying through five phases: becoming consciously aware, examining your strengths and weaknesses, taking responsibility, celebrating your strengths, and living purposefully going forward. The following pages illuminate each of these phases. You will pass through some more quickly than others and to a greater or lesser degree of comfort. Take the time to read through and reflect upon all five, because the journey itself has a tremendous impact on your job search and professional development successes. The next five sections also pave the way for all that follows.

Conscious Awareness

The first step is conscious awareness. All nurses have things about themselves that they like and are proud of; conversely, all nurses want to make certain changes about themselves. This is all perfectly normal. You are you: a unique, knowledgeable, talented nurse, capable of deep compassion. Show yourself as much compassion as you show to others by looking upon yourself with kindness, appreciation, and positive regard.

Another important aspect to this exercise is balance. In other words, you need to balance out your reflection of both strengths and weaknesses. How do you know if you're taking a balanced approach? Give them equal time and don't emphasize one over the other. There are millions of people out there whose first instinct is to focus on improving their weaknesses to such an extent that they practically disregard their strengths. This is characteristic of a person with low self-esteem. It is less likely that someone will be so taken with their own strengths that their weaknesses are hardly acknowledged internally, and if they are, shrugged off. Knowing and acknowledging how you see yourself and how you talk to yourself will allow you to move forward into acceptance of you as you are.

LAND THAT JOB!

How are you feeling right now, right this minute? Are you happy, energized, and engaged? Are you uncertain or doubtful? What are you saying to yourself in your head? Is your self-talk positive or negative? At this moment, how easy is it for you to accept you as you are?

Your sense of self is subjective. In other words, you are the one who places value judgments on all the things that make you who you are. At every given moment, you have a variety of thoughts and feelings in play. Paired with these thoughts and feelings are how you perceive them and the value judgments you place on them. If you are feeling happy, most people would think that is a good thing. But some people don't trust feelings of happiness, because they believe it can end at any moment. It is akin to "waiting for the other shoe to drop." From there, the feelings that they think are bound to follow happiness stress them out. This example illuminates how even feelings of happiness are subjective, as it is up to each person to judge if happiness is a good thing or not.

Though skeptics of the very premise of consciousness may argue that how and what we feel and think are an illusion, most people agree that perceptions, thoughts, and feelings seem very real—so real, in fact, that they guide our decision-making from moment to moment. It also stands to reason that such subjectivity lends itself to self-fulfilling prophesy. Worrying about when and how a current feeling of happiness is going to end will most certainly bring about the quick end of such an emotional state.

Conversely, you may believe that everyone has ups and downs and that such fluctuations are normal. In this example, while the feelings of what makes an "up" moment as contrasted by a "down" moment are indeed subjective, the key here is the weight placed upon those value judgments. In other words, while feelings of unhappiness may occur in "down" moments, the weight placed upon such an occurrence is relatively light as such an occurrence is seen as "bound to happen sometimes" as part of the "natural" rhythms of life. People who are severely depressed give far more weight to "down" moments—there is such heaviness to these moments that it can seem impossible to get back "up," and such perceptions seem very real.

The subjectivity of your consciousness directly impacts your job search and professional growth throughout your nursing career. The thoughts and feelings you associate with your job as it ranks within your career field are also subjective, and that subjectivity carries weight to a greater or lesser degree as you form judgments about them. Take a few moments to reflect upon the following questions:

> What is it about being a nurse that brings you the greatest sense of pleasure or satisfaction?
>
> What is the worst thing about being a nurse?
>
> How might nursing in different environments improve or impair your view of nursing?
>
> How do nurses rank in your mind compared to physicians or health care administrators?
>
> Who are the nurses you most admire and why?
>
> What makes you a good nurse?
>
> How might you improve your nursing skills?
>
> Do you readily tell total strangers what you do for a living?

> Do you ever hesitate to tell people you are a nurse and, if so, why?
>
> Did you want to be a nurse ever since you were a kid?
>
> Do you prefer a nursing environment within a structured organization?
>
> Can you envision working for yourself, as a private contractor?

A pattern should start to emerge once you analyze your responses to these questions. Discern your thoughts and feelings about nursing in general and then extrapolate those thoughts and feelings to your own career. If you love being a nurse and cannot imagine doing anything else for a living, that's great! That in itself has nothing to do with nursing; rather, it is how you subjectively relate to nursing. If the value judgments you made were more positive than negative, that means that your view of yourself and your career are in general alignment.

When your actual job is congruent with your desired career field, you are likely to find higher satisfaction or happiness with your situation. If your situation diminishes the value judgments you place on your career, you experience incongruence. In that situation, you need to determine if being a nurse elsewhere in a different environment would bring a greater sense of congruence.

Many new nurses seek out hospital medical-surgical environments when they graduate from college only to find the actual life-and-death pressure to be overwhelming and even downright scary. If you are experiencing more stress on the job than you can handle, it is critical to look at your coping mechanisms. Seek out a mentor or supervisor. Speak with your employee wellness benefits coordinator or the employee assistance plan hotline. Find healthy outlets such as exercise or meditation. But be on the lookout for poor coping mechanisms such as drug and alcohol use, avoiding patients, absenteeism, or taking frustrations out on loved ones. Such behaviors can derail your professional career as a nurse as well as your personal life.

The ways in which you view yourself as unique are also subjective. The word "unique" in itself can be perceived as positive as opposed to a feeling of being "different," which may be a more negative perception, even though the very idea of being unique also means that something about you is different from other people. Understand that how you view yourself is indeed subjective. The good news: If your subjective views of your thoughts and feelings are more negative than positive, you can change how you perceive them. Actions and behaviors are largely universal; however, how our perceptions and value judgments guide our actions and behaviors is a unique yet complex set of variables that is always in play.

Strengths and Weaknesses

Once you are aware of what aspects make you uniquely you, determine the strengths and weaknesses of each. All traits have pros and cons. Strengths are the things that you come by naturally and propel you forward to success. One of your strengths may be a strong sense of responsibility to others, so you feel compelled to check each of your patients one last time before the end of your shift. Or perhaps you are naturally strategic in how you approach problems and projects. In this example, you look at things from all angles and three steps ahead, which make you an asset on any special task force or implementation team.

An excellent resource for assessing personal strengths is the Clifton StrengthsFinder assessment (http://www.strengthsquest.com/home.aspx) and the StrengthsQuest book by Donald O. Clifton, Edward "Chip" Anderson, and Laurie A. Schreiner (2006) that accompanies the assessment. Curt Coffman and Marcus Buckingham wrote *First, Break All the Rules* (1999). Donald O. Clifton and Marcus Buckingham collaborated on *Now, Discover Your Strengths* (2001), which are both excellent resources for discovering and capitalizing upon your strengths. There are summary updates from 2010 as well as Marcus Buckingham's *Go Put Your Strengths to Work* (2010). All of these are based on over 30 years of research by the Gallup International Research & Education Center, http://www.gallup.com/home.aspx.

Each strength or attribute possesses asset and liability characteristics. This is an interesting premise as it infers that any given attribute is neither one nor the other. This idea goes beyond subjectivity, as value judgments are directly impacted by the immediate situation or environment. For example, a strong sense of responsibility that can defy healthy boundaries is an absolute strength or asset in the event of a natural disaster. Likewise, strategic thinking makes all the difference when having to manage through periods of intense change. Taking responsibility is a liability if it is expressed or perceived, primarily in the minds of others, as bossiness or martyrdom. And too much strategic thinking can delay or confound the act of actually getting things done.

LAND THAT JOB!

List what you perceive as your strengths and weaknesses. Then think about the relative weights of each. Finally, reflect upon how your strengths have been more of an asset versus a liability in specific situations or environments.

Good managers, who care about employee satisfaction as a way to drive results, can help show how a nurse's strengths are demonstrated on the job and the consistent, positive results that come from a strengths-based strategy. Seek out a current or previous manager or mentor to discuss how he or she has seen your strengths in action! When you (and your manager) focus on your strengths, any weaknesses tend to fade away in the background to become largely irrelevant.

After you have reflected further on what your strengths are, you can analyze which are primary strengths or liabilities in specific situations or environments. This distinction is an important one, as it is identifying specific situations that help you to understand how you can further develop and engage your strengths while allowing you to effectively manage around what may be primarily weaknesses.

The funny thing about strengths is that they can be perceived differently by different people. If you have a manager whose strength is responsibility, he or she may put in long hours to get the work done. This manager likely sees responsibility as a strength over the ability to be strategic. An individual with strategic strength strives to work smarter not harder.

Think of it this way: Different people have different strengths. Your strengths are powerful tools for success. It can be helpful to identify the strengths of your manager, then reflect upon how your strengths complement or clash with your manager's each day. For example, if your supervisor has belief as a top strength, it may run counter to your includer strength; your supervisor's enduring core values that drive how he or she approaches work in rather absolute terms may conflict at times with your strength in being able to see various viewpoints and your desire to engage others in decision-making. A manager who is routinely confident in his or her ability to identify the best course of action may have trouble appreciating your desire to be inclusive of others when making decisions.

You do not work in a vacuum but rather as part of a team; your strengths are not the only strengths in play, so it can be very helpful to not only appreciate strengths in others, but to recognize where their strengths may dominate or be the best fit in a certain situation (meeting an important deadline, staying absolutely focused in a chaotic, emergency situation). Having such perspective helps you to not necessarily align your strengths with others, but to understand how your strengths are just part of the picture instead. Doing so enables you to articulate how each person is especially valuable with his or her respective strengths.

Still, teams change over time. Your strengths can be seen and appreciated as a real asset in a given environment until a new supervisor comes onto the scene, at which point you will have developed the skills to better understand his or her strengths and articulate how your strengths fit into the team he or she is now charged with managing effectively. Situations can change for a variety of reasons, including how other people move in and out of the picture.

One of the reasons "change" within workplace teams can be hard to handle is that you may feel your strengths are suddenly called into question or somehow not as important when a powerful, new player enters the scene. You want to remember in these situations that your strengths are still your strengths, they are still important and valuable, and you can use your strengths to help ease potentially painful transitions until everybody gets better acquainted. Keep this firmly in mind if your main reason for job searching at this time is that you are uncomfortable or anxious about a new supervisor who appears to be quite different from you, has voiced taking things in a new direction, has different expectations of you, and so forth.

LAND THAT JOB!

As a nurse, are you more likely to roll with the changes and adapt as needed to maintain your situation? Or do you tend to "change with the changes," so that when an environment is changing anyway, you figure you might as well seek out an entirely new environment for yourself and your strengths?

By realizing who you are and what your strengths are across different situations and environments, you can create a set of guiding principles for your actions and behaviors. Though some might argue that "principle doesn't pay," that sentiment in itself is a value judgment based on the extent the perceived strengths are seen as an asset or liability when it comes to coping with change. Change is the one true constant. How you handle change says a lot about how you manage your career. Do you handle it actively or passively, as positively or negatively?

Reflect on the following combinations as you seek to identify which one most closely describes your own approach to change. How you approach change can change, so you can use this exercise to analyze your approach.

Active/positive: You cheerfully seek out change instead of waiting for it to happen. You expect it to happen versus being surprised. You are proactive and not only look for, but actually see opportunity where others don't. Because you recognize that things are always changing, you embrace changes as a path to career advancement. You tend to "have your feelers out" and continuously network with other professionals as naturally as breathing. You are likely motivated by challenge.

Active/negative: You seek new environments when you see change coming, because you foresee you won't like or trust what might happen if you stay put. You are compelled to make changes based on negative perceptions about how change will likely unfold in your current environment. This can also be viewed as forever running from one environment to the next, or believing that career advancement can only be achieved through movement from one organization to another versus promotions from within. You may be viewed as a "mover and shaker," but in your mind you are so because you have to be. Active/negatives may resort to getting fired as a way to force change. You are likely motivated by fear of losing control.

Passive/positive: You are passive about change, going with the flow and hoping for the best. You may not like or agree with changes taking place, but you are hopeful things will improve if you stick with it. You tend to take the path of least resistance. Your career will be slower to progress if you expect "good" things will happen if they are meant to be. You may believe it is better to be really good at a job, of being "the expert," versus the uncertainty or loss of expertise that comes with anything new. You're happy to attend a conference and mingle as part of your job but would not likely seek out such events on your own. You may wait for a promotion to come from above, a promotion that may never happen. You are likely motivated by the comfort found in familiarity.

Passive/negative: You don't like change to the point of finding it inherently offensive. Perhaps you have been characterized as "flying under the radar" at work or of just "wanting to be left alone" to work your shift. Others perceive you as unmotivated, which is true in that you are unmotivated to proactively seek opportunities in which to shine. Chances are you view your nursing job as a mere paycheck versus a calling; a sense of entitlement may be what keeps you locked in place. You may spend time finding ways to stay where you are no matter how much you dislike the place, including activities such as filing claims or needing frequent leaves of absence. You are motivated by the need to maintain the status quo for yourself no matter what the consequences may be.

LAND THAT JOB!

Which combination resonated most closely with you and your approach to change? How comfortable are you with your assessment? How does your approach to change align with your sense of who you are and how you describe yourself? Are your thoughts and beliefs congruent with your actions and behaviors?

No matter which of the four scenarios you chose as best representing your approach, you must decide whether to continue in that vein or make necessary changes that might make you uncomfortable. Change is easier where congruence is present. If you are struggling with ideas about yourself, take a step back and remove the value judgments you have placed upon them. Look at them objectively as basic facts about yourself. Realize they are what they are, and they evolved as they have for a reason. Determine if the reasons are still valid; chances are they are no longer valid or pertinent to your current situation. This is where you come to recognize how forces in your past are continuing to negatively influence your present. If so, let them go. Even if you identified yourself as an active/positive, you may have adopted past feelings of inferiority as perceived by others. The primary question is: What drives you to do what you do, to approach change as you do? This may be an ongoing reflective exercise of self-awareness.

Taking Responsibility

The third step in your journey is using your heightened self-awareness to take responsibility for how your self-talk is externalized. Your self-talk is yours and yours alone. Even if it has been unduly and negatively influenced by others, it is still yours for better or for worse. Therefore, you alone must take ownership of both the positive and negative aspects of yourself and recognize that you do show them off to the world whether you mean to or not.

You accomplish this step by saying your self-talk out loud and deciding which messages will enhance your success. Conversely, you must decide which ones hold you back, and oust those uglies from your repertoire. This relates to professional motivation to make active and positive changes throughout your career.

LAND THAT JOB!

Which aspects of your inner monologue are positive, healthy, and worth keeping? Conversely, which aspects would you do well to kick to the curb?

Motivation is that power or force that makes you want to take action about something, whether the activity is something you've done many times or is completely new. Taking responsibility is, in itself, an action. It is something that you do. Motivation is not thinking about doing something; it is the force that prompts you to actually do it. The key here is taking action. And you can break this activity down into three parts:

1. Decide what you want to accomplish.
2. Practice the art or craft you aspire to.
3. Achieve your goal.

Once you have decided upon a course of action that you feel good about and are motivated to pursue, determine what the "doing" will actually involve. Activity might include signing up for certification classes, attending a networking function, finding a mentor at work, refusing to gossip with coworkers, talking to your supervisor about your career path, polishing your professional appearance, or updating your resume. When it comes to actual activities, you have starter activities and maintenance activities. A starter activity might be to update your resume, whereas a maintenance activity may be to use it over and over to apply for different jobs of interest. You can sign up for a course as a starter activity; you also have to maintain that activity by actually attending the classes from start to finish, no matter what challenges arise along the way.

Reaching "success points" is critical to motivation. Determine them in advance so you know them when you see them. If you don't reach success points, you will be less motivated to try again or to try something new. Success motivates you to do more. This is why it is important to start with easier challenges than harder ones, quicker ones than longer-term goals. Success might be getting an interview, completing a certification course, landing a new job or promotion, getting three compliments on your polished appearance, making a fantastic connection with a hiring manager at a networking function, or reaching the 10th meeting with your mentor. Success can be anything you want it to be as long as you determine it in advance. Otherwise, it is too easy to fall into the trap of stopping at some arbitrary point and saying "good enough." Do not settle for good enough. That is not what motivation for success is all about.

LAND THAT JOB!

What are you feeling motivated about? What would you like to accomplish next, professionally speaking? How does that goal translate into the three motivational steps discusssed on page 36?

Think about it: You have worked this process before. For example, you decided at some point that you wanted to be a nurse. That was the first phase. Then you enrolled in college or took part in some type of training program where you practiced some element of nursing each day. Lastly, you graduated to actually be a nurse with a diploma and certifications to prove it. Mission accomplished. This shows you already have success under your belt when it comes to motivation and your career. This process gets repeated many times throughout your career. It starts each time you decide to get better at something you already do or to do something different, such as move from medical-surgical to pediatrics. Now that you have segued into and out of the topic of motivation, turn your attention back to the self-awareness exercises designed to expand your comfort zone.

LAND THAT JOB!

How have your reflections throughout this chapter helped to clarify your professional goals? What are one or two goals you have decided upon? How will you practice? What would success actually look like?

Celebrate Your Strengths

The fourth step in expanding your comfort zone is to assertively celebrate your strengths by putting them to work for you and to deliberately manage around your weaknesses. Treat strengths as ammunition in your arsenal. View weaknesses as potential danger zones and stay vigilant for when, where, and how they might get out of hand. This idea was touched upon in the section on motivation but deserves further exploration here.

How do you celebrate your strengths? You need to know what they are first, through identification and analysis. Once you can name them, think about ways those strengths have served you well over the years. Perhaps they helped you succeed on a hospital committee, gave you the insight on how to improve a process in your workplace to be more efficient, or gave you confidence to befriend colleagues at all levels within the organization. Appreciate what they have done for you, how and in what ways they have allowed you to grow. Think about what you are motivated to do next in your professional life and be grateful and appreciative of those strengths that you have in your corner.

Conversely, how do you manage around weaknesses? Again, knowing what they are through identification and analysis is your best starting point. Name them and think critically yet dispassionately about how perceived weakness has not helped you over the years, how such weaknesses have gotten in the way or impeded your progress. Recognize that they are still a part of you, but it is up to you to shrink them. You have more control here than you think.

Think about lessons learned over the years or when an approach you took backfired or flopped. It is possible you may readily identify such weaknesses through feelings of shame or guilt. Any memories that make you cringe to recall them are a good starting point. Now, it is important not to dwell on such feelings; rather, look at them objectively and tease out the feelings that prompted you to behave as you did at the time that still causes you to feel anger, resentment, shame, or guilt to this day. The trick is not to re-create or allow situations or environments in which weaknesses tend to take a leading role.

For example, think about supervisors you have worked with whose management style did not mesh well with your work style. Perhaps you prefer a good deal of autonomy but found yourself working for a micromanager, yet you were unable to stand up for yourself when his or her demands seemed unreasonable. Your weakness in this case may be in how you handle conflict.

Other weaknesses you discover about yourself may include, though are certainly not limited to: inability to exercise control over your emotions, procrastination, giving up too easily, authoritarianism, obsessive compulsiveness, self-consciousness, shyness, negativity, poor time management, foul language, lack of focus, hypersensitivity, easily influenced by others, willingness to engage in risky behavior, being contrary any chance you get, and more.

Identify yours. Write them down. Then think about ways to avoid or minimize being in situations where these tendencies are likely to take over. Unless you become a hermit and live in a cave, you will unlikely be able to eliminate the expression of all of your weaknesses. That is where heightened self-awareness comes into play, which allows you to recognize in advance the triggers that set such weaknesses in motion and learn to control them from the outset. And at the end of the day, remember, by focusing upon and further developing your strengths, your weaknesses will naturally become unimportant, even irrelevant. Let them!

LAND THAT JOB!

When is the last time you received constructive criticism at work? What were you told you do well? In what ways were you asked to improve and how? How did you handle this information?

It is a healthy exercise to think about constructive criticism received from others, including your colleagues and supervisors. Constructive criticism calls attention to a behavior you have expressed or demonstrated, articulates consequences of the behavior in a clear and understandable way, then recommends suggestions for improvement that are reasonable and warranted. There is nothing wrong with constructive criticism, especially when it is delivered with care and respect by someone who truly wants to see you succeed. It may be hard to hear, but it is crucial that you appreciate it for what it is; again, knowledge is power, and this type of information is worth its weight in gold. However, you have no reason to listen to or internalize plain old criticism that you sense is intended to demean, bully, or ridicule. Constructive criticism should provide clear suggestions for improvement. Negative criticism simply leaves you feeling awful and may serve only to motivate you to give up. It is crucial that you identify any such negativity from others in your life and do everything in your power to eliminate it. Elimination strategies may include a heart-to-heart discussion in which you provide constructive criticism or simply removing yourself from the presence of such individuals, temporarily or permanently.

Be Purposeful

Finally, strive every day to be purposeful in how you use your strengths and manage your weaknesses for the good of your career. Strategize how these elements translate into action steps that move you from one milestone to the next, ever closer to your goals. Be ethical and demonstrate integrity every step of the way.

Striving to be purposeful takes on several forms. One of these is to practice. You have probably heard the old adage "practice makes perfect," and it is through repetition that you build new skills. You don't master something doing it once, twice, or even 10 times. Practicing something diligently, day in and day out over a period of time, builds the activity into the natural rhythms of your life. For example, strive to polish your professional appearance by taking a little more time to get ready for work each day, or keep a journal and document after each shift what went well that day or moved you closer to a professional goal.

Another move is to set up or strengthen your support system. No one is an island unto themselves; you are a social animal, and we form communities around common needs. The need to succeed is universal; it is how we survive as a species. Survival by itself is a basic need; the goal here is to purposefully strive to succeed well. A strong, well-crafted support system can greatly enhance your successful accomplishment of professional goals. Such systems live and breathe in the background. You tap into them whenever you need them at a minimum, and regularly seek them out to be more proactive. This is what professional networking is all about and why we join professional organizations within which to learn from each other and create strategic partnerships. You have a personal support system as well, which can also enhance professional successes if your personal and professional supports are not at odds with one another. Look for congruency across these systems. Congruency can be further enhanced or diminished by geographic location, Internet access, belief structures, and personal behavior.

Your larger support systems are important, but as mentioned previously, they tend to exist more in the background. Therefore, smaller, more individualized partnerships are necessary to keep your goals in the forefront. You do this by getting a mentor or finding a partner who wants to accomplish the same goal so you can "buddy up," as two are often stronger than one. Reflect on who you might find to serve as a mentor. You don't have to be already acquainted with such a person, but simply start with the type of role they should hold to be of greatest value to you. You might identify such roles as charge nurse, nurse recruiter, director of human resources, or perhaps the president of a certain professional organization or CEO of a regional health care system. You should also seek out a partner with whom you can strive purposefully together. Look to your colleagues or fellow members of your professional organizations.

LAND THAT JOB!

Sketch out your support system and partners on a sheet of paper by placing yourself in the middle, along with a note about goals you wish to accomplish. Draw a circle around your name; then add two to three more concentric circles. Write partners' names in the first concentric circle outside of your name. Add names of people in your support system who actively support your goals in the next concentric circle. Add names of family, friends, and others who indirectly support or don't know about your professional goals to the next concentric circle. List anyone who actively does not support or disapproves outside of all the circles.

Additional ways to strive purposefully include activities such as keeping a journal, following industry trends, attending networking and social events, reading a self-help or inspirational book, enlisting the professional services of a coach or counselor, and setting aside the necessary time and space to make these activities possible.

All these steps, from conscious awareness to purposeful striving, serve to expand your comfort zone. By expanding your comfort zone, you expand the range of possibilities and opportunities available to you. By recognizing this, you will find you have more to talk about when networking with other professionals. Simply put, it all starts with you and what you are all about on the inside. Once you have a better handle on what is going on inside, you can take your knowledge and acceptance of strengths purposefully to those around you. Why? Because wherever you go, there you are. Bring your best and most purposeful self to the scene.

This chapter was geared to help you expand your awareness of just how much power you have through your strengths and how much control you can exert through self-awareness, reflection, and appreciation. There is much about job search that can leave you feeling powerless and without control if you let it. The point of this chapter is—don't let yourself be anything but your very best self as you go forward in your job search. You are an amazing and talented nurse; you know your strengths and can fully appreciate how your strengths and those of others create a work environment in which everyone can shine. In this, you can have real and lasting impact within the nursing community, so what are you waiting for? Turn the page to start exploring how you take all this personal and professional insight into the job market to enhance your search!

- ___ I have become consciously aware of my subjective sense of self and how it impacts both my behavior and my job search.
- ___ I have examined my strengths and weaknesses and understand how they impact my approach to change.
- ___ I have taken responsibility for my inner monologue and level of motivation.
- ___ I have identified my strengths and understand the importance of celebrating them regularly.
- ___ I know how to live purposefully going forward including active involvement of my larger support system.

3

The voyage of discovery is not in looking for new landscapes, but in looking with new eyes.

–Anonymous

Laying the Foundation for a Successful Search

You did a lot of work in the last chapter to identify and leverage your strengths, allow your weaknesses to fade into the background, and appreciate how everyone you work with also has a set of strengths to contribute to the cause. In job searching, a big piece to landing your next role has as much to do with your likeability as your nursing knowledge. This chapter shows you specific ways to apply what you learned in the last chapter for success in networking, interviewing, and more. In other words, you have strengthened the ongoing dialogue you have with yourself. Put that self-awareness to work with the people who can help you meet your job search goals. So, smile and jump in!

Knowing How Your Skills Fit Into the Market

Now that you have taken the time to discover the professional YOU, turn your attention to your skills. Nursing skills fall into two categories: technical and universal. Technical nursing skills include taking vitals, charting, working with electronic health records, using medical equipment, and interpreting medical information such as physicians' orders. Universal nursing skills include effective communication on the floor, organization and time management needed for timely patient care, and the critical thinking needed not only to spot errors but to note what is missing or not happening as it should.

LAND THAT JOB!

Make a list of the technical and universal nursing skills you possess. Don't hesitate to ask others for ideas or look online or in nursing journals to glean additional ideas.

After you have listed those ideas, rank them from strongest to weakest. The strongest are those you demonstrate daily if not hourly with a high level of proficiency. The weakest are those you do rarely or not well enough to claim expertise.

Make special note of the top five strongest ones in each category; conversely, cross off the weakest ones as moot, unless you will turn them into strengths within a year. For those you want to move from weak to strong, use the motivation exercise from Chapter 2 to map out a plan for success as well as a time frame for doing so.

LAND THAT JOB!

Write your top five strongest technical skills and top five universal skills. Add the strengths you identified in Chapter 1, such as responsibility, strategic thinking, and empathy.

You have now created your focal point for your next career move. What does this mean? Right in front of you, you have created a set of keywords to use on your resume, in any networking or interview setting, and as keywords in your search for job postings or professional development opportunities. These words are part of how you self-identify as a professional nurse. They serve as your guideposts, keeping your focus within the realm of your strengths and motivations. Doing so allows for greater authenticity within your job search and career development efforts. Greater authenticity helps to make the job search process more meaningful, as you are less likely to waste your time being too broad; it also paves the way for more genuine responses from you in both networking and interview situations.

Keywords can be used as a measuring stick of sorts to determine the strength of important terms within two-way communication. For example, suppose one of your professional keywords is pediatrics. You would use this word regularly in your conversations with others. You would use this keyword when looking for job postings of interest. The word pediatrics itself is commonly used and universally known in all medical circles. This would indicate a strong sense of alignment and congruence between your goals and passions with those in the health care professions. However, suppose you have a rather arcane or eccentric interest or passion around the now defunct and discredited field of phrenology, the study of the shape of a patient's skull to diagnose various ailments. No matter how fascinating and applicable you might find the topic, you would not find job postings along these lines, nor would you hear the topic broached in networking circles or as a point of inquiry within an interview. In other words, alignment and congruence would be very poor.

LAND THAT JOB!

Finalize and polish your list of the top 10 keywords you closely associate with your nursing specialty (technical skills) and your strengths (universal skills); create roughly five of each. Have this list handy as you read through the following sections on keyword usage.

Keywords When Networking

You will use your primary keywords often during networking opportunities. Repetitious use of your keywords creates a strong, direct associative link between you and those keywords so that within a relatively short span of time, others will think of you whenever they hear them. For example, suppose your primary keywords include pediatrics, rural hospital, public health, quality assurance, and management. Every time you introduce yourself to someone, you will use those keywords (or phrases).

With those keywords in mind, you might say, "Hello, my name is Sam. Isn't this a great event? I love being able to connect with other public health professionals with a passion for pediatrics and quality assurance in rural settings. That is what I am all about! What about you?" The conversational ebb and flow can then be steered toward projects you've worked on, again including primary keywords. You might share a story about specific ways your efforts combining pediatrics, quality assurance, and rural public health settings directly benefitted your young patients and their families (without divulging any identifying information, of course).

LAND THAT JOB!

How have you introduced yourself at networking events, workshops, or seminars? Do you take the initiative and introduce yourself or do you tend to wait for others to take the lead?

Practice combining your keywords into introductory and conversation-sustaining statements and questions. Create a "bank" of such approaches that you can use over and over again with every new person you meet. When you encounter the same individuals again in other settings, catch them up to speed on what you've done or worked on since you last spoke. To solicit new leads, ask them for the names of individuals, organizations, or projects they are aware of that fall within your job search and professional development activities. Be sure to ask for their business card and jot a note on the back about the people, places, or projects they recommend you look into. You can also supply them with your card. Do not hesitate to write relevant keywords directly on your card so that they can easily recall who you are and what you spoke about.

When you encounter them again, ask again. They might not have known of any people or projects the first time you asked, but your initial conversation likely planted a seed that has germinated over time. When they stumble across such information, they will think of you or perhaps even mention your name to those associated with the new information. Ask them to do so at the close of any conversation, in addition to setting up a time to follow up in the near future in order to keep the conversation flowing in other settings. Do the same for them in return. This is one of the ways to build partnerships within your larger support system.

How many networking events have you participated in over the past 6-12 months? Did you naturally use certain keywords or phrases each time you met someone new?

Keywords Within Professional Development Opportunities

You will use the same approach when networking within your professional organizations. If you do not already belong to at least three such organizations, start shopping around for the best, most relevant ones to support your professional objectives. Conduct an Internet search using your keywords along with the phrase "list of professional organizations" or "directory of professional organizations." Stop by your library and share with the reference librarian what it is you wish to accomplish. He or she can direct you, not only to organization names, but to their publications as well. Ask other professionals whom you stumble across in person or online about any organizations they can suggest.

Look for organizations that are highly active, are passionate about the same issues as you, and have a local presence that will enable you to interact directly with their members. There may be a cost, so do your homework to get your money's worth. Ask about trial memberships or attend a conference as a non-member first. Find existing members and ask how the organizations have directly supported their own professional objectives. Request concrete examples so you can evaluate to what extent their expectations are reasonable. For example, if someone paid a hefty membership fee then just sat back and waited "for something to happen magically for their career," they are not the best source of information.

Other tips that separate average organizations from exceptional ones include, but are not limited to, the extent that you hear their name come up again and again and in the most positive terms; other professionals talk about the organization as a "must"; its website is full of new and useful information that is easy to navigate; and its membership fee includes value-added components, such as networking events, a monthly newsletter or other publication, a career resource area, job postings, member bios, and more.

LAND THAT JOB!

Which professional organizations do you belong to already? Which ones have caught your interest and are likely candidates to help you move forward?

Once you are a member of at least two organizations, plug their events into your calendar and make sure you interact with them at least once per month. At a minimum, put a reminder in your calendar to visit their website and review new information relevant to your objectives.

Consider these approaches for building your keywords into correspondence and relationship-building opportunities:

- Personally thank contributing authors within an organization for their information, and state why or how you found their article so helpful.
- Offer to assist on current and relevant projects the organization or its members are working on.
- Make a point to introduce yourself online to any and all new members, along with a quick blurb about yourself.
- If the group has an online discussion forum, weigh in on the topics with your own expertise. Aim to contribute to the existing body of knowledge.
- Be sure not to antagonize anyone or disparage any ideas; that is wholly counterproductive, and you might not be able to recover from such a faux pas within that group.
- Be courteous, gracious, and wise at all times.
- Use your primary keywords within your discussions. Online discussion forums are an excellent networking opportunity.
- If you have the opportunity to build an online profile, be sure to do so in a professional way that, of course, incorporates and celebrates your primary keywords.

Keywords Within Job Postings

You have your keywords, and employers have theirs. Their keywords show up in many places: their mission statement, marketing materials, website, and job postings. Job posting keywords fall into four categories: the job title itself; the essential duties or functions; the environment/location in which they occur; and the qualifications, whether required or desired.

Job title keywords and phrases may include nurse, nursing, nurse practitioner, registered nurse, RN, LPN, nurse supervisor, charge nurse, nurse case manager, nurse advisor, nurse consultant, etc. Titles often include the shift to be worked or specialty in question, as well as whether such roles are full-time, part-time, on-call, or traveling.

Job function key phrases might include provide total nursing care, operate and maintain medical equipment and devices, ensure safety, follow physicians' orders, maintain constant vigilance, execute standards of nursing practice, develop and revise care plans, ensure compliance and ethical behavior, report issues or concerns, process admissions, promote excellent patient care, provide referrals, document care provided, answer unit phones, and provide excellent customer service to patients and their loved ones.

Environmental keywords are those that focus on the populations, settings, and location(s). If the nursing specialty wasn't a keyword in the job title itself, it will show up in this second category. Specialties include pediatrics, cardiac, geriatric, orthopedic, psychiatric, neonatal, emergency care, hospice, anesthesia, education, ICU, insurance, etc. Environments can include everything from the actual location to the setting, such as rural, suburban, urban, or inner-city. Environment may describe the place where nursing care is provided, such as hospitals, schools, military bases, or community agencies. It can include patient populations served or approaches emphasized, such as ventilator-dependent, addiction recovery, integrative health, healing arts, cancer care, IV therapy, assisted living, Medicaid, cosmetic/elective, ambulatory care, lifestyle and nutrition, vocational, end-of-life care, burn care, rehabilitative, nursing students, and much more.

Qualification keywords and phrases fall into required/essential and desired/preferred categories. Required qualifications may include a specific nursing degree, such as LPN, ADN, BSN, MSN, and DNS from accredited colleges; BLS, ACLS, and CPR certifications; and state licensure. Desired qualifications might include a minimum number of years of related experience, previous leadership or management roles, additional certifications, fluency in another language, and proficiency with specific electronic health record systems. However, it should be noted that it is the employer's prerogative as to which qualifications are required or desired. Five years of related experience might be a desired qualification with one employer, yet an essential requirement for another.

Job postings for nursing positions range from the most minimal information to extensively detailed descriptions. When job postings used to be featured primarily in newspapers that charge per line per square inch, a minimalist approach was understandably favored. Today, greater detail has become the norm, with unlimited space available online and a desire to provide more information to enhance an applicant's fuller understanding of the expectations. That doesn't mean you won't still come across plenty of minimalist postings, but such limited scope and depth are not proactive nor welcoming from a recruiting standpoint.

Your goal here is to align or create congruency between the keywords of prospective employers and your own. If you conduct an online search for "nursing jobs" and no other keywords, you will be inundated with 100 million results. Narrow your search by identifying the desired location, which yields fewer than 100,000 in Greenfield, Massachusetts, to 500,000 in Minneapolis, Minnesota, to 15 million in New York City. Further refine your search by specialty. Another strongly recommended approach is to search for health care systems, clinics, or other organizations that specifically meet two or more of your keywords, regardless of whether they are hiring. For example, you could conduct an online search for "hospital and pediatrics and Tampa," "directory of nonprofit health care organizations in Sacramento," or "list of burn centers in Toronto."

LAND THAT JOB!

Where do you tend to look for job postings? Are the postings you find detailed or sparse in terms of content? Why do you think that is?

No matter what approach you take, strive for alignment between your keywords and theirs. This practice is essential to finding the best fit for your needs and strengths. Job postings are an excellent source of information. However, focusing on the companies for which you'd like to work is more important. Even if they do not currently have an opening, they certainly will in the future.

Keywords on Resumes

The alignment or congruence mentioned in the last section comes to life on your resume through the interplay of your keywords and those of the health care companies that interest you the most. After you have determined your best keywords and found companies that share those keywords with you, it's time to capture them strategically on your resume.

Your resume is a strategic document that markets your strengths, skills, and experience specifically to the organizations you want to work for. Too often, resumes are "stuck in the past," by merely listing what a nurse has done with no specific goal identified or concrete evidence for that goal. This is called a backward-looking resume.

You want a resume that is forward-looking. Your keywords help you accomplish this in the way you weave them into your past as support for what you want to do going forward. Taking it a step further, your keywords become part of your professional profile that immediately expresses the type of role you are looking for and why.

LAND THAT JOB!

Do you have an existing resume? If so, what keywords have you emphasized within the document? To what extent are the keywords you listed aligned with your professional objectives? Does your resume seem more backward- or forward-looking? Ask a trusted colleague, mentor, or friend to review your resume with these questions in mind. Listen carefully to their feedback. Resumes will be covered in much greater detail in Chapter 4.

Keywords in Interviews

Interviews allow prospective employers to gauge whether you are ready, willing, and able to do the job in question. By analyzing and understanding what they expect of you on the job through keywords and phrases from job postings and other sources, you are in a far stronger position to convey that you are indeed ready, willing, and able to fit into their team and shine as a professional nurse in that environment. In an interview, you want to demonstrate the alignment or congruence that you initially captured in networking situations and on your resume. When you have the opportunity for informational interviews, be sure to learn which keywords they consider important. In formal interviews, take care to demonstrate how their essential keywords are yours as well. There is more to it, of course, and interviews will be covered in greater detail in Chapter 8.

Don't Guess—Find Out

You can guess which keywords are important, but you won't actually know. So, gauge to what extent your keywords are aligned with those of an employer. You can only determine this through investigation, which requires you to "do your homework" versus assuming they are the same or at least similar. Common (and faulty) assumptions in the nursing profession include but are not limited to:

> All nursing jobs and health care companies are basically the same.
>
> A nursing degree is all that is needed; just apply and get hired.
>
> Nurses don't need resumes or cover letters.
>
> Getting hired all depends on luck anyway.

None of the above is true, and assumptions only hold you back. Even if you think you "know" certain facts and essential keywords, every once in a while, you need to check your assumptions for accuracy. Reading this book helps.

Here is an exercise you can do with job postings you identify. You can use the results of this exercise in Chapter 4, which focuses on resumes. Follow these four steps:

1. Locate five job postings online that are close to what you are looking for in terms of specialty and location. Even if you are not currently looking for a new opportunity, it is a great way to test assumptions you plan to act on the next time you seek a new role. Print them off and lay them out side by side. Grab different colored pens or highlighters for the next step.
2. Identify common elements across each of the postings and mark them all the same color. To qualify as a common element, the same keyword or phrase should appear in at least three of the five postings. Circle all the common elements you spot. For example, they might all use the word "nurse" in the title. Nurse, then, would be a common element.

RN, nursing degree, and nursing duties are all keywords that could appear across all five postings. Perhaps they are all (or mostly) positions within a hospital system. Your nursing specialty may also be a common element appearing across all or most of the postings. Other keywords and phrases, such as quality or electronic health records, may serve as common elements.

3. Seek out important but uncommon elements with a different colored pen. Important but uncommon elements are keywords and phrases that appear in only one or two postings. Look for words and phrases (or acronyms) such as acute care, ICU, Alzheimer's, or overnights. You can likely spot recurring words easily; then, it is just a matter of determining if they are common (appearing across at least three of the five postings) or uncommon (appearing in only one or two of the five postings).
4. Sit back and visually scan the "larger picture." Compare the amount of one color with the others. More of the common element color indicates that the postings you chose are well-aligned with your focus. If the dominant color reflects uncommon elements, it could reveal a lack of focus on your part. It could also suggest that companies are intentionally striving to differentiate themselves from their competition, even if they use the same job titles.

   If you determine that your focus isn't clear enough, revisit your strengths and try the exercise again using new postings with a clearer common focus. If the latter, reflect on how your keywords and approaches in different scenarios should differ with each unique organization.

Based on your observations, you should now know and be able to make a list of the keywords and phrases most important to positions and employers you want to target. You can use your list for searching job descriptions, exploring professional organizations, and in networking situations. Keep your highlighted descriptions handy for use in Chapter 4.

Company Insiders Are Your New Best Friends

A primary goal throughout your job search or career development effort is to build relationships with other health care professionals both within your geographic area and your specialty. Why? Company insiders within hospitals, clinics, insurance companies, and nonprofit health care organizations are your best sources of information. Getting to know them will make your job of "digging deeper" for facts versus relying on assumptions far easier, and company insiders are more accessible than you think.

The first step is to find them—in hospitals, clinics, schools, insurance companies, public health agencies, nonprofit health care organizations, and more. Identify all the local professional organizations they might belong to. Create a list of at least 25 such places if you reside in a metropolitan area. Find at least 10 in outlying or rural areas.

Next, identify at least one person associated with each facility. This can be accomplished in a number of ways. Be sure to work all angles rather than relying on just one approach. In order to "get a name" for each place on your list, ask everyone you know for the name, job title, and contact information of anyone they know who works or belongs there. Review membership lists to glean useful insights. Explore professional networking websites such as LinkedIn, which allows you to search industries, companies, and individuals within any geographic location. Connect with them through shared groups and introductions. Although Facebook is considered "social" versus professional, it is another promising tool for job searching, because it allows you to connect to professionals through people you already know. Clue your network into your job search status and see job postings in the Marketplace. Look for management team biographies on company websites.

Now you are ready to make contact with those you identify. Apply your critical thinking skills here and determine the best approach. Send a customized connection invite in which you state why you wish to connect with them that suggests a mutually beneficial discussion. Introduce yourself online to members of groups you have joined to discuss shared interests. When introduced to other professionals, make the most of the opportunity by finding out more about them and what their professional objectives include. Attend conferences and networking events that cater to your target market and get conversations off to a strong start.

This step compels you to find a common link with those professionals with whom you want to connect.

LAND THAT JOB!

Have you ever used social media to help you meet your professional objectives? Which social media resources have you tried? Have you identified successful strategies? When was the last time you participated in a professional discussion or forum online? Are you comfortable attending workshops and seminars by yourself, or do you attend with others whenever possible?

Developing Confidence

Networking is a form of sales and marketing. The product is you and your talents. Does the idea of "selling yourself" feel uncomfortable? If so, your feelings about networking may result in diminished confidence. Always remember that networking starts by simply being able to talk to others and establishing common ground. You do this now when working with patients and their loved ones. Why is it so easy to do with patients and those who love them? Because you are addressing a need they have.

In sales, this is called "finding their pain" and easing it with a solution you are able to provide: the perfect analogy for health care professionals. You already know all about easing one's pain. You intuitively sense discomfort. You know which questions to ask to get at the root of patients' discomfort. You know what solutions exist to help make them more comfortable. In short, you practice this type of skill every day.

The trick is to shift to a different audience and apply the same skills for their benefit. You have an added edge in that your audience of professionals is busy addressing other people's pain. Often their own needs are put on the back burner. To have someone assist in easing their own professional pain can be a great comfort, indeed. You know this intuitively, and you can probably recall a time when someone has helped you with a professional need and the feeling of relief that washed over you. Your goal is to create that sense of professional relief for others, who can help you in turn.

LAND THAT JOB!

How comfortable are you with the ideas of networking and marketing your skills? Think back on recent conversations you have had with other professionals, and identify concerns or needs. How can you take what was complained about and turn it into a positive by offering your services?

Now that you have a more positive picture of networking than you may have previously held, turn your attention to confidence-building exercises that will help you "make the sale" or "close the deal."

Start with the list of companies and organizations you identified. Round out this list to include as many entities as possible as a way to diversify your target market. Diversification is an investment term. The idea is to create multiple investment options versus "putting all your eggs in one basket." The more options you have, the stronger your position and the greater likelihood of success. Don't limit yourself; in fact, rule everything in at this point versus out. There is no room for judgment at this stage of the game. Any idea you find yourself saying "no" to should be added to your list without a second thought.

Now think about the types of professionals and the positions they hold at each place on your list. This includes nurses, nursing supervisors, health care directors, and recruiters. Looking at it this way, you are immediately encouraged to find not just one name for each place, but to take a more dynamic "approach and investigate those in all such roles, as they will interrelate and support one another in various ways. Think about the "professional pain" people in each of these roles might feel and how you might ease such discomfort. Evaluate the ways in which you can form a common bond. Other nurses may be in need of moral support within a stressful, demanding role. You could indicate that you are looking to build up your network of professional nursing contacts and resources within your peer group. You can ask about "wish list" items they may have in terms of their own professional development or how they successfully maintain a healthy work/life balance. Find out who is also attending a particular conference or networking event and offer to "buddy up." Ask for their opinion and advice on best job search resources in your area. Find other nurses to start a weekly coffee group to share additional ideas and concerns.

If you feel it is easiest to talk among your peer group, start with them. Get as many conversations going as you possibly can. Once you establish contact with them and get a feel for how open they are to continuing a dialogue, you can build a stronger rapport. Once you've established solid rapport, you can press for them to recommend a health care search firm, put you in touch with their favorite nurse recruiter, give you a tour of their facility sometime, or arrange an informational interview for you with someone at their company. This interaction provides additional networking practice, which builds further confidence.

LAND THAT JOB!

Identify at least 10 nurses and health care professionals you already know. How often do you chat about common professional interests? How might you formalize such discussions and be more proactive about furthering such interests together?

Employ this same approach of establishing contact, starting a dialogue, building rapport, and making specific requests (and honoring theirs) with nurse recruiters, nursing supervisors, medical directors, public health directors, officers and board members of professional organizations, and more. In each case, find out what their "pain" looks like. This is a common sales approach that you can use just as effectively as anyone selling a product or service in a business-to-business environment.

Nurse recruiters have open positions to fill and must do so quickly as a matter of demonstrating solid job performance. Remember that nurse recruiters work for health care entities, not you, so approach them as a potential partner with whom to build a mutually beneficial relationship. Learn what positions they need to fill and, if none are right for you, recommend potential candidates or offer to send someone their way (and make sure that person references your name to demonstrate that you made good on your offer). Also, ask nurse recruiters to describe the kind of nurse that dominates the top of their candidate pool. In other words, find out how you can become the first nurse they call when something opens up that matches your talents.

Nursing supervisors also have open positions to fill and work in tandem with recruiters to do so. But supervisors also have quality-of-care concerns, performance issues to deal with, special projects to complete, cost constraints to work within, and more. They are always pressed for time. Find out which recruiters they work with and if they have a favorite. Request a brief informational interview to learn what makes an ideal candidate in their eyes. Demonstrate alignment between their needs and what you have to offer. Find out what is making their job more stressful right now or what is coming down the pike that will require them to change their approaches. They might not have anything for you at the moment, so offer to stay in touch and then do so regularly. This helps you to stay on their radar as someone ready, willing, and able to help out wherever and however needed.

Public health directors and medical directors of nonprofit organizations often need volunteers. Find out what their needs are and offer your services. You may help serve a particularly challenging population, promote an awareness or educational campaign, or collect data.

Professional organizations also need volunteers. Volunteerism can include holding an officer role, organizing their next conference, driving membership campaigns, or assisting with all kinds of needs. All of these organizations look to their volunteers first when paid positions become available. Volunteer opportunities exist for all skill levels, from current nursing students looking to strengthen their resume for better employment prospects when they graduate to retired professionals with more time to give back.

Although no single strategy is completely foolproof or guaranteed to work every time, by diversifying your targets and your contacts you can work this process over time and gain momentum toward your desired results.

Not everyone responds, and don't take it personally if they don't. Some may not respond right away, yet you'll hear from them weeks later. Networking is a process, and it does not happen overnight; rather, it can take weeks or months, but once developed, it takes on a life of its own and will become as natural as breathing. While you may hit shorter-term job search objectives along the way, this approach and the momentum it spurs will benefit your career development efforts over the long term. Once started, don't stop. Continue to grow and strengthen your network.

The No. 1 mistake job seekers make is to let all that hard-earned momentum come to an immediate halt as soon as they land a new job. Don't be shortsighted. Well-developed contacts and a strong professional network are worth their weight in gold. When you do land your next role, you can turn your attention to helping others as they helped you. You may find you still have needs, but the focus has changed to adapting in your new role. Mentors can come in handy while you get up to speed. Either way, your needs will surface again, sooner or later, and when they do, you will be loathe to have to start over from scratch.

Networking Events for Nurses

Networking events can happen in person or online. If in person, you need to add your location to the search terms. If online, it may help to note your specialty. Networking events can include job search support groups, local events hosted by a professional organization, hospital or health care-related fundraisers, book signing events for local health care authors, meetup groups, job fairs, topical workshops and seminars, health care organization open houses, and more. Narrow your search by year (e.g., 2013) to see what is to come and to eliminate events that have already passed. There may be a fee associated with them, and it is up to you to determine if only free events are viable or if you believe that "you get what you pay for." A nominal fee to cover basic costs to promote the event or provide food and drink is not uncommon or unreasonable. Tip: Set up Google Alerts to "save" your search terms and receive an e-mail as soon as a new entry is posted online that meets your search criteria.

As explained in Chapter 2, the conversations you hold internally are reflected in those you conduct externally. Keeping your inner monologue healthy and positive paves the way for proactive and successful networking opportunities and outcomes. Career development exploration for nurses is a skill set in its own right. Coupled with the reflective and hands-on exercises in this chapter that are designed to spark new approaches based on your strengths and the needs in the workplace, your own job search and career development initiatives are bound to flourish. Use your skills well and often!

Best Candidate Checklist

___ I have identified how my skills directly and indirectly fit into the nursing job market.

___ I have created a focal point for my next career move.

___ I have determined the essential keywords that drive my job search communications with others.

___ I have prepared a bank of opening lines and objectives to communicate across a variety of networking situations.

___ I have identified and joined at least three professional organizations that directly relate to my career.

___ I have analyzed the contents of five similar nurse job postings and identified both common and unique elements.

___ I have created a list of 25 or more places where I would like to work and have started to reach out to company insiders at each location.

___ I have started to actively network with other nursing and health care professionals to aid my job search.

___ I have developed an organizational system in which to store and track my contacts and networking results for each company of interest.

4

Be yourself. Above all, let who you are, what you are, and what you believe shine through every sentence you write, every piece you finish.

–John Jakes

The Heart of Resumes and Cover Letters

Many health care systems make robust use of online applications. Modern day recruiting makes use of a combined approach whereby you fill out database fields within an application online and then upload your corresponding resume and cover letter. In some cases, the online application will "read" your uploaded resume and populate the database fields for you, and all you need to do is check it for accuracy. Your resume and cover letter are marketing materials designed to command attention. An application form (paper-based or online) is a legal document that all employers ultimately need to show they have done their due diligence throughout the hiring process. Chapter 4 shows you how to navigate both routes to achieve the same end.

Follow-up Starts Sooner Than Later

Now that you're comfortable with networking, you can slide seamlessly into how resumes are used to support your networking efforts instead of the other way around. What?! Yes, it is a novel idea for most people and highlights yet another common misconception in job searching. This is one of the surest ways to set yourself apart from your competition: Start with networking, and follow up with a resume and cover letter. In other words, your resume should not be your first point of contact with a prospective employer. Rather, it should be one of the follow-up activities to your networking efforts. Because your career development goals may not include job searching at this time, this section provides examples to use for any professional goals.

Your networking activities are more important than writing your resume —believe it! Think about it. Whenever you start and maintain a dialogue with other nursing and health care professionals, your focus is on one or more professional objectives that you want to accomplish. Whether your goal is to build up your professional acquaintances, gain professional advice, join a project, volunteer at a future event, advance within your organization, or land a new position, it all starts with talking. Talking is a two-way communication activity in which information and ideas are exchanged through questions and answers. It is through such exchanges that you determine critical knowledge such as how strong an ally or partner the other person is in helping to meet your goals, what their needs are, and how you can assist them in meeting their own short- and long-term objectives.

Without this additional and critical knowledge, you also won't know which details to capture in your resume or cover letters that will command their attention. Unless you get them to stand up and take notice, your resume and cover letter writing efforts are for naught. Do not waste your time. The task of writing becomes much easier when you have a clear idea of who your audience is, what they are like, what is most important to them, and other information that you and other job seekers could never glean from a job posting alone.

Imagine your audience expecting your resume and cover letter—indeed, looking forward to seeing it because you have paved the way through your networking activities. You know instinctively that this is a more effective approach than blindly sending out your materials.

Paving the Way

There are numerous avenues that "pave the way" for your follow-up materials to take root and flower into something productive.

First, learn about project or hiring needs whenever you are at any event, function, or environment in which people are exchanging ideas. Before parting ways, be sure to specify how and when you will be following up. Then, follow through with confidence. Do as you promised. Following up can include sending your resume and cover letter, sending a schedule by which you can contribute to a project, or forwarding them the name and contact information of someone you know who can help them.

Second, you can ask someone to speak on your behalf. For example, maybe you can't get a direct audience with someone important, but you know someone who can. Work with that intermediary person on what to say and the context in which that exchange should occur. In other words, take control and be specific about the objective at hand. Such exchanges that occur without you should not go unrehearsed or be vague in their intent. Literally practice with that person the exchange that is to take place. Don't simply say, "Find out if they are hiring." Rather, ask them to speak personally with the individual in question. Have them "set the stage" by indicating they know of a pressing need and how to help solve it. They should introduce the idea of you from a position of strength, in positive and glowing terms. Have your intermediary indicate that you will be sending a resume and cover letter within the next 2 days, or that you will be calling them to discuss the project, or to give/receive advice. Your intermediary can indicate that you wish to schedule an informational interview by phone, e-mail or in person—whichever is easiest or more convenient for the person granting the interview. You want your go-between to do just enough to set the stage so you can take it from there.

Third, you can reach out directly. For example, professional networking sites such as LinkedIn allow you to invite other professionals into your network. Do not fret about whether the places you'd like to approach are hiring right now;

in fact, use this technique with those that are not presently hiring. Once you have invited them to join your professional network (using a custom invitation versus the canned one provided), and they have accepted, you are free to continue a dialogue with them. To encourage a productive conversation, you can write: "Hello ___________, I've been following your company for a while now, and I believe you are a clear leader in alternative health in the metro area. Although it appears you are not hiring right now, I'm taking this opportunity to introduce myself to pave the way for an interview when the time is appropriate. Thank you." This is especially effective, as the recipient can simply click to review your profile to get an idea of your strengths and talents. In turn, you help them to build a candidate pool for future hiring needs. You can also call them on the phone and say roughly the same thing.

If you are not job searching right now, you can use this same approach to help realize whatever your goals may include. For example, you can write: "Hello ___________, I noticed on your profile that you are involved with developing creative new approaches for improving geriatric quality of life. As I share similar interests, I'd like to add you to my professional network." Similarly, you can join groups with other like-minded nursing or health care professionals, and you can weigh in on questions in which your professional expertise provides valuable perspective.

The objective is to get an initial response that paves the way for further dialogue. For example, you send an introduction, and they respond by "accepting." You can then send a follow-up message such as, "Thank you for accepting my invitation. It appears we have similar interests within the geriatric care community. I'm interested in connecting with others to see if there are common project themes underway. May I ask what projects you are working on?"

You can focus on any idea of interest so long as it follows the formula of a) make contact by inviting them to join your network by establishing a common bond/interest or have someone reach out on your behalf, b) get an initial, positive response such as having your invite accepted, and c) ask a follow-up question to start a dialogue. Here are additional examples that follow this formula:

Make contact	Get initial, positive response	Follow-up
Meet someone at a networking event and discover common interests.	Tell them you'll call them tomorrow with specific dates you can help them on their project and they say, "Great!"	Call them tomorrow after consulting your calendar to find dates you can commit to. Go forward.
Ask HR to help you connect with an internal mentor who will help you successfully navigate your new role.	They say, "Sure!" and suggest you connect with someone in particular; they will help pave the way with an e-mail introduction.	E-mail them asking about their availability to connect for 30 minutes each week at a place of their choosing. Go forward and never miss a meeting.
Reach out to 10 group members on a professional networking site with a custom connection invite.	Count how many of the 10 accept your invite; for example, you hear back from four of them within the first few days, and four more a week later, but no word from the last two.	Thank each one as they respond, and let them know how their advice helps you. Ask another related question if appropriate, invite them to join your network, or find other ways to maintain and strengthen your new connections.

Make contact	Get initial, positive response	Follow-up
Find a job posting of interest and connect with someone you know who already works there to indicate your interest. Ask them for information about the hiring manager.	They tell you the person's name and title with correct spelling, as well as what projects they are working on, what they're passionate about on the job, and more. They also say they are happy to put in a good word for you and to tell them to watch for your resume and cover letter to come to their attention.	The next day, route your customized materials to the hiring manager, along with a duplicate set to the person who recommended you and to HR. Incorporate everything you learned from your contact into your materials to show that you will be an excellent fit for the role and within the hiring manager's team.

You won't get a response every time, but don't take it personally. They may have already identified an internal candidate who has proven himself/herself ready for a promotion; there may be a temporary hiring freeze; or they've decided to take this opportunity to restructure the position. The hiring process could simply take longer than anyone anticipated. Maybe strong competition for the role beat you fair and square. In an online outreach scenario, an intended recipient might not have the time to take on anything more at this time. There are a thousand reasons.

Ways to improve your response rate include being very professional in your approach, demonstrating excellent writing skills free of typos and grammatical errors, keeping it simple, showing your willingness to help them versus making it all about you, following up again in a few days if you don't hear anything at first, and being gracious and respectful.

LAND THAT JOB!

Whom do you know who can positively and professionally get someone's attention on your behalf?

Make a list of 10 people you know, along with a note about someone they know whom they could connect you to with a specific objective in mind. Noteworthy others could include their supervisor, someone further up the chain at work, someone within a professional group, a networking or social club, a well-connected neighbor or family member. Different connections can help you meet different objectives; that said, try to focus on no more than two or three at a time, lest your activities become too fragmented.

The Anatomy of a Successful Resume

Resumes are living, breathing documents that have an anatomy just like other living things. They are ever-evolving, never static. Your resume should work for you, never against you. Strive to keep your vibrant, dynamic, glowing resume in the very best of health. The anatomy of a resume is comprised of the following parts, which will vary a bit based on your experience and certifications.

Name and contact information

Title bar

Professional profile

Customizable skills area

Education and certifications

Clinical rotations

Preceptorships

Clinical nursing experience (work history)

Non-nursing experience (if applicable)

Volunteerism

Publications

Honors and awards

Where to learn more

One hallmark of a great resume is experience. There is nothing like writing a resume to make you doubt and find holes in your own experience and skill sets. New nurses are especially vulnerable to "resume doubts" and can't do enough to strengthen their resume. More experienced nurses, by contrast, run the risk of doing too little, especially if they assume that simply being a nurse is all you need to change jobs. Nothing beats experience. That said, experience can be made moot by arrogance or passivity. All experience is strengthened through networking activities.

Do not assume you are an automatic shoo-in for any job you desire because you have 20+ years experience—never underestimate the competition. However, your excellent credentials, networking skills, resume, and interviewing skills will put you above most if not all of your competition. For those of you approaching semiretirement, leverage your incredible experience to craft a position that you will enjoy and that will help you meet your retirement objectives. This is where networking pays off. Talk to everyone and anyone about the role you'd like to craft for yourself and enjoy for the next several years. Chances are you have seen so much, survived just about every triage situation one can think of, and been able to calm down the most hysterical patients and irate or untested physicians; you could nurse a small city with your eyes closed and one arm tied behind your back. Look for organizations that need exactly that level of competence and confidence within an autonomous role that allows you some flexibility and creativity while earning a paycheck and socking away retirement savings.

What does that mean for nursing graduates and newer nurses who don't have 20 years' experience? It's all about balance. Offset your weaknesses with strength and a willingness to start anywhere.

Nursing students must develop professional nursing contacts, work in-field as a certified nursing assistant, and volunteer in caregiver situations as much as possible while in school. Become a student member in professional nursing organizations; join a student chapter on campus and take on a leadership role. If you graduated from school and have not landed your first professional role yet, you have some catching up to do. Develop professional nursing contacts, work part-time or apply for roles in settings that need help, even if it is not part of your long-term plan, and/or become a nurse volunteer to round out your experience.

Once you have at least 2 years of experience, you are certainly on stronger ground, but that doesn't mean you can rest on your laurels. Rather, you must move into a growth phase where you refine your day-to-day skills with an eye toward your development and advancement within the field. This is when you acquire additional certifications, keep up on your continuing education requirements, join additional professional organizations, and make networking a weekly endeavor.

Nurses with 8-12 years of experience may be looking for senior-level management roles or leadership roles on a board of directors or within a professional organization. At this level, you may be seeking a creative outlet for your talents, such as writing an advice column or book. Networking continues to serve as the catalyst for new and intriguing endeavors. And as discussed above, once you have 25+ years of nursing experience under your scrubs, you can craft career plans to move into semiretirement at a point of your choosing.

Now that you've strategized your experience level, turn your attention to the anatomy of your resume. The following sections walk you through how to approach each one, from your name to how you wrap up your document at the very end.

Name and Contact Information

The first thing anyone sees on your resume is your name. Therefore, use a 14-point, bolded font here. Your name should be followed by professional designations such as RN, LPN, etc. If you go by a nickname, you can insert it in quotes between your first and last name or leave it out until you meet the interviewer in person.

Your contact information should be current and the same font size as the body of your resume, no bolding. You can include as much or as little contact information as needed. For example, if you are looking to relocate but haven't moved yet, you might want to omit your mailing address and simply provide a phone number and e-mail address instead, so that you don't appear "anchored" outside of the hiring area. If you do list your mailing address, include your ZIP code, as this can be a helpful search tool for recruiters. You can also save space by listing your address on just one line versus two, with a spacer (•) inserted between your street address and your city, state, and ZIP (see examples). A spacer is simply a text symbol inserted to create a visual break between two pieces of information on the same line. In Microsoft Word, go to Insert > Symbol and pick a simple one that appeals to you.

Your name and contact information should never be in the header of your resume, nor should it be tabled or have graphics attached, as it can be harder for automated applicant tracking systems to read information that isn't text-based. So, beware of using any resume templates such as those you can download from Microsoft or other sites. Many of those were created before the conception and explosive use of applicant tracking systems (ATS). The following are examples of how you might show your contact information.

Lisa LaRue, RN
1212 Galaxy Way
Memphis, TN 55555
789.456.1233
Llarue45@gmail.com

Lisa LaRue, RN
789.456.1233
Llarue45@gmail.com

Lisa LaRue, RN
1212 Galaxy Way • Memphis, TN 55555
789.456.1233 • Llarue45@gmail.com

Title Bar

Although the first thing your audience sees on your resume is your name, you want them to associate your name with what you are about. That's where a title bar comes in. A title bar appears just below your name and contact information, is centered, and appears in bolded text or all capitals. It contains one to three keywords or key phrases, including the job title you are targeting. If you have included a professional designation just after your name, such as RN, you would actually spell it out in your title bar. Suppose you saw a job posting that highlighted the need for an RN to provide exceptionally compassionate care while ensuring high quality and accurate documentation. Your title bar might look like this:

Registered Nurse • Compassionate • Accurate

Your title bar should illuminate whatever is most important to your audience. Since your audience changes with each application, the title bar becomes an easy point of customization. You can pull ideas for your title bar from keywords or phrases used repeatedly in a posting, in a networking encounter, or in an informational interview session. You can also look to the desired qualifications area of a posting to show how you exceed minimums at first glance. Whichever two or three you pick are entirely up to you, so long as they are relevant to your target audience, and what you choose can be comprised of skills or attributes.

Professional Profile

Your profile gives your reader a brief description of what you can bring to a nursing role in the here and now. You want a profile that highlights the relevant skills you can bring to the job today, but that will also grow with the job. It is not all about your past. Direct your profile toward the future.

Remember that exercise in Chapter 3 in which you gathered five similar job postings of interest and analyzed them for common elements? Those common elements are exactly what you want to highlight in your professional profile, so long as they are also true for you. For example, if four of the five postings indicate that experience with a specific type of health records management system is desired, then that type of software is a common element. If you also have experience with that software, great; list it in your profile. But if you have not worked with it, then you should not list it, even though it is a common element. Why? Because it would not be true for you. It is not one of the elements you have in common with nursing postings you reviewed and compared.

Suppose for a moment that you have conducted the exercise from Chapter 3 and determined that the common elements across most if not all of the postings you surveyed include the following: RN degree, BSN preferred, BLS and ACLS certification required, experience with EPIC desired, case management experience required, hospital setting, state licensure, able to work independently and exercise autonomous judgment, and ability to handle complex behavioral situations. If all of these common elements were true for you, your professional profile might look something like this:

> *Registered nurse with earned BSN and 14 years' experience caring for individuals across a full spectrum of medical needs in hospital settings and case management roles. Hold current BLS and ACLS certification as well as TX state licensure. Over 1 year of daily experience with EPIC; demonstrated ability to ensure accuracy and timeliness of all entries. Recognized ability to work independently and exercise autonomous judgment while handling complex behavioral situations.*

Notice the emphasis is on the common elements. This means your profile rarely requires customization, because you already show the attributes of the nursing roles you're targeting. Looking ahead, you will want to support each of your profile statements within the work history section of your resume. Remember when you had to write a paper in school? Your resume is similar in that your title bar serves as a sort of thesis statement, and your profile is the introduction. The body of your resume serves to support your main ideas. You may be asking yourself, "But what if I want to apply for something for which this profile doesn't fit?" Be cautious here and treat such a question as a potential red flag. Why? The postings you chose were to cater to your strengths and experience and to align with your professional goals.

However, say your experience has a cross-over element that would enable you to work as a nurse educator rather than as floor staff. If that is the case, you want to go back and identify five similar postings specific to nursing education. Repeat the exercise of analyzing postings for all common elements and determining which elements are also true for you. You will then craft a second resume specific to nurse educator roles.

The lesson here is not to use one resume for all goals. Instead, craft separate resumes that can stand on their own with a specific audience. Don't make one resume do double or triple duty. Doing so results in a fragmented resume that is too broad or generic. Instead of appealing to all targeted audiences, you will appeal to none of them.

Allow your professional profile to keep you focused. If your profile doesn't fit a position of interest, consider moving on to a more suitable posting. If you still want to apply, determine how it plays to your strengths and experience. If it doesn't match your strengths and experience at all, don't waste your (or their) time. However, if you still want to apply, first search for more information so you can best customize your materials to suit the audience. To clarify, you may quickly find your resume just doesn't support a role you wish to apply for. This can happen if you come across a posting that is really interesting, something you never would have thought about before, but has completely captured your imagination. Go for it! But also realize that you should create a copy of your resume and edit it for the specific needs of the opportunity. The other situation you might find yourself in is an opportunity that really isn't what you're looking for, but is one of the few that exist at the moment. You may choose to go for it anyway.

Customizable Skills Area

This area is a subset of your professional profile, and it falls between the profile and education areas on your resume. Whereas you want to leave your profile intact, there is enough difference from role to role to require some customization. This customizable area consists of four to six distinct or uncommon elements that may only be relevant for a specific position of interest.

Suppose you apply to a role that specifies all the common elements mentioned earlier but further states a need for supervisory or management experience, project management skills, training and development, and creative approaches to complex medical needs. Your profile would remain intact, and just below it you would add (again, using inserted symbols if using Word) the four specific items for that role, as follows:

> *Registered nurse with earned BSN and 14 years of experience caring for individuals across a full spectrum of medical needs in hospital settings and case management roles. Hold current BLS and ACLS certification as well as TX state licensure. Over 1 year of daily experience with EPIC; demonstrated ability to ensure accuracy and timeliness of all entries. Recognized ability to work independently and exercise autonomous judgment while handling complex behavioral situations.*

- Supervisory experience
- Project management skills
- Creative approaches
- Training and development

Notice how this quick bulleted area calls out specific elements most important to a particular organization for a position they are seeking to fill. There is no guesswork for a recruiter or hiring manager; they don't have to wonder whether you are qualified, which makes it easier for them to make a favorable decision about you. Again, your work history must clearly support your claims. You cannot list "project management skills" in your subprofile without clarifying later in your resume exactly what you meant by that or when/where you developed such skills on the job. You are advised to use no less than four elements in your subprofile and no more than six. For six items, you would continue to list directly below the previous four. For example:

- Supervisory experience
- Project management skills
- Creative approaches
- Training and development
- Emphasis on quality
- Recruiting, hiring, and staffing

Education and Certifications

On nursing resumes, education and certification information should appear sooner rather than later. In many other industries, only new graduates list their educational summary above their work history. After relevant work experience is gained, said work experience trumps education, and the education section would fall further down the resume over time.

However, in nursing, one's education and certifications remain relevant and serve as an absolute requirement for all nursing jobs. It is not to be left to question. This is not to say that if you are a nurse with over 20 years of experience you cannot move your education section to the end of your resume. You can. If you worry about "dating yourself," you might be tempted to move education to the end to make your veteran status less obvious. However, talented and experienced nurses continue to enjoy high demand. Be proud of your history and accomplishments.

Clinical Rotations

This area is specific to students and recent graduates. It demonstrates the settings and populations in which you have gained at least some basic familiarity. As an added benefit, it is helpful for you to see which settings and populations you prefer to work with, versus those you can tell right away are not the best fit for you, which lends greater focus to your job search. For new nurses, clinical rotations were an important part of your nursing education. So, do this section justice: Indicate where and when, populations served, and the presenting symptoms and diagnoses/treatment plan/outcomes, as applicable. Once you have two years of experience, this section can drop off completely. Here is a formatting example:

Medical–Surgical, University of Minnesota Medical Center Riverside, Minneapolis, MN Feb 2012

- Conducted MSSA assessment and dosing per protocol
- Assessed falls risk precautions on patient and initiated safety precautions
- Collaborated with OT in assessment for discontinue of a discharge order
- Identified patient's goal of remaining sober and collaborated with patient to develop plans and interventions for reaching his goal

Adult Medicine, Hennepin County Medical Center, Minneapolis, MN
Nov - Dec 2012

- Performed medication administration safely and correctly—IV, IVPB, Subq, and Oral
- Communicated therapeutically to patients' developmental age and cultural background
- Integrated critical thinking skills into the nursing process to care for complex patients
- Initiated rapid response for a patient with dangerously low BP
- Assessed patient's decreased urine output, collaborated with primary nurse, and inserted Foley catheter per patient order, and prioritized care for multiple patients

Preceptorships

Preceptorships are clinical experiences designed to get your nursing career off to a strong start with expert help available through coaching and role modeling. This arrangement is time sensitive, so specify time frames as well as where you worked, doing what, and under whose guidance. Once you have 2 years' experience, this section can drop off unless doing so leaves a big void on your resume.

Clinical Nursing Experience (Work History)

Actual nursing experience is critically important. Experience should be listed in reverse chronological order, starting with your current or most recent position and working backward for up to 10 years. While it is easily the No. 1 element that will help you advance in your career, experience alone will not work miracles. When it comes to experience, your focus is typically on "how to" capture your experience depending upon your goal: how to gain initial experience, how to gain additional experience, how to specialize, or how to generalize.

Gain initial experience by jumping at every opportunity to show off your newly developed nursing skills and knowledge in verifiable ways. Volunteering for a well-known organization is beneficial. Participating in student chapters or obtaining a student membership in a professional nursing organization helps, but don't stop there. Become an active member, so the leaders can get to know you and serve as excellent references. Use such venues to build your professional contacts and network with others at every level, at every opportunity.

Do not fool yourself into thinking you are "too busy" with school and other responsibilities to invest time and energy into your emerging career. It is never too early to get serious about networking and building professional relationships. Ask professors to invite you to events as a student guest. Connect with your career services office to learn about upcoming employer events, who has hired past graduates, when on-campus interviews will be held, how to get your resume on file with them, and more. Negotiate additional preceptorship hours if possible.

Gaining additional experience requires discipline and intentionality. Reflect on your career path often. Write out clear goals and note specific milestones to be reached and by when. Having a plan helps to ensure you actively meet your goals versus taking a wayward, lackadaisical approach that may or may not get you anywhere near where you want to go or as quickly as you would like.

Specialization is another intentional activity, and you want to seek out specific opportunities to delve ever deeper into your emerging specialty nursing area. For nurses who have held more general roles, you may wish to specialize in one of the areas within which you have a working knowledge. For example, family practice experience could translate into pediatric nursing. To make this transition, you might obtain specialty certifications, work with a specialty mentor, become a more active member in groups and organizations that cater to your specialty, move into management within your specialty, and contribute to the existing and emerging body of knowledge in your field. Such contributions can include writing articles, books, and manuals; speaking engagements; mentoring; teaching specialty classes; and more.

But perhaps you have the opposite issue in that you've been highly specialized up to this point and now wish to pursue a more generalist role. Generalization is used to move you away from an entrenched specialty or to help you bridge your skills and abilities toward a more generalized role such as management. Generalization allows you to take on broader roles, creating stronger flexibility along your career path. It can enable you to balance work and family needs or move into semiretirement. Volunteer work is useful here, as is joining public panel discussions about how specialty areas need a more generalized focus to be a stronger, full-spectrum partner within the health care community. Use your connections to meet and build relationships with health care professionals whose worldview is widespread, all-encompassing, and holistic.

After you have determined which experience quadrant relates to your goal, frame your work experiences to support your current direction. As a student, obtain the most relevant job possible while you are in school. This might include becoming a certified nursing assistant, medical assistant, personal care assistant, health unit coordinator, or records technician. In other words, find part-time work while in school that will get your foot in the door with a prospective nursing employer or at least show that you have experience caring for others in a professional or private setting. Aim high. Don't settle for babysitting or general caretaking. That said, any job is better than no job at all. Just make sure it is verifiable through pay stubs and an employer reference.

As a new graduate, non-nursing jobs in your background are perfectly acceptable. No one is born a fully fledged nurse. Whether you have worked in retail, marketing, fast food, education—anything—you need to focus on the universal or transferrable skills you developed at those jobs that are directly or indirectly relevant to the nursing field. For example, customer service translates to patient care. Filing, answering phones, using a database, and following directions are all skills that also need to be handled effectively by nurses. If the tasks you performed cannot be associated to nursing competencies, then focus on the attributes you developed on those jobs. For example, in any jobs you've held, did you use communication skills? Time management and organizational skills? Project or case management abilities? Social skills or other persuasive talents? The chances are quite good that you did, so highlight those on your resume.

Whether specializing or generalizing, as the two are opposites along a continuum, you want to craft statements around your experience that support your direction. If specializing, pick and highlight those items across positions that show how you have been specializing in this area along the way. In the family practice to pediatrics example, you would downplay care for adults and emphasize work you've done with children. The same premise holds true when generalizing: Pick and highlight the more generalized skills you developed within your specialization. In the nurse to nurse manager example, emphasize your participation in the hiring process, where you've trained or mentored new nurses and taken on charge nurse duties, versus talking primarily about your nursing skills.

And perhaps your roles have been a hybrid in that a third of your time was providing direct care on the nursing floor, another third was spent training and mentoring new nurses, and a final third was spent being the charge nurse. If you want to move into a role more dedicated to patient care, highlight that skill set and minimize or ignore the rest. You wouldn't say much if anything about taking on charge nurse duties, because that is not what you are looking for. Conversely, if you are looking for full-time charge nurse roles, show what you have taken on and the impact you had in those roles. Include information about how you trained and mentored new nurses. Or, if the training and mentorship aspects appealed to you, highlight specifics to help you move into teaching or a preceptorship coordinator role. This approach is also effective when applying for leadership roles within your professional organizations.

Now that you have determined your direction and decided what to highlight or minimize, you're ready to craft actual statements around your work history to support your objective. Use this formula when drafting your work experience section:

Action Word + Detail + Impact

Action words help to "prove" what you can do. They illustrate the level and scope of your activities. Therefore, action words need to be congruent with your experience level, and there is some natural overlap between each. Nursing students will use action words such as learn, develop, follow, monitor, answer, file, work, recognize, apply, care, help, assist. Those with a few years' experience will use action words such as provide, monitor, develop, implement, modify, educate, facilitate, contribute, cover, train, perform, administer. Nurses with many years of experience can easily craft statements with action words such as manage, direct, specialize, hire, train, mentor, coordinate, authorize, supervise, ensure, lead, champion, model, promote, prepare.

Details are the "what" that is directly associated with the action words. Using the same action word examples from above, you can see how the action word + detail portion of the formula might play out. Nursing students could learn procedures, develop rapport, follow orders, monitor complaints, answer phones, file paperwork, work within a team, recognize patient distress, apply protocols, care for others, help as needed, assist as directed. Those with a few years' experience will likely use action words + details such as provide information, monitor equipment, develop care plans, implement physicians' orders, modify notes, educate patients, facilitate communication, contribute on care team, cover shifts, train others, perform direct patient care, administer medications. Nurses with many years of experience can easily craft statements with action words + details such as manage caseload, direct nursing staff, specialize on obstetrics, hire new nurses, train on new equipment, mentor students, coordinate care plans, authorize drug refills, supervise nursing assistants, ensure smooth operations, lead special projects, champion alternative health initiatives, model best practices, promote emerging industry standards, prepare budgets. Again, you can see how the scope and depth of each level is brought to light with action words and their associated details. But don't stop there!

Impact is where you set yourself apart from your competition. With each action word + detail you craft, take it further by asking yourself why or how it is important, who benefits, what has been made better as a result, how many were impacted, how such actions could be measured. Continuing with the same examples above, watch how each action word + detail fragment is rounded out when impact is added. Nursing students could write learn procedures to ensure child safety, develop rapport with chronic pain patients, follow orders accurately at all times, monitor complaints to make needed course corrections, answer phones professionally and efficiently, file paperwork according to current standards, work within a team to provide excellent service, recognize patient distress and alert the appropriate personnel immediately, apply protocols for patient safety and security, care for others with Alzheimer's, help as needed every day and with enthusiasm.

Those with a few years' experience can round out impact statements in a variety of ways, such as provide information to families, monitor equipment for validity of data, develop care plans as part of an interdisciplinary team, implement physicians' orders in pre- and post-operative environments, modify notes within Cerner application suite, educate patients on medication management for heart disease, facilitate communication between hospice care and family members, contribute on care team to enhance quality of life for AIDS patients, cover shifts independently and with autonomous judgment, train others on EPIC, perform direct patient care in the pediatric ICU, administer medications across a full spectrum of patient diagnoses.

Nurses with many years of experience can easily craft impactful statements with action words + details, such as manage caseload of 40 diabetes patients; direct nursing staff of 12 full-time, 18 part-time, and four on-call professionals;

specialize on obstetrics within rural settings with critical health care delivery challenges; hire new nurses on an average of 20 per year; train on new equipment such as obstetric beds and fetal heart monitors; mentor five students per year at Western Governors University; coordinate care plans for 17 mobile dialysis patients in Northern Maine; authorize drug refills across a seven-county metro area; supervise nine nursing assistants through Doctors Without Borders in Columbia and Venezuela; ensure smooth operations on a 32-bed, level 1 trauma center burn unit; lead special projects, including internal audits of visiting nurse organizations; champion alternative health initiatives, including vegetarian diets and relaxation, to treat heart disease in Houma, Louisiana; model best practices in emergency nursing; promote emerging industry standards in nursing informatics; prepare annual budget of $13 million. You can see how your objective-relevant skills and accomplishments are elevated with not only action words and their associated details, but by showing the impact of your work.

Non-nursing Experience (If Applicable)

There are two primary reasons for noting non-nursing experiences on your resume. One, you are a new nurse and your pre-nursing work rounds out your resume. Two, you have moved in and out of nursing and include non-nursing activities to close what would otherwise be gaps in your resume. Otherwise, once you have 3 or more years of nursing experience, with nothing in between that was non-nursing in nature to highlight, and you wish to remain in the nursing field, those pre-nursing work experiences can drop off your resume.

If you list non-nursing experiences on your resume, follow the same reverse chronological order you use for nursing experience. However, if you are filling out an application, all work experience needs to be noted. While a resume is a marketing document, an application is a legal document. You can omit irrelevant information on a resume but must construct a full and accurate picture of your past experiences on a nursing application form.

Volunteerism

Volunteer activities can be formatted much the same as work experiences, in reverse chronological order. Include your role, the organization served, dates of service, and notations that follow the action word + detail + impact formula.

Publications

List any publications that you have authored, co-authored, or contributed to in APA style, latest edition.

Honors and Awards

Mention these if you have them and if they directly or indirectly support your objective. List the award name, the awarding organization, and when you received it or which year it represents.

Where to Learn More

Years ago, it was common to end all resumes with the phrase "references available upon request." This outdated catch-all phrase has been replaced with a more dynamic approach that encourages the reader to see more, to dig deeper while making it easy for them to do so. Reference checking itself has gone to a new level and is generally handled by third-party verification services.

However, you can set yourself apart from the competition in three ways. The approaches are the web link to profile, the web link to portfolio, and a fully annotated reference page.

"Link to profile" is where you provide the URL address to your profile on a professional networking site such as LinkedIn or NurseTogether.com. Avoid linking to purely social networking sites on your resume unless your (intended) role merits it. This might be the case if you are a nurse involved in a public health marketing campaign that makes heavy use of Facebook or Twitter. At the very end of your resume you can insert a centered line that reads, "To learn more, please visit <insert URL>." If your profile includes public recommendations, the line should read "To learn more and review recommendations of my work, please visit <insert URL>." The URL is simply the "address line" of a particular webpage. For example, the LinkedIn profile URL of this author is www.linkedin.com/in/lisamaurithomas. You find this URL on your profile page in the main area that features your name, photo, etc.

"Link to portfolio" is where you provide the URL address to your e-portfolio. Portfolios can be useful to illustrate your work and competencies as a stand-alone display or as an addendum to your resume. Nursing portfolios can include a 30-second video clip introduction, a short set of PowerPoint slides that quickly summarizes where you have worked, special projects you have been involved in, equipment you've used, a quick video clip that shows you in a training/teaching environment, graphic captures of certificates you have earned, and more. Let your creativity shine! At the end of your resume, you can insert a centered line that reads, "To learn more, please view my portfolio at <insert URL>." To see a nice collection of nursing e-portfolio samples online, simply do an online search or check out the gallery put together by San Francisco State University at http://sfsueportfolio.myefolio.com/sfsugalleries/nursing. Ask your school's career services office if it has space available for you to use for free—many do.

"Annotated reference page" is a page entirely separate from your resume or cover letter where you craft a list of professional references, as well as the ways they can vouch for your skills and abilities. You should list three to six professional references on this page. Their formatting should be consistent, but they don't have to be identical, because you will only list the contact information they prefer. One reference might only provide a phone number or e-mail address, whereas another may provide you with a full mailing address and more. Here is an example of an annotated reference entry:

Sue Johnson, RN
Charge Nurse—Pediatrics
EverLove Healthcare Systems – Springfield Hospital
321.555.1212 • sjohn9999@springfield.org

Sue has been a mentor and colleague of mine for over 5 years, and she can speak to my abilities around direct nursing care, time management, and patient rapport. From Sue, I have learned how to find ethical cost containment opportunities within my role without sacrificing quality. She and I have also worked together tirelessly on JHACO projects and accreditation initiatives.

Imagine a recruiter or hiring manager receiving a full page of four to six such entries, all focusing on verifiable evidence that you have what they need. The content of such entries should directly support what a prospective employer or organization will expect of you in a new role. If you are applying for direct nursing care roles, select references who will speak to those abilities. If you are seeking nurse case manager roles, your references should be able to vouch for the associated skills for such positions.

Be specific and understand that it is perfectly acceptable to use different references for different prospective roles; no matter what, customize your annotated reference page as appropriate. Although reference checking might be handled through a third-party verification vendor, a good reference page will spark interest and trust in you as a potential candidate. It creates a very good impression. You can supply the annotated reference page as part of your resume and cover letter materials, bring it along to an interview, or send by e-mail as part of a thank-you note after an interview.

Best Resume Format Ever

Figure 4.1 is a resume format that makes necessary and essential resume customizations a breeze. Imagine being able to make quick, easy, and effective customizations to your resume for each position desired. Increase your visibility and command attention with confidence and ease. This resume template is available to download and customize from the *Landing Your Perfect Nursing Job* page at www.nursingknowledge.org/sttibooks.

Figure 4.1: Best Resume template

YOUR NAME
Street address (if needed)
phone • e-mail

TITLE 1 • KEYWORD 1 • KEYWORD 2 (customizable area)
Marketing tagline (optional)

Insert professional profile that is forward-looking, captures what you bring to the proverbial table in the here and now that hones in on what is most commonly sought out by prospective employers for the type of nursing job you are seeking. Limit to no more than five to six lines of text. Focus on skills and abilities foremost, and attributes second. Use fully justified formatting for a cleaner look. Use information gleaned from earlier exercise where you analyzed postings for common elements.

- Custom keyword/phrase
- Custom keyword/phrase
- Custom keyword/phrase
- Custom keyword/phrase
- Custom keyword/phrase
- Custom keyword/phrase

Education

Degree acronym; DEGREE written out as appears on your diploma; school name, graduation date (must be verifiable)
2nd Degree acronym; DEGREE written out as appears on your diploma; school name, graduation date (must be verifiable)
Certification acronym; written out as appears on your certificate; name of organization, date earned (must be verifiable)

Clinical Nursing Experience (for new grads only)

Specialty area, name of organization, location, dates
Annotated information about population served/observed, treatment plan/outcomes
Specialty area, name of organization, location, dates
Annotated information about population served/observed, treatment plan/outcomes
Specialty area, name of organization, location, dates
Annotated information about population served/observed, treatment plan/outcomes

Professional Nursing/Health Care Experience

JOB TITLE; mo/yr – mo/yr
Company name; location
- Action word + detail + impact (quantified if at all possible)
- Action word + detail + impact (quantified if at all possible)
- Action word + detail + impact (quantified if at all possible)

JOB TITLE; mo/yr – mo/yr
Company name; location
- Action word + detail + impact (quantified if at all possible)
- Action word + detail + impact (quantified if at all possible)
- Action word + detail + impact (quantified if at all possible)

JOB TITLE; mo/yr – mo/yr
Company name; location
- Action word + detail + impact (quantified if at all possible)
- Action word + detail + impact (quantified if at all possible)
- Action word + detail + impact (quantified if at all possible)

Additional work history (non-health care) available upon request

You are invited to learn more at: list LinkedIn URL, e-portfolio URL, or indicate reference page

This resume template is available to download and customize from the *Landing Your Perfect Nursing Job* page at www.nursingknowledge.org/sttibooks.

Speak the Language of Your Audience

Customization sculpts your resume to show prospective organizations that you meet their needs. Show them what an excellent fit you are. Demonstrate you are clearly ready, willing, and able to address their needs. The use of one generic resume is not in your best interest when you are actively seeking a new role.

Here is how to know if you are speaking their language: Place printed copies of a job posting and your resume next to each other. For each line of the posting check your resume for corresponding support. Use a highlighter to illuminate the congruent items on the posting. Once you have evaluated the entire posting against your resume, see how much of the posting is highlighted. If at least three-fourths is highlighted, then your resume speaks their language. If less than half is highlighted, your resume misses the mark, and you need to strengthen your resume with more customization. If you cannot incorporate nonhighlighted items of the posting on your resume because they are not part of your skills, abilities, or history, realize that the posting in question may not be a good fit for you after all.

Customizing Your Resume for Specific Roles

Explore several examples of how a base or master resume can be customized for similar yet different positions. Seeing how other nurses have customized their resumes will make building your own far easier. Use the information in the last section about speaking the language of your audience. That section showed you how to determine if what you are targeting meshes well with your resume. This section shows you how to strengthen alignment between them with two specific visual aids. Figure 4.2 is a professional nurse's resume created from the Best Resume Ever template, provided in Figure 4.1. Figure 4.3 shows both a job posting and the customized portion of the professional resume in Figure 4.2. Note how the nurse customized it to tie into specific phrases in the job posting. Focus on postings that align well with the talents you bring to the organization.

Figure 4.2: A professional nurse's resume based on the Best Resume template.

PROFESSIONAL NURSE, RN, MSN
555 Main Street ~ City, ST Zip
Phone ~ e-mail

Registered Nurse ~ Oncology Nurse Manager ~ Clinical Expertise
Championing cancer patients to survive and thrive in Third World countries

Dedicated and proven oncology nursing director with RN licensure, OCN and CNML certifications, and 20 years' experience caring for cancer patients; seeking new international projects in developing countries. Highly professional and seasoned nurse leader who has contributed to the field of oncology through publications, teaching, development of best practices, and professional development leadership. Served as volunteer in Alaska, Guam, Nigeria, the Falklands, Borneo, Syria, and Peru.

- Nurse manager and leader
- Radiation procedures
- Research analysis
- Chemotherapy and alternatives
- Cancer in childbirth expertise
- Passport, all vaccinations current

Education

MSN, Master of Science in Nursing; School of Nursing, 2006
BSN, Bachelor of Science in Nursing; School of Nursing, 1996

Licensure

RN, Registered Nurse; My State, 1990

Certifications

CNML, Certified Nurse Manager and Leader; October 1995, current
OCN, Oncology Nursing Certification; June 1992, current
ACLS, Advanced Cardiac Life Support; September 1990, current
IV Therapy Certification; IV Tech, June 1990, current
BLS, Basic Life Support Certification; American Red Cross, March 1990, current

Professional Nursing / Health Care Experience

Nursing Director, Oncology; September 1996 – current
Carlton Cancer Care; City, ST

- Oversee all aspects of managing oncology department, which began with the preparation for opening the new cancer center in 1998
- Championed the launch and ongoing growth of community-focused cancer screenings, detection, and prevention initiatives that have served over 5,000 local residents since their inception in 2002
- Manage a budget of $45M and supervise 6 charge nurses with 30 second- and third-level employees
- Guest lecture an average of 10 times per year at local community colleges on oncology nursing topics for past 7 years
- Volunteer staff nurses from the organization to serve in Doctors Without Borders every year for past 5 years

Charge Nurse, Oncology; September 1992 – September 1996
Richardson Cancer Care; City, ST

- Ensured intensive care focus of bone marrow transplantation that contributed to an 87% successful transplant rate over a 2-year period
- Assisted with ongoing community-focused cancer screenings, detection, and prevention initiatives that served over 1,000 local residents
- Performed executive functions as requested, which included data collection, nursing diagnosis, planning, intervention, and evaluation; served in charge nurse capacity
- Participated in nursing research studies, consulted with and educated patients, and strived to contribute to the field each day

Oncology Nurse; July 1990 – September 1992
Samaritan Cancer Clinic; City, ST

- Completed patient assessments with patient consultations, including assessing patients for radiation therapy side effects, and provided appropriate nursing interventions for an average of 15 patients per week
- Assisted in coordinating the scheduling of patient consultations, simulations, and follow-up visits
- Assisted with scheduling of required outpatient lab tests, x-rays, scans, etc., as needed in a busy, fast-paced clinic
- Maintained comprehensive and accurate records of all patient activities, including exams, diagnostic testing, medications, infusions, injections, and more throughout each shift

Publications

Cancer in Pregnant Women (co-authored with Rebecca Moore)
Baltimore, MD: The Johns Hopkins University Papers, 2011.

Bringing It All Back Home: Cancer Care
London, United Kingdom: Care Press, and Boulder, CO: Westlake Press, 2009.

Economic Ramifications of Cancer (co-authored with Steven Grady)
Alberta: Alberta University of Economics and Health Care, 2007.

Class and Cancer Care
Minneapolis: Minnesota Press, 2005.

Professional Organizations

Doctors Without Borders, 2009–current; active member with critical and community care experience in 6 countries
International Nursing Association, 2007–current; active member; served on board of directors 2009–2011
Frontier Nurses of America, 2004–2008; led efforts to improve rural health care in Hentley, ST, population 1,400
Care Nurses Association, 2000–2004; was an active member; presented at 4 annual conferences

You are invited to learn more by visiting: www.linkedin/ *[insert your LinkedIn profile here]*

This resume template is available to download and customize from the *Landing Your Perfect Nursing Job* page at www.nursingknowledge.org/sttibooks.

Figure 4.3: A job posting and the customized portion of the resume (shown in Figure 4.2). Notice how the job posting (below) was already in alignment with the nurse's skills. It's quick and easy to customize a resume when you have already developed one based on your core abilities and strengths.

Overview:

(1) ABC Hospital is dedicated to providing nurturing, compassionate, humane, interdisciplinary, and personalized care to patients and families. (2) At ABC you are empowered to take ownership of and drive the hospital experience from the patient's perspective and create healing partnerships between caregivers, patients, and family members—guiding patients as active participants, true self-advocates. (3) Caregivers who work at ABC are committed to providing a truly extraordinary experience for patients and families, especially children. If you are this kind of caregiver, consider us as a place to share your valuable talent. Our employee experience complements the patient experience—working in a beautiful, nature-inspired environment as a member of a team committed to excellence while using state of the art equipment and communication tools.

Responsibilities:

(4) Coordinates care referrals from physicians and health care facilities to the Cancer Center. (5) Provides education related to patients' illness and planned treatment.

Qualifications:

Required: Current RN license, BSN. Must have excellent communication and computer skills and have the ability to work with physicians in many specialties. Three years' experience in medical and radiation oncology. Preferred: OCN certification.

PROFESSIONAL NURSE, RN, MSN
555 Main Street ~ City, ST Zip
Phone ~ e-mail

Registered Nurse ~ Oncology Nurse Manager ~ Clinical Expertise
Championing cancer patients to survive and thrive in Third World countries

Dedicated and proven oncology nursing director with RN licensure, OCN and CNML certifications, and 20 years' experience caring for cancer patients; seeking new international projects in developing countries. Highly professional and seasoned nurse leader who has contributed to the field of oncology through publications, teaching, development of best practices, and professional development leadership. Served as volunteer in Alaska, Guam, Nigeria, the Falklands, Borneo, Syria, and Peru.

- (1) Family and child-centric
- Radiation procedures
- (2) Healing partner
- Care experience engineer (3)
- Referral coordination (4)
- Patient education (5)

Resume Critique Worksheet

Appendix A, Nurse Resume Critique, on page 229, will help you polish a customized resume. Use it as a quality-assurance measure to evaluate your efforts before submitting your resume.

Crafting a Cover Letter That Commands Attention

Some job seekers hold a misconception that the resume requires more work than the cover letter—not so! Between two equally qualified resumes, the cover letter can act as the tiebreaker. While many cover letters go unread because the resume failed to impress, an impressive resume must be accompanied by an equally impressive cover letter. Think about it: Your cover letter serves to introduce your resume when you are not there to do so in person. This is why you would not bring a cover letter to a networking event or job fair or interview. In those scenarios, you are live in person and can discuss your resume yourself.

A cover letter also strengthens the bridge between their posting/need and your resume. It serves as the mini-story that brings your resume (and your personality!) to life. Your cover letter shows how you connect the dots in satisfying a particular employer's need. You have this page that demonstrates how you are right for them, and they are right for you. Most job seekers focus on just the first half of that equation, and the result is a cover letter that appears to be all about them. The trick is to balance your letter so that it blends what you have to offer in terms of their needs and acknowledges what it is about them that appeals to your professional senses.

Figure 4.4 shows a basic yet balanced cover letter and showcases in italics the parts you would customize for yourself. Notice how the top of the letter that contains your contact information is a mirror image of how it is showcased on the resume sample, creating a "matched set." Do the same with your resume and cover letter; create a "matched set" if you are submitting your materials via the postal service or as e-mail attachments. You may also embed your cover letter into the body of the e-mail message and attach your resume. In this scenario, you would not mimic the top of your resume nor include the date as your e-mail will be dated and time stamped.

Notice how this letter is formatted. For example, none of the paragraphs is indented. This is business letter formatting, and you are indeed writing a business letter, not a social one. The paragraphs themselves are fully justified, and there is consistent spacing between paragraphs. There is adequate room for a signature, though you do not need to sign in ink when submitting electronically unless you have the ability to do so via an electronic signature or by scanning the document after printing and signing it. You will want to be especially attentive to your spelling, grammar, and punctuation within your letter. Use complete sentences, not fragments. Use capital letters only where appropriate. If you have any doubts or questions about your writing skills, have others proofread your letters before sending them. Poorly written letters create a poor impression.

Finally, notice the content of the letter. The first paragraph is your opening. It gets right to the point by stating which position you are targeting and why that company interests you. The second paragraph is your "proof" that you are an excellent fit for their needs. If the posting states you need at least 2 years of experience in emergency services, you would use this area to explicitly state that you have 2 years of experience in emergency services. By indicating your years of experience, you are quantifying your evidence. Do this whenever possible. If the posting requires supervisory experience, use this area to indicate that you have this experience and to state the roles, ranks, and number of direct reports you've managed. Quantify your proof whenever possible. The last paragraph is your close. It serves to create a pathway to "next steps" that you'd like to see happen. Next steps can include a follow-up call you will make within the next few days or a request for a formal interview.

The letter should be addressed to a named individual. This might require you to do a bit of research if you don't already know the contact person's name and title. Use your network. Use your research abilities. If you know someone internal to the organization, learn the exact spelling of the hiring manager's or recruiter's name and what their exact job title is. You can simply call the receptionist and ask, too. Use professional networking sites such as LinkedIn and do a People search of employee names and titles within your target organization. Since not everyone keeps profiles up to date, it is helpful to make a quick call to the receptionist and ask if so-and-so is still the (state title) of the company. This allows you to choose a name with confidence. The recipient will notice that you addressed him or her by name versus "dear recruiter or hiring manager" or "to whom it may concern." It also gives you a specific name to follow up with a day or two after submitting your materials. Again, you want to establish a connection and keep the dialogue going forward.

Figure 4.4: A basic and balanced cover letter

YOUR NAME
Street address (if needed)
phone • e-mail

Date

Contact Name
Title
Company Name
Street Address
City, ST xxxxx
(OR e-mail address in lieu of mailing address)

Dear *Contact*,

With over # years of proven success in the nursing profession *(state what you're best at that the prospective company also needs)*, I am submitting my materials for your *Job Title* position. I am well aware of the *(List two relevant details about the company. Indicate region in which they operate, the industry they are in, or related information regarding what they are known for. This shows you clearly know who they are, and can be gleaned from personal observation, news blurbs, and informational interviews or your networking contacts). If someone has referred you to this position, state here their name and how you know them as well as what they referred you for or why.*

My resume is attached for your review. Specific and relevant qualifications include:

- List several things that are important for the job in question AND true for you, and give an example if possible

The combination of *(cite something from their mission statement or their corporate values that you can find on the About Us section of their website)* that *Company Name* fosters every day is of great interest to me, personally and professionally. I would like very much to lend my *(list three qualities about yourself that will be important to them for this role)* to support your continued success.

Please contact me at *your phone number* to schedule an interview so that we can further discuss concrete ways that my talents will directly benefit *Company Name*, both short- and long-term.

Sincerely,

Your Name

In summary, this chapter has showcased the importance of resumes and cover letters as a means to demonstrate your skills and abilities in a manner that solicits a person-to-person meeting. Even if you tend to complete an application form for each role, you can attach your resume to the application for an extra professional touch. Crafting a resume and cover letter also serves as a pre-interview exercise because it forces you to think through what you want, how you can benefit the organization, and why you are targeting that organization. Lastly, if you are interested in doing so as a creative and strategic exercise, you can craft the resume you WANT to be true for you within the next 1 to 5 years as a way of plotting the trajectory and associated milestones of your career development plan. No matter what, you cannot go wrong with any of these approaches.

Best Candidate Checklist

___ I have come to understand the interplay among resumes, cover letters, and applications.

___ I have developed an appreciation of how resumes should follow networking and not be expected to stand on their own.

___ I have started asking about projects I can assist on, ways I can volunteer, and people who can introduce me to hiring managers.

___ I have created at least one online networking profile, such as LinkedIn, and am actively learning how to use such tools effectively.

___ I have made a list of 10 people I know, reaching out to them to introduce me to recruiters and hiring managers they know.

___ I have updated my resume using the template provided and followed the advice for each section in this chapter.

___ I have customized my new resume in order to be responsive for postings or opportunities.

___ I have written a cover letter that will serve as my own customizable template.

5

If you look at what you have in life, you'll always have more. If you look at what you don't have in life, you'll never have enough.

–Oprah Winfrey

Confronting Negativity and Turning It Around

If job search and career development efforts were easy to accomplish, everyone would do them. They don't. However, other people's struggles in this area don't have to be yours. Common challenges include lack of motivation, an expectation of quick results, and poor confidence levels. This chapter is dedicated to helping you succeed with gusto! This chapter applies a variety of tried and true techniques to staying positive throughout your job search.

Clear Away What's Holding You Down

Job searching can be draining. You may feel tremendous pressure to succeed quickly. Why? You may be anxious about finances if you are unemployed or underemployed, or if you haven't truly started your nursing career yet. You may feel desperate to leave a toxic work environment or a bad boss. Or you sense you should be more successful by now. No matter what your situation, this section explores ways to stay positive and achieve balance by incorporating career development activities into your regular routines.

If you feel good about yourself and your situation, you are better positioned and motivated to launch your plan. If you are happy in your current role yet feel ready to take on new challenges, you are in a healthy, positive place from which to go forward. However, you might feel some trepidation about your search. Whatever you believe is holding you back likely falls into one of two camps: internal or external. In short, you feel that either you are holding you back or someone else is. These two areas represent how you view your assets and liabilities.

If you are embarking on a job search or career development goal out of anger, desperation, disappointment, or another negative state, or if your current situation is colored by blame or shame, whether directed internally or externally, you will feel far less motivated or in control. What is important is that you identify what's holding you back. Take a look at the following lists to see if one better describes your situation. Check off all the statements that you believe apply to your job search or career development goals.

Internal/Self

- ❐ I can't wait to get started.
- ❐ I have a clear plan and can visualize success.
- ❐ I want to succeed but doubt that I can.
- ❐ I am not good enough/don't have what it takes.
- ❐ I feel like a fake or a fraud.
- ❐ My current situation is all my fault/I hate myself.

External/Others

- ❐ I am excited to meet other nursing professionals.
- ❐ I have a large professional network to lean on.
- ❐ I could succeed if others would actually help me.
- ❐ It is _____________'s fault that I am in this situation.
- ❐ It is just no use/it is awful out there right now.

If you are challenged by internal negativity, understand the toll it will take on your job search and career development efforts over time. Internal negativity is hard, but not impossible, to combat. First, look at why self-doubt exists in the first place. When you feel self-doubt, you literally doubt yourself and your abilities. You also doubt how well you can assess personal risk. While there is always some risk involved in what we attempt, a quick assessment can usually determine if it is a relatively safe risk or can be made safer with the addition of a few extra resources. An inability to understand reasonable or calculated risk leads to chronic fear of failure. If you are convinced you will fail, you will. Over time, self-doubt turns into self-hatred and self-loathing. If you checked boxes under Internal/Self that speak to self-hatred, you will need to seek professional help. You do not deserve such self-inflicted hatred and loathing and will need specialized assistance to root it out of your system. Self-hatred is like cancer—it won't go away on its own. You will need to take radically different approaches. You need to see that taking risks is necessary, that there's nowhere to go but up, and that by maintaining your status quo, you will be "stuck" until you do make significant changes. So why not start now? Why not do something radically different yet healthy today? Get a counseling referral or actually reach out on one you've received. Go for a brisk walk no matter what the weather. Call someone who has always been supportive of you, ask her advice, and follow her lead, even if you feel utterly disinclined to do so. Whether or not you seek out help for internal negativity, the choice is yours.

Realize that everyone experiences some degree of self-doubt, arranging along the healthy to unhealthy continuum. Healthy self-doubt stems from self-awareness. It allows us to see, acknowledge, and correct our mistakes and learn from them. It helps us to see ourselves as others see us and recognize how we can improve and be a better partner or colleague going forward. A healthy sense of self requires us to continually assess where and how we are in this world and to realize we'll never know all the answers; we're not right all of the time. Healthy self-doubt is what makes you an excellent nurse.

Understand that chronic self-doubt holds you back because so much time and energy are spent worrying. Once you have internal negativity under control, you free up energy to move forward. This opens up a world of possibilities to explore. When you can appreciate and pursue possibilities, you do so from a position of strength. This in turn feeds your sense of purpose and capacity to take additional yet reasonable risks. You will be far less worried about failing and be more willing to make mistakes and learn from them along the way. This can inspire you to reach out to others, strengthen your supports, lean on others a bit when needed, and enjoy the career development journey.

But what if the problem isn't you? What boxes did you check from the external/others list—any of the last three? Look at each of them individually for a few minutes. There are typically three reasons why others won't help you. One is that you don't believe they will help you, which speaks to the relationship you have with them; you expect support from them but rarely receive it. If this is the case, you need to re-evaluate the people in your support system. A second reason why others won't help you is that they can't. In this situation, you need to seek out those who can and incorporate them into your support network.

The third scenario, and infinitely the most difficult reason, is when they won't help you because you've burned bridges, abused their trust, or deeply disappointed them. In this case, give them breathing room and find success with others. Turn your life around and then come back to those you've let down with proof that your changes are entrenched and sustainable. If you checked the box indicating an individual or group is to blame, scrutinize why or how you've given away your personal power. This is not to say you've never been wronged by others. But while you cannot change what has happened in the past, you can decide to go forward despite their wrongdoing. This is a difficult challenge. Some people have a natural ability to forgive and move on. For others, it is far too easy to hold a grudge, bemoan their fate, and stay mired in blaming others for their misfortunes.

When you blame others for your mistakes or failures, you learn less and perform worse, as researchers Fast and Tiedens proved through a series of experiments. They summarized their findings in an interesting paper featured in the *Journal of Experimental Social Psychology* (2010) titled, "Blame contagion: The automatic transmission of self-serving attributions." Think about that in the context of your job search or career development efforts or within your nursing career as a whole. Why? If you're busy blaming others, you have less time to look at how to take responsibility for yourself going forward. That may be because it seems too hard or daunting, or it seems too overwhelming and you don't even know where to begin. Start by recognizing that the only one who can change your life for the better is you. However, that doesn't mean beating yourself up. Instead, practice any one or all of these self-care strategies to support your job search, career development, or personal development journey.

Look to the rest of today and do something positive.

- Take responsibility for your current state and make plans for a better, healthier, and more powerful tomorrow.
- Do something positive and productive for just 15 minutes or during the next few hours.
- Get out for a change of scenery, take this book to a public park or anyplace that calms you, and revisit the reflective exercises in Chapters 1, 2, and 3.
- Avoid unhealthy or potentially destructive outlets such as watching TV, sleeping excessively, drinking alcohol or using drugs, spending money, or hanging out with unsupportive people.

Whatever it takes, get yourself in a good, better, or healthier place today. Quick, healthy fixes include walking, riding a bike, making and eating a salad, drinking water, smiling at yourself in the mirror, weeding your garden—anything immediate that helps you break out of your funk.

Do these funk-busting activities every day until they become healthy habits. Notice how they serve to elevate your mood, help you see things more positively, and make you more enjoyable to be around.

Think about it! You are in the best position to succeed when you are already in a good situation, so it behooves you to work on getting there sooner rather than later. Life is about finding your purpose, making good friends, knowing you are a good person, and helping to make the world a better place. Your attitude toward your current job makes all the difference. Think about what made you become a nurse in the first place, and find ways to reconnect with those ideals in the job you have now as a way to stay positive throughout your search.

Explore! Once you have a more positive outlook about your current job (satisfying, pays decently, with an enjoyable supervisor and great coworkers, and in a role where you feel connected to your patients, etc.), you are in the best position to further your career development efforts and to explore what else is out there. Whenever a new opportunity is identified, you have the enviable position of evaluating it against an already good situation. If it doesn't measure up to how good you already have it, you may opt to turn it down. The process itself, however, is a good way to practice your interview and negotiation skills in a relatively safe environment.

Be creative! Career development activities can be broader and more varied at this stage. Perhaps you'll consider going back to school for an advanced degree or certification. Meet with a financial planner to make sure that your current efforts are on track with meeting future objectives. You might look for ways to carve out a flexible position for yourself should you desire to start a family. You could be bold and start a professional networking group for local nurses if there aren't good options in your area. Write an article for your local paper on what you love about being a nurse. Teach a nursing class at the local community college. Connect with a nursing organization that offers community service opportunities, locally or in another country. No matter what, if you are feeling jazzed just thinking about the possibilities, you are in a great position to see them through and fully realize your career dreams.

LAND THAT JOB!

What is going well for you right now? What do you like about your job? What small steps can you take to make your current situation even better? In other words, what "low-hanging fruit" can you pluck and benefit from with little additional time or effort?

Note of caution: Don't make the mistake of settling into a good situation and ignoring the need for further career development. There is a cycle to all things. What is good now can change quickly. Your clinic could be bought out, you might get a new supervisor, you could be injured on the job or laid off, or any number of other common events. Use your current positive climate to make new connections, or use a less hectic schedule to create a satisfying volunteer opportunity for yourself. You'll be more confident because you are approaching new contacts from the perspective of getting to know them organically over time. You won't approach them in a desperate rush; if they sense you're approaching only because you're desperate for a new role, they won't be so helpful. (Think of the typical used-car salesman.) When you're in a good situation, you can engage in career development activities without worrying about an immediate job search.

LAND THAT JOB!

While volunteering may not appear to be connected to career development and job searching, it is! Did you know that some employers look at volunteer activities as a direct reflection of a candidate's investment in the community? Or that volunteering helps build confidence, connection, and a broader understanding of the needs of communities, cities, and the world? Do you volunteer? Think about what you've learned by volunteering and consider adding it to your skills list. If you don't volunteer now, seek opportunities that will allow you to inspire others or be inspired.

But what if you are suffering a bad boss, massive budget cuts, or unemployment? These require different strategic approaches before you can really get into the business of job searching or career development. Specifically, here are activities to help you make sense of a tough situation and pave the way for a new path: Join a job search support group, obtain unemployment funds and/or eliminate debts, seek individual counseling, read self-help books such as Crowley and Elster's 2009 title, *Working for You Isn't Working for Me.* Feeling strapped for cash these days? The book is available in most local libraries, there are a number of debt-counseling resources available at no charge, many job search support groups are free, and each state has specific resources to guide those experiencing unemployment. And while maintaining a positive attitude takes time and energy, there need not be any financial cost associated with it. One particular challenge when unemployed is making use of government services can take up a lot of time, be tedious in nature, and feel downright demeaning and dehumanizing. You cannot control the approach taken by others, including services, but you can recognize up front that such difficulties exist and steel yourself accordingly. It will be up to you to know that you are not just a number. You have much to offer. You have loved ones who will help you as best they can, and that this too shall pass. Work the process but also recognize what triggers your mood and attitude such as long lines, snide comments, disrupted schedule, and fears of not making ends meet. Know that all of these things will happen, so think proactively and in advance about how to help yourself through them when they do.

Such approaches help you to see that a) you're not in this alone, b) you're better than you give yourself credit for, c) you can quell your financial anxieties, and d) there are ways to take back your personal power from a destructive, diminishing supervisor or from a demeaning unemployment experience. Each of these approaches helps to strengthen your position so you can go forward with greater confidence than you would without these supportive measures.

Accessing these activities on behalf of your career development can help to recharge you, and you can use them to your advantage. Although you cannot control what prospective employers want or need in a candidate, you can control how you put yourself out there and to what extent you learn and leverage useful information about nursing trends, prospective companies, who the recruiters and hiring managers are, who your competition is, where things may be opening up versus slowing down, and more. Making the most of what you can control is a great way to stay positive and achieve balance throughout your career.

LAND THAT JOB!

What funk-busting activities can you engage in for the next hour? Refuse to worry about the current weather conditions, what you're wearing or how you look, or if anyone will think such activities are stupid. Seriously, take a walk or weed your garden in the rain, do stretching exercises in the park, or meditate on the kitchen floor. Choose healthy and readily available activities to support yourself in this moment—and—do it!

Forming Your Plan to Get Ahead

There's an old adage that says "you have to start somewhere" for any project or goal. This means that no matter what it is, where you are at, how big or small the goal is, you have to find some kind of starting point. Perhaps your starting point is reading this book or engaging in the quick and healthy funk-busters. Once you are in a good mood and positive frame of mind, you are ready to get started on your plan.

To determine your starting point, keep two questions in mind. What information do you already possess, and what information is missing? By answering these two questions routinely, you can guide your way from any starting point.

Information is power; you leverage information to meet your goals. Information you already possess is an asset. Conversely, information you are missing provides concrete and immediate next steps to turn the unknown into the known. Remember to bring up your mood and energy level before assessing information—a bad mood or unhealthy frame of mind will negatively impact your judgment.

LAND THAT JOB!

What do you know about job searching that plays directly into an action plan? In other words, what informational assets do you already possess? What information are you missing, and how might you obtain it? Who or what can you turn to for help in filling in your informational gaps? As suggested throughout this book, resources include job search support groups, recruiters, and other nurses who have recently concluded a successful job search.

Information aids decision-making, and you can break up decision-making into manageable parts as you would a project; indeed, job searching and career development are projects. Break your all-encompassing goals into manageable micro goals that you can finish in a reasonable amount of time. Completion of the micro goals brings the larger goal into fruition. Simply put, there are larger, macro goals (such as getting a new job) and smaller, micro goals (such as attending networking events). Too often, people focus on the larger goals, which can be overwhelming. Every day that passes where the individual does not land a new job can feel like a failure. Don't do that to yourself!

You can manage such projects successfully if you are SMART about them: specific, measurable, achievable, relevant, and timely (Doran, 1981). Let's walk through these and develop your plan of action along the way.

Specific. Be exact versus vague in defining what you want to accomplish. You can also look at the S part of SMART to mean significant or even simple. The idea is ultimately the same: Choose something meaningful and break it down to its essence. In terms of a job search, you might choose to "identify local companies that hire surgical nurses" or "apply for nursing jobs." In terms of career development, you might choose to "identify professional nursing organizations" or "meet more nursing and health care professionals."

LAND THAT JOB!

In the simplest sense, identify a current job search or career development goal. It can be anything. Just make it specific and meaningful, something concrete that you really want to accomplish. Write it here:

Measurable. At this stage you should attach a metric to your goal. You want to give it a number, so to speak. Numbers help you manage your goal by enabling you to assess if you are meeting it, which is important because it allows you to make course corrections along the way. In the examples above, you can add metrics such as "identify 10 local companies or 10 professional nursing organizations" and "apply for 12 nursing jobs or meet 20 professionals."

LAND THAT JOB!

Whatever goal you specified above, make it quantifiable so that you can measure your success. Write it here:

Achievable. Assess what is attainable. Form an agreement with yourself (or others) on what is actionable and useful. Determine which tools, resources, or space you need to accomplish your specific, measurable goal. In terms of the examples given above, you would now determine the "how-to" necessities, such as whether you will search online or visit your local library to identify companies or professional organizations. You might need to identify or create a calm, uncluttered workspace in which to concentrate without interruptions. Organize your approach and track your findings and progress.

What tools and resources will you need to make your specific, measurable goal truly achievable? Write them here:

During the Achievable stage, you might decide to modify your original goal; don't be surprised if you do. You must have adequate tools and resources to achieve your goals, or you will have a harder time succeeding. Remember, you are clearing a path for success. You are identifying goals to define what success looks like on both the micro and macro levels. At this point, you might realize that your micro goal isn't small, simple enough, or realistic. If your goal begins to look too challenging at this point, take a step back and reformulate. You might also realize that in order to accomplish your goal, more steps than expected are needed. Such realizations are normal and acceptable. Take your time, go back, and take another run at it. It will be a quicker endeavor each time you do.

LAND THAT JOB!

Do you need to alter or modify your specific, measurable goal? Rewrite your goal as needed by repeating the last three steps: Specify a better micro goal based upon your reflective activities, assign a measurable metric to it, and determine how to make it achievable by identifying the tools and resources you'll need. Write it all out here:

Relevant. This is a secondary assessment point at which you test your goal by ensuring it is important, reasonable, and results-oriented. It should resonate closely with your macro goal of getting a job or developing your career. If your micro goal doesn't fully support your macro goal, repeat the previous steps to refocus your approach. Misalignment can be the result of knowing you need to accomplish the larger goal but also dreading it, so you create distractions to help you feel or look busy. The problem is, and you know this at a gut level, you'll never achieve that larger goal unless you take concrete, well-aligned steps. Whether or not your goals are realistic may also come into play here.

There are two ways to measure relevancy after misalignment has been ruled out. One, ask yourself what would happen if you worked the micro goal to the end. If working the micro goal would result in something of tangible value, great! However, if your result would be vague or intangible, strengthen it. Two, ask yourself if the goal truly suits you. This is not the same as asking yourself if you want to do it; job search and career development activities are expected to expand your comfort zone as discussed in Chapters 1 and 2. Few people want to go through the process of finding a new job, but they need to, so they do it. It is a relevant endeavor. Perhaps your specific, measurable goal is to land a nursing job that pays at least $100,000 per year. If you are a nurse anesthetist in a major city, this could be reasonable. If you are an LPN at a rural family practice clinic, it could be unreasonable or irrelevant to your situation.

LAND THAT JOB!

How well does your specific, measureable, and well-resourced goal pass the relevancy tests?

Timely. You are ready to attach a schedule to your goal. By attaching a schedule or time frame, you will know when your micro goal should be accomplished so you can let it go, move on to the next one, or repeat it as needed. Make your goal and micro goals time-sensitive or measurable. For example, your micro goal might take place hourly, daily, or weekly. Map it on a calendar.

If the time frame is longer than 1 week, you might want to revisit the specific step and simplify it.

One of your first micro goals might be to identify, within 1 day, 10 companies that hire for your nursing specialty. You can craft another micro goal to immediately follow this one, such as identifying and reaching out to one person at each of these 10 companies within 1 week. Accomplishing micro goals creates momentum in the form of smaller successes. If all goes well, by the end of the week, you have met TWO goals! Even if you are only able to identify and contact six of the 10, you are still much closer to your goal than you were at the start of the week. You could also reassess whether you can meet your goal with a bit more time, or determine if you need a different approach with those remaining four companies. You would make a reasonable course correction and continue forward.

Maintenance goals are larger, macro goals. They may include the goal of getting a job and an added time frame of within 1 month. If you focus only on the maintenance goal, there's nothing more specific for you to work on other than what you have spelled out until the end of the month. The odds that you will have a job lined up are 50-50 without further action. On the other hand, effective maintenance goals reflect milestones you seek to meet over the long haul of career development or job searching. These goals can incorporate monthly check-ins, such as attending networking events, or major accomplishments, such as completing semester-long courses.

SMART goals are fluid and flexible. After you create one or two, you can create dozens over time with ease. Perhaps you're planning to take a week off of work in which to further your goals. You can create goals to accomplish before, during, and after that week.

You can develop your SMART goals in any order you want. The last example showed how you can start with timely if you have a known time frame; then you develop SMART goals that work within that time frame. Similarly, you might craft micro goals that can be accomplished within 1 day so you can see tangible results on a daily basis, the slow and steady approach to meeting your macro goals.

Or you might start with the achievable phase by looking at your resources and tools and developing SMART goals around those assets and liabilities. For example, if you are a single parent with little time at home and a full-time nursing job, you may need to start by identifying a calm, uncluttered space in which to work your goals (or even to start the planning process itself). Your immediate SMART goal might be to use 15 minutes per day during your lunch break to jot down ideas in a journal to pursue and to review previous notes to determine which ones could be accomplished sooner. You can create goals that run consecutively or simultaneously.

Take things a step further with a SMARTER goal, adding evaluation and reward to the mix. Evaluate each goal once met to determine how easy or difficult it was to accomplish. Apply your conclusions to your remaining or evolving SMART goals, and modify them as needed. Or craft new SMART goals to address gaps or to improve strengths for greater success going forward. Find ways to reward yourself as you meet each goal. For some, the very act of successful accomplishment is enough. For others, additional positive reinforcement is needed, especially if the goals are more challenging.

LAND THAT JOB!

Craft five micro goals that are well-aligned with your job search and/or career development macro goals. Write them in a journal or post them on your refrigerator or bathroom mirror or in your locker at work. Turn them into a checklist, if desired, and check them off as you accomplish each one. Or put them into a 1-month calendar so you can keep track of your project by reviewing your calendar each day. Add evaluation and reward steps as desired.

Here is a list of possible SMART goals for job searching:

- Identify calm, uncluttered space for job search activities: 2 days. Create strategy to organize contacts: 1 week.
- Identify 10 companies that hire in your specialty: 48 hours.
- Identify at least one individual associated with each of the 10 companies: 3 days.
- Outreach to all 10 individuals identified: 1 week.
- Conduct at least one new informational interview: weekly.
- Add two new, strategic allies to contact list: weekly.

- Identify at least five positions to apply for: weekly. Join three professional nursing or health care organizations that directly support your career: 1 week.
- Locate and attend one monthly event, one quarterly event, and one large regional/national event: 1 year.
- Follow up on all resumes or applications submitted, depending upon method of submission, to ensure materials were received and to inquire about the interview process: 48-72 hours.
- Create two outfits that are suitable for interviews and are ready to use: 1 week.
- Review and practice responses to 25 common interview questions, out loud, in front of a mirror or recording device, at least four times each: 1 month.
- Enlist specific help from at least five people in your support group who could encourage your efforts through daily accountability check-in calls; share your goals.
- Find a job search buddy (someone whose activities parallel your own), share information: weekly.
- Reach out to potential references to discuss how they can support your job search goals; craft your annotated reference page: 1 week.
- Reach out to five new recruiters asking for a description of their ideal candidate for positions they routinely seek to fill. Determine whether their feedback aligns with your strengths and goals. For every good fit, arrange for an informational interview, submit your resume, or hold a follow-up phone conversation to sell your skills: ongoing.

Here is a list of SMART goals for career development you may want to use in part or in whole. Career development is a sometimes slow, steady progression of ongoing activities including networking, building your experience and expertise, study of literature in your field, and more. Keeping your SMART goals in mind, you can apply specific deadlines as the need arises.

- Define what is most essential to your career: advancement, recognition, money, flexibility, autonomy, charity, adventure, knowledge sharing, mentorship, etc.

- Identify at least three professional organizations and join them, with at least one being an active, local chapter.
- Create and maintain a professional bio on sites of the organizations you have joined and professional networking sites such as LinkedIn.
- Engage in discussion and answer questions in forums as a proficient nurse, knowledgeable in your field, and contributing to the greater good with professionalism, graciousness, and tact for at least 30 minutes.
- Maintain at least one or two interview outfits suitable and ready to use at any given time.
- Observe and analyze job postings in your field and community.
- Update your resume so that you can customize it quickly and effectively.
- Conduct a salary survey online or at your library, and use at least three different sources of information to gauge how your salary compares with the regional average.
- Attend at least one networking event every month.
- Start a career development journal in which you track ideas and make progress notes.
- Strike up a conversation every day with someone you don't know to become more comfortable doing so.
- Read one book, article, or white paper written by fellow nurses every month to follow industry trends or emerging issues.
- Establish yourself as a knowledgeable nursing resource by gleaning and sharing insights from your reading with others.
- Attend and participate in a college course, certification program, continuing education class, seminar, or workshop.
- Visit your supervisor and/or human resources department to discuss career options within your organization.
- Visualize and write about your dream job (or dream retirement), and map out a plan that will get you to that dream.

- Reach out to a colleague, faculty member, classmate or nursing professional asking them about their professional expertise and career development strategies to get where they are. Consider how this informs your own strengths, weaknesses and goals for the future.

Ready, Willing, and Able

Three little words have never meant so much to a prospective employer. In other words, prospective employers want to know to what extent you are ready, willing, and able to take a job, relocate, switch companies, take on a new project, or move up to the next level. These questions are not only asked within formal interview settings. Such assessments are being made about you (and being subtly asked) within your current job, at networking events, and among your peers and supervisors. Therefore, it's important to learn how to speak (and really mean) the language they love to hear. As you move through the job search and career development phases, there are points at which negativity can come out sideways, or you can be caught off guard by the very questions themselves.

This section shows you how to use the words "ready, willing, and able" to diminish negativity and stay on your "A" game throughout your job search or career development efforts. Take heed: This section is not about fluffy responses or telling employers what they want to hear. It is about what you are conveying, who you are, and what your deal breakers are. Knowing these up-front and practicing them keep you from getting caught off guard when the questions arise. This section also helps you to recognize when and by whom such questions are being subtly asked of you.

Ready. Readiness is about being fit for duty and is strongly associated with timing. Are you ready now? Will you be ready soon? What would you need to become ready? To what extent are you fit for duty? How prepared are you in terms of education, experience, personality, and strength of character? More importantly, consider these questions for demonstrating your readiness:

- Do you have the requisite education and experience based on your analysis of common elements?
- Do you have transcripts, diploma, and certificate copies ready in both paper and electronic forms?

- Does your resume reflect readiness in concrete, understandable terms? Are your references in order?
- Have you recently practiced your responses to common interview questions?
- Have you done your homework in terms of company research and salary surveys? Have you identified if, where, and when you could relocate if need be?
- Have you compiled a portfolio in which to showcase what you have done to prepare for the next step in your career?

On a resume, you can show readiness by indicating your expected graduation date; showing a clear career progression toward your goal; showcasing relevant keywords and phrases to show you speak the language; and providing dates of employment. You can highlight strengths and use impactful statements to demonstrate readiness. You can list publications, research, and volunteer experiences that show you are well-versed in the culture and climate of nursing roles.

In networking situations, show readiness by being up-front about your goals and describing the steps you have taken to get ready. Talk about current or past projects you've tackled that demonstrate your achievements. Discuss how your strengths contribute to your sense of readiness. Discuss articles read, workshops attended, and information gleaned that gave you additional insights that support your goal.

What if you are not ready yet or are unsure about it? Reviewing the questions and statements in the previous few paragraphs will help you to assess readiness to some degree. You may be more ready than you think, or it may take a bit more preparation to get you there.

Willing. Willingness is about consent, desirability, and happily anticipating whatever you are trying to achieve. Assess your enthusiasm and define your potential deal breakers. Ask yourself these questions to determine your degree of willingness:

- Are you willing to invest in membership fees or tuition costs?
- Are you willing to expand your comfort zone for a better working situation than you have now?

- Are you willing to take a calculated risk on a move from a current, stable job to something unknown but potentially more rewarding?
- Are you willing to do whatever it takes to make your dreams come true and increase the value of your new organization?
- Are you willing to relocate, take a short-term pay cut, or move to a bigger or smaller operation?

On a resume, willingness is conveyed through your choice of action words and in how you exceed the required qualifications. Caution: This is not to be confused with being "overqualified," but rather that you can spell out how you not only meet the required qualifications, but also the desired ones.

In terms of the action words on your resume, think of how you show willingness and enthusiasm for your current role when you change "Manage 10 nurses on a 30-bed unit" to "Champion 10 highly capable nurses to meet and exceed the needs of a 30-bed unit." Show that you love what you do and want to do even more. In your profile, state that you "have recently obtained XYZ certifications" to help you prepare for the next level. Discuss projects and committees on which you have participated and cheerfully share the "wow factor" of your results or impact.

In networking situations, smile warmly with genuine excitement shining in your eyes as you talk about what you're doing now and what you'd like to do next. Demonstrate your passion for your work, for your patients, for your team. Show your audience that you are the very embodiment of a terrific, accomplished, hard-working nurse with personality plus. Treat problems as puzzles that you thoroughly enjoy solving. Eagerly brainstorm to solve common problems with others. Show your creativity balanced with compliance needs.

LAND THAT JOB!

A note of caution: Try not to appear desperate or too eager to jump ship after you just finished talking about how great a ship it is. You don't want to create a sense of disconnect between what you describe versus the reality of the situation. Keep the old adage in mind: "If you can't say anything nice, don't say anything at all." In other words, find safer topics you can speak well of and make the most of them.

If you have little to no nursing experience, demonstrate your willingness to learn, your excitement about being a nurse, your desire to get your feet wet. If you are moving into semiretirement, discuss your willingness to help in any way that is needed since you have so much experience, so long as you have enough flexibility to take on more personal pursuits.

Issues around unwillingness arise when you obviously aren't excited about the prospects before you, or you won't commit to a particular pursuit. Enthusiasm is hard to fake, so take time to identify what you get excited about, because that will translate to greater success in your micro and macro goals.

If you are unemployed and anxious about your dwindling finances, you might feel pressure to consider jobs you are not excited about. You may require short-term, albeit disheartening or painful, solutions to get you to a position of greater strength. If you find yourself in this situation, look for the silver lining. Find the positives and work with what you've got for the time being. Such situations need not be permanent; view them as a necessary stepping stone to get to your dream.

Conversely, don't settle for something you don't want just because it's easier, quicker, or because you don't know what all your options are. Job seekers routinely underestimate their options. Be mindful that you are not selling yourself short without a good reason. This is where calculated risk taking helps you to assess where your tipping point is. However, you also don't want to limit what you are willing to do so narrowly that the only things you will do are unrealistic. If you suspect this is the case, revisit your SMART goals with an emphasis on realism.

Able. Ability speaks to your capacity and competence to complete tasks, whether physical, financial, ethical, emotional, or intellectual. It speaks to your special skills and talents. At the least, all nursing jobs require a nursing degree because competency tests are built into the curriculum; prospective employers are assured that your competence has been assessed at multiple points along the way. Certifications are a further test of competence. Experience goes yet further to strengthen your competence and prove your abilities in many real situations.

Ability can refer to your capacity to handle yourself in a particular culture or climate or with a certain management style or patient population. For example, there are excellent nurses who are wonderful in a family practice but wouldn't last a day on a burn unit. Others work wonderfully with children but find those same care characteristics fall short when working with chemically dependent populations. Nurses who specialize in anesthesia are naturally calculated risk takers and have a strong stomach for potentially life-threatening situations. Some nurses find the hectic pace of emergency medicine exhausting, whereas others find it exhilarating. Being in tune with your abilities and capacities will serve you well over the years. You may expand your comfort zone over time and even surprise yourself along the way. Beware, however, of thinking of your abilities in such concrete or universal terms that you wind up falling short of expectations. Remain humble as you grow as a nurse.

On a resume, ability is showcased through your education and experience, not only in what you've done but also in terms of where you've done it. This is why it is helpful to work as a certified nursing assistant or health unit coordinator while in nursing school, so that you can develop related on-the-job abilities and capacities prior to graduation. It's also great for your resume. Different nursing schools take different approaches or are better known for certain specialties than others. Providing direct nursing care in a purely outpatient clinic setting is vastly different than an inpatient setting with chronically ill patients and complicated treatment regimens. On your resume, emphasize scope by indicating type and size of units, whether you have worked as part of a large or small nursing team, types of equipment you've used, procedures performed, etc.

If you are targeting new roles that are similar to what you have done recently with a few key differences, such as facility size or the supervision of a greater number of nurses, your goal is congruent with your experience. Your education and experience must directly support your goals.

In networking settings, ability is demonstrated by describing how you handled yourself in different settings, how you resolved challenges with a good attitude, describing both what you are good at and sharing a bit about your limitations to show that you have a clear sense of what you can and cannot do well. Talk about where you went to school and what you found most valuable about the experience. Talk about related jobs you held while in nursing school. Describe the work environments and management styles in which you thrived. Talk about how you continue to grow as a nurse, how you're expanding your comfort zone, and how you stay positive when the job gets stressful.

You must be ready, willing, and able because all three are necessary ingredients in any job search or career development endeavor. You cannot operate fully without them all. Readiness is about preparation and the steps you take to get prepared (such as going to nursing school). Willingness is about commitment with enthusiasm (such as excitement about being a nurse). Ability is about how you are actually able to perform going forward, which is largely predicated on how you have performed in the past (that is, proving you can perform well as a nurse). If you have readiness and ability but not willingness, how will you find the motivation to make changes (common among job-seeking nurses)? If you have readiness and willingness but not ability, how will you convince others you can do the job, especially in demanding environments (common among recent graduates)? And lastly, if you are willing and able but not ready, how will you get started with either job search or career development pursuits, considering you don't have the requisite prep work completed or don't know where to begin (common among those currently employed and just starting to contemplate a change)?

LAND THAT JOB!

Of the three ingredients—ready, willing, and able—which one is strongest? Weakest? What can you do to leverage the stronger and bolster the weaker? How can you optimize all three on your resume and in networking situations?

Raising the Bar

Shine in all ways! Here are tips and tricks to present your best self to the world. You are visible. People are watching. Show them your brilliance. Take a look at each of the following situations and apply them, as appropriate, to your own world.

In your current job while developing your career:

- Follow your organization's dress code with the highest professional standard. Even if you have to wear the same scrubs as everyone else, clean shoes and neatly groomed hair reflect professionalism.
- Know the rules where you work before you wear jewelry to work.
- Check your personal baggage at the door, including negativity or apathy.
- Practice what the health care community preaches to patients and show it by organizing an exercise club—walking, running, Zumba, yoga, etc.—a smoking-cessation group, or by bringing veggies to share.

- Introduce other healthful ideas to your unit.
- Network at work by introducing yourself to those you don't know and re-introducing yourself to someone whose name you can't remember.
- Ask your supervisor to help you make a stronger connection to his or her boss or the boss's boss. Meet your counterparts on other units. Connect with the nursing staff in another clinic in your building.
- Sign up for work-sponsored events and workshops as a way to grow professionally and extend your work-based network.
- Be mindful of your words; you are always making an impression whether you are greeting someone or having a conversation with other nurses. Stay focused and commit to using a positive tone.
- Be a mentor to a junior nurse, and keep your supervisor in the loop.
- Find a senior nurse to serve as your mentor. Again, speak to your supervisor first, so he or she can make recommendations or pave the way for you.
- Track how and where you spend your time, so that you can identify and eliminate time wasters.
- Refrain from engaging in rumor, gossip, or any type of subtle or direct attacks. Be the very picture of positivity and graciousness. Apologize to anyone you have intentionally or unintentionally harmed.
- Make and maintain a list of on-the-job accomplishments, and reflect upon them often to help you through times of stress.
- Save copies of performance reviews, complimentary notes from supervisors and colleagues, and thank-you notes from patients. These can refresh your motivation and help you understand how your performance is viewed by others.
- Don't miss breaks or mealtimes by working through them. Taking a breather, a walk, a stretch, or a veggie break helps to maintain your sanity.
- Follow through on your word; honor commitments and don't slack off. Be proactive and think ahead. Don't put off until tomorrow what you can accomplish today.

- If you feel overworked, practice saying "no" in a polite but firm manner, so you can carve out some breathing room for yourself and maintain a healthier balance.
- If you have the time, find ways to help others.
- Ask your boss for an additional assignment that allows you to develop new skills.
- Understand the performance appraisal and review process well, stay on top of goals that have been set, track your progress to use for self-evaluations, and ask about promotions.

In your job search as part of your career development activities:

- Dedicate yourself to job searching and networking activities.
- If you are unemployed, consider your job search to be your job and work at least part-time hours toward your goal. Stay focused with daily and weekly goals that move you forward while keeping your efforts consistent.
- Prepare your interview clothing and accessories so they are ready for action.
- Participate in healthy activities to keep your motivation and energy up, especially during slower stretches. Pursuing healthy activities reinforces career changes.
- Create and regularly update your professional profile on networking sites.
- Strike up conversations with people you meet over the course of your day as a regular practice of networking.
- Practice positive affirmations every day to keep your mind and attitude strong.
- Set up and facilitate regular informational interviews.
- Stay mindful of how your spend your time, minimize time wasting that doesn't serve you.
- Grow your personal support network.

- Actively network. Research and reach out to companies of interest, learning about their mission and organizational culture and meeting employees who presently work there.
- Stay positive, focused, and committed to your micro and macro goals.

No matter how you go about it, be a shining light for others. This comes naturally with your patients, but remember to extend your light to your team. Bring light and clarity to your daily life. Maximize those things that enhance your light; eliminate those things that diminish your light. One of the many benefits of developing your career is that you improve your personal life along the way. By actively taking care of your career, you take better care of yourself. With shine comes polish. Increase your visibility and savor the spotlight when you get it. Let others shine, too. You'll shine brighter together!

References

Doran, G.T. (1981). There's a S.M.A.R.T. way to write management's goals and objectives. *Management Review*, *70*(11), 35-36.

Fast, N.J., & Tiedens, L.Z. (2010). Blame contagion: The automatic transmission of self-serving attributions. *Journal of Experimental Social Psychology*, *46*, 97-106

Best Candidate Checklist

___ I have cleared away what is holding me down or back in my continued job search efforts.

___ I have tackled internal negativity and replaced it with positive affirmations.

___ I have identified what I can control with a plan while letting go of things beyond my control.

___ I have determined who I consistently tend to blame for my situation, why I blame them, and how to take back control by letting go of blame.

___ I have found creative, positive, and funk-busting ways to sustain my job search activities.

___ I have made a list of my information gaps—things I need to learn more about so that the answers can propel my job search forward.

___ I have developed a clear set of S.M.A.R.T. goals to keep my job search on track.

___ I have demonstrated on paper how I am ready, willing, and able to make my next career move.

___ I have come to understand all the ways I can truly shine in my current role and throughout my job search.

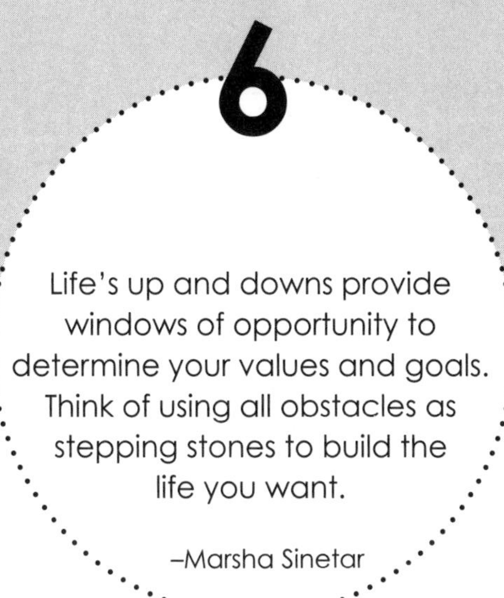

6
Life's up and downs provide windows of opportunity to determine your values and goals. Think of using all obstacles as stepping stones to build the life you want.
–Marsha Sinetar

Your Short- and Long-Term Goals

How do you spend your time? How do those choices impact your job search? This chapter takes a hard look at what you are actively choosing to do that either enhances or diminishes your job search strategy. This is one of those areas mentioned in the introduction that will challenge you, expand your comfort zone, and ultimately make your job search approach stronger with successful milestones embedded along the way.

Doing Versus Dreaming—Letting Go

Once you have a plan, you are ready for action. Seize the day! This chapter provides active steps to take every day to reach your goal. All goals require adequate planning to be successful; the trick is not to get so caught up in the "planning" that you never get to "doing." This section covers the actual doing of everything from immediate job search needs to long-term career development desires.

By now, you should already have your plans and micro goals on paper, in your journal, in a notebook, on your calendar, on your refrigerator or bathroom mirror, on the dashboard of your car—anyplace readily visible and upon which you can track and evaluate your progress. Experiment over the course of a week to find the best method for you. Think about how you spend the bulk of your time. If you are often on your feet and running around, you need something portable such as a small notebook or smart phone. If you are at the computer a lot, look at tracking and maintaining your plans on that. If you spend a good deal of time commuting, find ways to organize and record new information and feedback while in your car or on the bus. Ideas for commuting include recording your thoughts and notes via voice notes, gathering information through podcasts, and listening to inspirational CDs or resources. Ultimately, you have to find a way to quickly store, organize, and retrieve all new bits of information on a daily basis.

LAND THAT JOB!

What organizational tool and process have you decided upon? Are there strengths and limitations to your choice? How can you manage around any apparent weaknesses of your tools? What might you use as a backup plan that meshes well with your primary system?

Next, determine how much time you can set aside and commit to using for the sole purpose of meeting your job search or career development goals. How much time can you create? Face it, you probably don't "have" the time already, so you must intentionally make the time, which may also mean choosing to give something up for the duration. If you are already busy or even overwhelmed, simply adding to your list of daily tasks and not eliminating something else is a recipe for loss of energy and enthusiasm. Make the time and the requisite sacrifices to foster true, sustainable success. Start by making a list of everything you do in a given day. You can use a calendar blank, if desired, or create something in Word or Excel. You can use the following list and note in the margin of this book the amount of time you spend on each.

The immediate objective is to identify what your daily life looks like, as it is, right now before making any substantive changes. Be sure to include time you spend on:

- Sleeping
- Meal prep and eating
- Getting showered and dressed/personal care, including haircuts
- Exercise or mediation
- Pet care
- Transporting children or others in your care from one place to another
- Supervising children or others in your care
- Commuting to and from work
- Actual work hours
- School/in class or doing homework/studying
- Social time with family and friends
- Personal errands and phone calls
- Watching TV and playing on the computer
- Gardening, taking care of your property, and cleaning your living space
- Special projects, hobbies, or clubs
- Networking or other recurring professional events
- Anything else you can think of

It is easy to question how you will ever find time to job search on top of everything else. Yes, it can be done! Once you have a clear picture of how much time you spend on routine activities, you can make necessary adjustments. Chances are your plate is already quite full; therefore, simply adding new tasks to support your job search or career development goals simply isn't going to happen as desired. You have to make time. How much time? If working a full-time job, you may not be able to make more 1 hour per day, and you'll have to keep yourself highly organized for that 1 hour per day to be productive and meaningful. Think about all the ideas generated in Chapters 4 and 5, in terms of plans you'd like to make and in the ways you'd like to shine. How much time is needed?

If you need an additional 10 hours per week, what can you radically cut for the next 3-6 months to achieve your goals? For example, if you watch TV or gravitate to your computer for personal pursuits for more than 2 hours per day, cutting those would easily provide the extra 10 hours per week. Before you balk at the injustice of it all, ask yourself how TV or personal computer time compares to advancing your career, making more money, and becoming the best nurse you can be.

If you find the idea of giving up personal pleasures for a few months so distasteful that you would sacrifice your professional growth, you may need to revisit Chapter 4, seek counseling, or read self-improvement books that help you focus on getting out of your own way. It could be that you simply are not yet ready, willing, or able to take on professional growth activities right now. This happens for a variety of reasons: depression, grief, feeling overwhelmed and stressed, chronic fatigue, chemical dependency, and other issues. If this is the case for you, map out a timetable and sources of professional support to get you back on track. Giving up TV altogether (including video games) for the short term should not be problematic.

You take on other tasks simply because they are expected of you or you feel they are your responsibility. Perhaps you believe your way is better than someone else's. Let go of any outdated perceptions that no longer serve you. Someone else can likely get things done just as well, or you can loosen some of your perfectionist standards for a while. Let go. Here are examples of different approaches to take.

Find someone else, delegate, pay for professional services—whatever helps you let go of routine tasks for the short term. Ask unemployed neighbors to help you out, and pay them for their time or "swap" childcare time in ways that allow you a bit of free time to pursue projects independently. Tell your spouse, partner, children, or parents that you need them to step up to the plate and do more for a while. Give them a time frame. Share what you are trying to accomplish during the specified time. This will all serve as motivation to stay on track and make your efforts and accomplishments visible along the way. It can help to point out how if your career improves, your family's life will improve, too. By involving others in your plan, they can see how they are indeed part of the solution, that their actions are an investment in the family.

For each of the routine tasks, determine which changes can and should be made. Here are some possibilities:

Activity	Possible timesavers/ changes	Your chosen approach
Sleep	Getting enough? Too much?	
Meals	Too much? Too little? Healthy foods?	
Personal care	Looking your best? Cut something out? Move certain items to weekends only?	
Exercise/ meditation	Getting enough? Streamline routines?	
Pet care	Can someone else handle this now?	
Dependent care	Can someone else handle this now?	
Commuting	Can you take the bus and use time making notes or working on your computer? Can you adjust your work schedule to commute outside of rush hour? Can you ride your bike or walk to offset time spent on another exercise routine? If driving, can you listen to a motivational or informational CD and reflect upon it?	

Activity	Possible timesavers/ changes	Your chosen approach
Working	Many employers allow you to take paid or unpaid time for professional development activities. Find out what is available and take advantage. Take a quieter shift. Job share. Use all/full break times to reflect.	
School/ studying	Find out if you can get credit for alternative activities. Take a career development course. Visit career services regularly while at school. Study/do more homework at school versus at home.	
Social time	Determine how much is truly needed for the short term. Plan specific activities versus just "hanging out." Try to avoid alcohol/happy hour. Exercise with friends as an alternative.	
Errands/phone calls	Set aside a block of time each week and do them all at once. Enlist help. Get a hands-free device and make calls while commuting.	
TV/computer/ personal	Be intentional and healthy about the amount of time spent on these activities. Get TiVo or rent a streaming service and limit TV to Sunday afternoons as a treat.	

Activity	Possible timesavers/ changes	Your chosen approach
Housework/ yard work	Can someone else handle this now? Stick to the basics for a while. Hire a service for 3-6 months.	
Projects/ hobbies/clubs	Limit participation as feasible. Finish one project and delay starting the next.	
Networking/ pro events	Continue. Do more. Make sure choices here are good, active, useful events.	
Other	Can someone else handle this now?	
Other	Can someone else handle this now?	

Finally, calculate how much time you're able to create for your job search or career development goals. Once you have determined how much time you have, decide how to effectively organize your tasks.

LAND THAT JOB!

How much time were you able to create? ________
For how long? __________ weeks/months

How can you best fill the time you've made with job search or career development activities? Which micro goals will you work on first?

#1:

#2:

#3:

#4:

#5:

Strategize Constructively

In addition to having a plan and a clear set of action steps or micro goals, a larger strategy or macro goal will keep you on track and help you make course corrections along the way. This section focuses on how to align your plan and action steps with the larger picture.

If you focus entirely on the large goals, it can be very challenging to see gratifying results in a timely manner. It may dampen any enthusiasm you have for risk-taking. Frustration can also serve to fuel self-doubt. Conversely, if you focus entirely on smaller, micro goals, you stop being able to see the forest for the trees. You end up too close to it all with a microscopic perspective that leads you off track from the larger goals. The key is balance. You need to balance the bigger with the smaller, the macro with the micro, the forest and the trees.

Think back to Chapter 4, where you read about resumes. The title bar and profile area represents the larger goal—it states what you want to obtain. Your education and work experience represent the smaller goals, the steps you took to be ready for the larger picture. Your resume, then, represents a healthy sense of balance.

Suppose your larger goal is to become a published author of articles on a professional networking site for nurses within 6 months. Smaller goals over the course of 3-6 months might include:

- Completing a writing workshop designed to help you organize your material, write concise headlines and content, and clarify your message
- Becoming a member on each of the sites you identify and locating their publication guidelines
- Identifying the top 10 articles on the various sites in terms of most public feedback, commentary, or views and analyzing each for common elements across topic, content, tone, and length
- Identifying and reaching out to the website communications coordinator or editor directly involved in publishing articles
- Submitting an initial article for feedback
- Re-submitting the article after incorporating feedback
- Repeating the process with 10+ sites until you get an article published

- Evaluating what approaches have worked, eliminating what hasn't worked, and modifying your micro goals to more strongly align with the macro goal of getting an article published on a professional networking site for nurses

Suppose your larger goal is to become a keynote speaker for a national nursing organization within 5 years. Smaller goals over the course of 1-5 years might have you:

- Identify topics about which you are already passionate and at least somewhat knowledgeable
- Complete one or more public speaking courses to learn all the ways to wow your audience
- Research your chosen topics
- Form a compelling thesis statement for each of your chosen topics that will grab an audience's attention
- Start seeking out and speaking to small, local groups on any of your chosen topics
- Analyze evaluation results and find common themes to adjust (remember that there will always be one or two negative comments; carefully consider whether these are valid or need no response on your part)
- Obtain recommendations from group organizers; ask them to refer other event organizers to you, and have them post a review of your speech on professional networking sites
- Continue to hone your speaking skills and persuasive power by delivering your well-rehearsed speeches to ever larger audiences from local to regional to statewide events while soliciting evaluations and recommendations
- Be prepared to accept speaking engagements on a national or international scale when they are offered to you
- Evaluate what approaches have worked, eliminate those that didn't, and modify your micro goals to more strongly align with the macro goal of becoming a keynote speaker for a national nursing organization within 5 years

LAND THAT JOB!

One of the best ways to balance the macro with the micro is to define the macro goal and work your project backward. Identify micro goals in reverse order until you arrive at a solid starting point. This ensures all of your micro goals lead to your macro goal.

For example, suppose your macro goal is to land the role of charge nurse in the neonatal unit of a brand new hospital that's set to open in 1 year. Recruiting for the top positions of medical director, chief financial officer or controller, and director of facilities is already underway. Working in reverse chronological order, you would start with the end goal in mind—starting your first day on the job as charge nurse in that brand new neonatal unit.

For that to happen, consider the steps that need to precede day one on the job. Working backward, you would get something like this:

1. You hired and prepped all staff nurses.
2. You understood what was expected of you in your new role.
3. You had several meetings with your boss and your management peers to determine what needed to be implemented and how.
4. You got to know your boss and team.
5. The job was offered to you.
6. You interviewed well and did your salary research.
7. Your resume, cover letter, and initial screening call impressed the recruiter and hiring manager—and got past the "eyes" of their automated applicant tracking system.
8. You had a well-crafted, keyword-rich, and visually pleasing resume and cover letter.
9. You knew how to customize your resume and cover letter based on what you learned from the posting and other sources.
10. You did not rely solely on the posting. You conducted informational interviews; networked for more intelligence on the needs of the emerging facility; and had strong, reputable, and credible references.

11. You strengthened your networking contacts through proximity and frequency; conveyed a singular message about your desire to advance; were clear about which role you sought (charge nurse); and showed your readiness, willingness, and ability to take on that role.
12. You ensured you were ready, willing, and able to every extent possible.

With this list in hand, work steps, then wait for the job offers to roll in!

Since you have seen clearly how the micro goals cascaded down from the macro goal, you are assured of balance. Macro and micro goals can be of size, so long as they are proportional to one another. Goal size does not necessarily lend to nor detract from a sense of balance; rather, you must show how they tie together and reinforce each other. Once you identify a macro goal, create a set of supporting micro goals. Then, with each micro goal, ask yourself how well it supports or feeds into the macro goal. Adjust as necessary. If you find disconnects, use the reverse chronological order technique.

Try the reverse chronological order technique yourself:

List Macro Goal Here:
For that to happen, I need to have done this:
For that to happen, I need to have done this:
For that to happen, I need to have done this:
For that to happen, I need to have done this:
For that to happen, I need to have done this:
For that to happen, I need to have done this:
For that to happen, I need to have done this:
For that to happen, I need to have done this:

Add more lines as needed until you arrive at a reasonable starting point you can initiate today or this week. Determine if you found it more helpful to keep things strictly sequential or if you prefer to tackle micro goals concurrently. Each micro goal becomes a milestone with its own measurement of successful completion.

Calendar Exercise to Stay on Track and Timely

This activity helps to turn the previous ideas and techniques into reality by embedding them into whatever calendar system you already use. With a calendar, you can better estimate time to completion for each milestone. Calendars or planners can be paper-based or electronic. The best choice for your purposes will be a) whatever you are already and consistently using or b) whatever best adapts to how and where you spend the bulk of your time. Consider whether you need a system that is mobile and has the infrastructure to support effective management such as while driving or requiring wireless Internet access.

Review the following sample calendar that reflects a variety of job search and career development projects. Further sample calendars are available in the appendices. Choose the one that best reflects your own situation and adapt it, or create one of your own from scratch. With every calendar, work your plan for 60-90 days, then take a week off and determine whether you should continue your plan or redirect your efforts elsewhere.

Figure 6.1 is a calendar is for a currently employed nurse and single parent in a facility with a Monday-through-Friday work schedule who is launching a job search for a new role offering a better salary. The first day reflects what the norm was before launching a job search. You will notice that "exercise" is noted frequently. For you, exercise might look like an actual workout, a brief walk, stretching, running a folded pile of laundry up the stairs, or anything else that can easily be worked into your routine. Exercise gives you an active outlet that can clear your head and keep nagging worries at bay. It can be anything that helps you maintain forward momentum.

Figure 6.1: A job search calendar for a currently employed single-mother nurse working in a health care facility.

Monday	Tuesday	Wednesday	Thursday	Friday	Saturday	Sunday
Get up/ exercise	Get up/ exercise	Get up/ exercise	Get up/ exercise	Get up/exercise	Get up/ exercise	Get up/exercise
Personal care/ eat	Personal care/ eat	Personal care/ eat	Personal care/ eat	Personal care/eat	Personal care/eat	Personal care/ eat
Commute	Commute/ reflect	Commute/ reflect	Commute/ reflect	Commute/reflect	Make list of all known professional contacts and determine whom to reach out to as a direct or indirect strategic ally	Craft new master/base resume and construct a cover letter template to speed customizations and submission time for the month ahead
Work 8 hours	Work 8 hours	Work 8 hours	Work 8 hours	Work 8 hours	Create annotated reference list	Laundry
Commute	Commute/ reflect	Commute/ reflect	Jot down notes during break	Jot down notes during break	Play with kids	Kids do housework and yard work, then decide to hire a service
Dinner/kids	Dinner/kids	Dinner/kids	Commute/ reflect	Commute/reflect	Dinner/TV/ TiVo	Dinner/TV/ TiVo
Watch TV	Watch TV/ set up TiVo or service	Jot down reflective notes, make a plan	Dinner/kids	Dinner/send kids to a sleepover	Sleep 8-9 hours	Sleep 7-8 hours
Sleep 7-8 hours	Sleep 7-8 hours	Sleep 7-8 hours	Ask neighbor for help with kids 3 eves/wk for 2 months	Identify list of companies to target, types of roles to pursue		
			Locate job postings to analyze	Sleep 7-8 hours		
			Sleep 7-8 hours			

Monday	Tuesday	Wednesday	Thursday	Friday	Saturday	Sunday
Get up/ exercise	Get up/ exercise	Get up/ exercise	Get up/ exercise	Get up/exercise	Get up/ exercise	Get up/exercise
Personal care/ eat	Personal care/ eat	Personal care/ eat	Personal care/ eat	Personal care/eat	Personal care/eat	Personal care/ eat
Commute/ call to set up cleaning and yard services for 2 months	Commute/ listen to inspirational or informative CDs	Commute/ listen to inspirational or informative CDs	Commute/ listen to inspirational or informative CDs	Commute/listen to inspirational or informative CDs	Explore LinkedIn or other professional networking site fully, add to your contacts, participate in forums, answer questions, post your master resume, apply for 5 jobs	Follow up with everyone who accepted your invite and start a dialogue
Work 8 hours	Work 8 hours	Work 8 hours	Work 8 hours	Work 8 hours	Play with kids	Apply for 3 jobs
Network at work	Network at work	Network at work	Network at work	Network at work	Dinner/TV/ TiVo	Locate upcoming local events to attend
Commute/ reflect	Commute/ reflect	Commute/ reflect	Commute/ reflect	Commute/reflect	Sleep 8-9 hours	Update your notes/record your activities to stay organized
Dinner/kids	Dinner/kids to neighbor	Dinner/kids to neighbor	Dinner/kids to neighbor	Dinner/kids		Play with kids
Identify additional ways to save time for 2 months, conduct a salary survey	Create a LinkedIn or other networking site profile, explore the site, join 12+ nursing groups	Locate 1 posting and apply, then reflect on milestones so far	Locate 2 postings and apply, record activities to stay organized	Identify 20+ hiring managers and recruiters to invite into LinkedIn network		Dinner/TV/ TiVo
Sleep 7-8 hours	Sleep 7-8 hours	Sleep 7-8 hours	Sleep 7-8 hours	Sleep 7-8 hours		Sleep 8-9 hours

Monday	Tuesday	Wednesday	Thursday	Friday	Saturday	Sunday
Get up/ exercise	Get up/ exercise	Get up/ exercise	Get up/ exercise	Get up/exercise	Get up/ exercise	Get up/exercise
Personal care/ eat	Personal care/ eat	Personal care/ eat	Personal care/ eat	Personal care/eat	Personal care/eat	Personal care/ eat
Commute/ listen to inspirational or informative CDs	Commute/ listen to inspirational or informative CDs	Commute/ listen to inspirational or informative CDs	Commute/ listen to inspirational or informative CDs	Commute/listen to inspirational or informative CDs	Explore LinkedIn or other professional networking site fully, add to your contacts, participate in forums, answer questions, post your master resume, apply for 5 jobs	Follow up with everyone who accepted your invite and start a dialogue
Work 8 hours	Work 8 hours	Work 8 hours	Work 8 hours	Work 8 hours	Play with kids	Apply for 3 jobs
Network at lunch	Network at lunch	Network at lunch	Network at lunch	Network at lunch	Dinner/TV/ TiVo	Locate upcoming local events to attend
Commute/ reflect	Commute/ reflect	Commute/ reflect	Commute/ reflect	Commute/reflect	Sleep 8-9 hours	Update your notes/record your activities to stay organized
Dinner/kids to neighbor	Dinner/kids to neighbor	Dinner/kids to neighbor	Dinner/kids to neighbor	Dinner/kids to neighbor		Play with kids
Locate 2 postings and apply, find 5+ new LinkedIn contacts, record activities to stay organized	Locate 2 postings and apply or attend a local event, record activities to stay organized	Locate 2 postings and apply or attend a local event, record activities to stay organized	Locate 2 postings and apply or attend a local event, record activities to stay organized	Locate 2 postings and apply, find 5+ new LinkedIn contacts, record activities to stay organized		Dinner/TV/ TiVo
Sleep 7-8 hours	Sleep 7-8 hours	Sleep 7-8 hours	Sleep 7-8 hours	Sleep 7-8 hours		Sleep 8-9 hours

Repeat the previous weeks for the next month, adjust as needed, and evaluate your efforts along the way.

Figure 6.2 is a blank calendar for your own purposes. In the space provided, briefly describe your situation and job searching goal. Use the first day to reflect your current schedule. Build from there the strategies you will need to carve out time for your job search or career development efforts.

What have you got to lose? You won't lose friends during this metamorphosis; if you do; they aren't really your friends, are they? Enlist your pals as a direct mode of support versus a gang to hang with when there isn't anything else going on. Ask your family for help. Go ahead and mix things up for a while. Chances are that one of the reasons you are seeking a professional change is because you're bored, and you sense there must be something more to gain, a way to stretch your horizons. You could also take up rock climbing, but that is not what you had in mind when you picked up this book in the first place.

LAND THAT JOB!

What have you chosen to give up in to create time for pursuing job search or career development goals? If you anticipate any "pushback" from them, think about how you might proactively combat any potential negativity or confusion from family, friends, and neighbors, to make them supportive partners in your job search project.

Your time is valuable; make the most of it. Recognize that sacrifices are temporary. Stay focused on what you hope to gain yet realize it won't happen overnight. Understand that simply adding tasks to your plate almost guarantees they will not be sustainable for more than a day or two unless you remove unnecessary activities. Keep healthy activities intact; increase them as needed to keep your energy and attitude strong. Recognize what can bring you down and avoid it. You will likely craft healthier routines for yourself across the board, benefitting yourself personally as well. You can do this!

Figure 6.2: Use this blank to create your own job search calendar.

Situation/Goal:						
______day	______day	______day	______day	______day	______day	______day

Best Candidate Checklist

- ___ I have transitioned from thinking about taking action to taking active steps every day to propel my job search forward.
- ___ I have analyzed how I spend my time and how my activities can be restructured to benefit my job search and career development.
- ___ I have constructed both micro and macro professional goals and know how to balance them.
- ___ I have projected the appropriate series of tasks to tackle based on my ultimate goal.
- ___ I have created a calendar or schedule to follow until I have achieved my goal.
- ___ I have given up activities that I know will directly and negatively impact my job search success.

7

Success is almost totally dependent upon drive and persistence. The extra energy required to make another effort or try another approach is the secret of winning.

–Denis Waitley

Fine-Tuning Your Approach for Job Search and Career Success

There is far more that you can control along your path to a new job and career success than you think. Though there is much that is subjective and influenced by others, how you handle yourself across different environments and scenarios says a great deal about who you are. How well you stand up for yourself, handle adversity, take advantage of new opportunities, and give back to the nursing community is a reflection of who you are. How you are perceived correlates directly to how much influence you have over other people's subjectivity.

You have seen this in action anytime you persuaded someone to reconsider you and your abilities or to see you in a positive light in the first place.

Continue reading to discover how you can fine-tune your approach and bring consistency, graciousness, and etiquette to your job search or career development efforts, yet still be unique. Bringing your best self into the light, every day, reinforces your own strong sense of self, which brings confidence and personal power for all the world to see.

Consistency

Consistency is the degree to which your standards conform to behavior. In other words, to what extent do you practice what you preach to yourself or others? Consistent practices and behaviors vary little over time. Consistency can be positive or negative; a person might be routinely late or punctual for every shift. It can be measured or quantified by the number of times a person behaves the same way in the same set of circumstances.

LAND THAT JOB!

Have you started strong in any number of projects only to watch your dreams and energy slow to a trickle? Have you taken a strong stance on a topic only to be quickly persuaded to change your tune? Do you see yourself one way yet have to regularly defend opposite perceptions of yourself by others? If you answered yes to the first three questions, try to identify the point at which things changed from a stronger to a weaker or less certain position.

If you were to make a list of people it's easier to be nice to, would it contain a list of only certain names, or would it be a very short list that simply read "everyone"? Have you sworn you were going to make good on a promise to yourself or another and then not followed through? Do you stand up for yourself in some situations but not others? Again, try to narrow down the point at which things changed direction, and reflect on the how and why as best you can. You may come away with deeper clarity and be able to know the moment the opportunity presents itself to keep things going strong.

The common theme across each of the questions is inconsistency. Being inconsistent can negatively impact your job search and career success. Instead of looking at possible causes of inconsistency, concentrate on where you have noted inconsistency in your own actions, and look for ways you can create consistency going forward. However, as with all things related to job searching and career development, be your own best advocate and focus on your strengths. It is easier to be consistent where you are already strong. As discussed in Chapters 2 and 3, it is far easier to improve an existing strength than a known weakness. One of the ways to manage around your weaknesses is to find workable solutions that you can consistently apply.

What does consistency look like in terms of job searching and career development? Finding what works or is beneficial and doing those things repeatedly. For example, routinely attend networking events. Always follow up on submitted resumes and applications within 48 hours, even if you don't always get the desired response. Proofread all materials carefully before sending them into circulation. Never fail to genuinely thank someone for help along the way, even if the job lead or advice provided didn't have the desired effect.

When your positive behavior and performance vary little over time, others notice and attribute to you traits of reliability, trustworthiness, credibility, and personal power. Intuitively, you know that consistently negative behaviors have the opposite effect.

LAND THAT JOB!

Make a list of the top five positive things you do consistently and note the benefits of each. Then, list five things you are not consistent about and identify the consequences of each. Where can you make small yet meaningful changes that will help you meet your job search and career development objectives?

People commonly rationalize inconsistency by attributing causes to other people or external situations. The trick is to remember that it all comes back to how you perceive yourself and others. You control how you perceive other people and situations. You may perceive someone to be preventing you from advancing in your role, and you may very well be right about that. But you might then perceive, incorrectly so, that there isn't anything you can do about that person or this circumstance. Such hopelessness can leave you feeling stuck.

You may be dealing with a situation in the workplace where your supervisor has inconsistent reactions to normal, day-to-day issues. This can be a difficult situation, especially if you try to accommodate your superior's inconsistency. It is important when you notice such inconsistency to call attention to it, tactfully and without rancor. Your supervisor might acknowledge your claim favorably, dismiss it out of hand, or vehemently deny it. Those are his or her choices. You, in turn, have a choice as to how you will react further. The trick is to persuade him or her to be positively consistent with you. Otherwise, such inconsistency builds pressure over time, causing you to seek needed changes, healthy or unhealthy. An excellent resource for difficulties with your direct supervisor is Crowley and Elster's book, *Working for You Isn't Working for Me* (2009). The best action you can take is to maintain a consistently positive self-image as discussed in Chapter 2. To be consistent on the inside, you need to have a strong grounding in your own self. This means that you must have a firm hold on and acceptance of your values and beliefs about yourself, as this directly affects your behavior, which in turn is displayed in a consistent or inconsistent manner. Don't worry about anybody else at this point. Focus on you.

Table 7.1 is an exercise to help you articulate what is important to you and how that translates into consistently positive behaviors that you demonstrate across situational variables. The first line provides an example.

Table 7.1: Articulate your priorities and translate them into positive behaviors.

A strong belief or value you hold about yourself as a nurse	How you demonstrate positive behavior associated with it	Situations you might be tempted to be inconsistent about it for any reason
Everyone deserves care	*Jump in to help*	*Too busy, overwhelmed*

There are many ways to maintain a strong, consistent sense of self. This next section offers six ways to do so. As you read through them, assess to what extent you do these well and consistently. You can use a scoring rubric of 1–5 to assess your level of positive consistency: 1 being positive but highly inconsistent and 5 being positive and highly consistent. The point is to assess to what extent you handle each of the following in truly positive ways. Or you may assess a -5 to +5 scale with plus numbers in the positive realm and negative numbers in the negative realm. For example, anything you do consistently and positively would be a +4 or +5. Conversely, for any of the following items that you handle consistently but in negative ways, the score would be a -4 or -5. Either way, write your chosen values for each item in the corresponding boxes below.

Trusting Your Gut

To what extent do you consistently listen to and trust your inner voice? How well do you recognize your first instinct that someone or something is good or bad, healthy or unhealthy, consistent or inconsistent, right or wrong? This is not about whether those snap value judgments are a good thing or a bad thing, but rather that your innate sense of the world around you actually works in conjunction, or in congruence, with your beliefs and values. You may recall a time when you met someone and knew immediately you really liked and felt close to him or her. Or you were presented with an opportunity, and you sensed without hesitation that it was just right for you.

Conversely, what do your inner warning signals actually feel like? For instance, you might feel your head get warm, experience a sinking feeling in your stomach, or feel an immediate desire to physically step away. How often do you listen to these signals versus tamping them down? Do you ignore them for personal convenience and social or professional comfort? Do you hope the discomfort will resolve itself on its own or tell yourself it is nothing to worry about? Have you sensed immediate, inner hesitation yet gone forward anyway? Even if you are not entirely sure which beliefs and values had been fully or potentially compromised in a given situation, you can still "trust your gut" by stepping away and reflecting on the best decision and action for you to make.

Trust your gut score: _________

Doing and Looking Your Best

You want to do your best. You hold yourself to a set of expectations as to how you conduct yourself at work, school, and home and in social situations. How would you articulate those expectations? To what extent do you regularly assess the importance of those expectations and your level of consistency in demonstrating them?

Simply put, to what extent do you consistently put forth your best effort? Are your best efforts consistent across different situations and environments? Your efforts can be bolstered by your daily approach, which correlates to how you dress and groom yourself. Your clothing is a uniform, such as your scrubs. Beyond clothing, your hairstyle, fragrance, shoes, jewelry, and other details are also a part of your uniform for the roles you play throughout your life. Regardless of which role you are playing at any given time, it is interesting to explore the common elements of your approach to such roles. In addition, whether you are a consistent early riser or a regular night owl plays into how consistent your patterns are in other areas.

Do your best score: ________

Look your best score: ________

Handling Pressure

Everyone experiences pressure in life. In some cases, that sense of pressure is more acute based on situational factors such as being short staffed, having to pick up extra shifts, juggling school and family while working a full-time nursing job, or simply getting through the holidays unscathed. What positive ways have you devised to handle anticipated work and social pressures? When confronted with pressure or conflict of any kind, do you express it outwardly or hold it in? Outward expressions may be healthy or unhealthy, positive or negative. For example, you might take the opportunity to talk things out then and there to find an appropriate compromise. You might step away and go for a run or get in a vigorous workout to release some pressure, so you can better organize your thoughts and map out a plan of action. Try to avoid sudden expressions of anger or rage, lashing out, or taking comfort in unhealthy or unproductive patterns and behaviors.

Different phases of your career have different stressors and pressures. For example, as a recent nursing graduate, you are trying to navigate a whole new world of sights, sounds, attitudes, and problems that may be life and death in nature. When you change jobs or get promoted, you are trying to navigate a new landscape with different personalities and hierarchies in play. As you get further credentialed, you work new proficiencies into your routines and apply a deeper level of critical thinking skills. And as you move toward retirement, you need to find a sense of balance between your professional role and income and a burgeoning sense of freedom and adventure. Are there instances when you believe your best approach is to tell small lies to get through uncomfortable moments? Do you step away when a situation becomes tense until things have calmed, or have you devised a healthy approach? Are you consistently more proactive or more reactionary? Reflect on the times and situations where you stood firm, held your ground, or maintained your beliefs. Conversely, think about when you have wavered, switched tack, or followed someone else's lead.

Handling pressure score: ________

Budgeting Your Time

As a nurse, you have to learn to manage your time and to know when it is safe to multitask versus concentrating intently on one critical thing at a time. If you are well-versed in your role, you will be able to competently tackle several things at once. If you are just learning your role, you may need to focus on each new task to get it right.

How well do you manage your time? How regularly do you assess how you spend your time and to what extent you are appropriately on task? For example, you might rely on a calendaring system or use checklists. Such techniques help you to stay focused—to be on time as well as organized. Lists also provide a natural feedback loop, helping you assess how well or how quickly you were able to complete tasks. Perhaps you compartmentalize your time into buckets that are earmarked for work versus professional growth activities, or family time versus job search project time. Are you consistently satisfied with how you spend your time and the extent you get things accomplished with the time you have?

Spending your time score: ________

(Not) Taking Things Personally

Sometimes, you need to reflect honestly about how you impact your environment and the people around you. Other times, you need to let someone else's bad attitude roll off your back. This can be tough in a culture where compassion for others is an occupational requirement.

Do you realize you are not responsible for anyone else's attitude and behavior? Recognize that other people's habits and moods have nothing to do with you. You can choose to feel a certain way—calm or angry, complacent or excited, hopeful or sad—and so can other people. Taking things too personally can easily lead to grudges, acting out, or projecting your hurt and anger onto others. It may leave you unable to see opportunities to find a common bond, compromise, grow as a person, or see other options and solutions.

Often, the extent to which you take things personally has much to do with healthy boundaries. This is easier said than done without getting defensive. You may not see that you're taking things too personally on your own; it may take someone else pointing it out. When they do, do you think, "Wow, I guess I am," or do you get even more defensive about the latest bit of constructive criticism? On that note, do you handle constructive criticism in a positive manner? Does it depend upon the situation or the environment?

Not taking things personally score: ________

Being Fair and Ethical

Fairness is a basic, human construct within the workplace and essentially is a platform from which you operate without prejudice, injustice, or bias. Workplace norms have been in place a long time; this is hardly a new concept. Fairness is inherent to the public interest. Yet, can you say without any hesitation that you are unequivocally fair to others?

To be fair, you already listen to diverse viewpoints, watch for and step in to help level whatever field you are playing on, and take into account the needs of others, including yourself. Ethics is a set of socially defined parameters of personal or professional morality that guide your actions and behaviors. There are clear ethical guidelines for nurses and other health care workers. The American Nurses Association has a well-established Code of Ethics for Nurses. Similarly, many organizations, including Sigma Theta Tau International, have a Code of

Conduct for Nurses. These codes serve as prescriptive modes for interactions with others as you represent a larger group in a professional manner.

In nursing, you are expected to uphold standards or virtues around beneficent care, nonmalfeasance, and more. Your role as a nurse is not to cure but to care for those in need. It can be easy to direct that ethical sense of care to your patients, yet overlook the need for care among your newer colleagues. Always strive to be fair and ethical, in all situations and with all people, so as to contribute to the greater good on a daily basis.

Fairness score: ________

Ethics score: ________

Now, look back over your scores. Which items did you identify with a score of 3 or less (areas where you may not demonstrate consistency?) For those areas, map out a plan to be more positively consistent to strengthen your sense of self. Why? Because positivity and consistency are essential hallmarks of job search success and ongoing career development gains. Negativity or inconsistency can come out unintentionally, impacting or preventing you from reaching your objectives. Mapping out goals to strengthen yourself in the identified areas and continually striving to improve upon them will show up in ways that will communicate ongoing positive intent, sincerity, and genuineness, along with a heightened credibility.

LAND THAT JOB!

What is the No. 1 item you would like to address from the statements above? Why did you choose it? What is your plan to become more consistent in this area? What benefits do you envision will come with the success of your plan?

Graciousness

Since job searching and career development start by talking to people, here are tips to show how genuine your hopes and dreams are through the use of graciousness and goodwill toward others.

Graciousness is the art of being kind, courteous, and pleasant-mannered to everyone, especially when you think such treatment of others is not necessary. While your code of ethics or conduct is highly prescriptive with a particular audience or population through representative interaction, graciousness is especially directed at those who may be somehow lower than you in terms of rank, socioeconomic class, age, or some other variable. Think about when you have shown genuine graciousness toward someone experiencing homelessness, or a teenager, a younger sibling, or those working service and hospitality industries. Does such a quality exude from you every day like a warm glow toward everyone in your path, or is it more sporadic and specific, such as when you have something to gain from others? Are you truly approachable and accommodating to others? Do you share information and tips easily? Are you quick and forthcoming with a helping hand or a quietly discrete caution that will save another from potential downfall, disgrace, or embarrassment? Do you tend to be polite and sociable yet also tender and gentle with all whom you encounter?

As a nurse, you have myriad opportunities to be gracious in your workplace. Think of the Golden Rule, which is to treat others as you would like to be treated. Work from the premise of how alike people are. Remember the Platinum Rule, which is to treat others the way they wish to be treated, bringing to light the fact that differences exist and are perfectly acceptable.

One of the biggest reasons graciousness is dearly needed is because you do not live and work in a vacuum. You do not do every little thing all by yourself; you are part of a team, and your team was created to serve a larger purpose. Graciousness can be underrated as you think about how much work you have to do, or how you rarely get a break, or you wonder why it seems you work so much harder than someone else. Consider the following practices as ways to be gracious or promote graciousness in others.

Graciousness practice: Believe that all people are doing the best they can. Even when you think people are acting in an ungracious manner; try to take the perspective that they are really doing their best. You don't need to excuse behavior or even understand the motivation for it, but you can graciously set boundaries to let them know their actions or words require attention. You can also take poor behavior as a cry for help; realize the person probably isn't aware he or she is making such a cry, which is why offers of help may initially be rebuffed. Taking this perspective may bring just the clarity needed to know how you might navigate the situation further. Caution: If what you are seeing in another is actual incompetence, the solution is not graciousness but appropriate and diplomatic action as dictated by the organization's policies.

Graciousness practice: Create a climate where it is safe to be uncertain, ask for help, and take the lead. Practice by taking a few minutes each day to try to understand other people's perspectives, their passion for what they do, and what makes them tick. Openly acknowledge your common bonds and delightful differences. Encourage them to do the same with people they encounter. Remind yourself that perspective is relative, so you will tackle problems and arrive at different solutions, accordingly. You might want to focus on continuous quality improvement so that a particular incident doesn't happen again, whereas another professional on your team might look at mistakes as critical for deeper learning.

Graciousness practice: Approach each person as if you deeply care for him or her. This is a difficult concept in an era of automated self-service with specialized roles and an increasing administrative concern that time is money. Understand that re-work and problems left to fester are harder and costlier to resolve. While not the most cost-effective approach, take a few extra minutes to explain and show someone how to do something, or walk a patient to the next person they need to see. Don't underestimate the power of such simple phrases as "please," "thank you," "you are most welcome," "as you wish," and "I'm here to help you."

You may feel that you could practice graciousness with ease if only others were so inclined. So what do you do when you encounter a lack of graciousness in others? And where do you draw the line between ungracious behavior and outright bullying? Unfortunately, examples abound in nursing, which is why you see articles, blogs, and training sessions with titles such as:

"Why nurses eat their young" (nursetogether.com)

"When the nurse is the bully" (*NY Times*)

"Hospital bullies take a toll on patient safety" (msnbc.msn.com)

"Disruptive physician behavior contributes to nursing shortage" (findarticles.com)

"Why nurses quit" (healthleadersmedia.com)

"Survey finds doctors and nurses still behaving badly" (nursezone.com)

"Recognizing and overcoming toxic leadership" (rnjournal.com)

"Nursing practice – lateral violence" (minurses.org)

"Beware of bullies" (news.nurse.com)

"Nursing against the odds" (digitalcommons.irl.cornell.edu)

"When the nurse is the problem" (workingnurse.com)

"What the nursing board really cares about" (legalcounseltoprofessionals.wordpress.com)

These are just a handful of the articles you can discover in a quick online search.

Is it a jungle out there? It can be. But take heart because there are just as many articles defining how to stand up for yourself, navigate toxic waters, or defuse the bully on your unit. The trick is to do so with graciousness, creating a professional culture that transcends base improprieties going forward.

As Gandhi said, "Be the change you want to see in the world." There is a great blog, the PositivityBlog, published by Henrik Edberg, which includes "Gandhi's Top 10 Fundamentals for Changing the World." The precepts presented resonate strongly with the essential elements of this book. So, the short answer on how to deal graciously with ungracious behavior is that it all starts with you. You are the one who is in control, able to forgive, take action, practice humility yet persist in consistent and authentic ways by making changes in yourself first and letting others follow suit. Take the lead.

To take a gracious lead as a nurse, it is helpful to understand the notion of nursing, cultural, and interpersonal competence. Patricia Benner's stages of clinical competence are nicely summarized by Shonta D. Collins (2008) at minoritynurse.com. A nurse moves through five stages: novice, advanced beginner, competent, proficient, and expert.

As a novice, you can take a gracious lead by being courteous and kind with all you meet. Even in the earliest stages of your nursing career, cliques and stratification occur, and you have to decide how to navigate these waters. You have made it through nursing school and achieved a baseline professional goal by becoming a bona fide nurse. But your work has just begun as you encounter a wide range of beliefs; some make sense, but many do not and will challenge you to understand them all to excel as a caregiver.

As an advanced beginner, you begin to truly articulate your principles as a nurse. At this stage, you establish fairness and ethics that you will maintain over the course of your career, unless you have to create action plans to change them for specific reasons (such as the consistency exercises discussed earlier in this chapter).

By the third stage, competency, you have gained a solid sense of familiarity and comfort in your day-to-day role and can demonstrate graciousness by being ready, willing, and able to step in and support your team, which helps you grow professionally, too. You learn to show respect through sensitivity and effective communication, which you demonstrate on the job and model for others around you. Your graciousness will be paired with humility; you know a good deal at this stage but not everything. You have a ways to go and can appreciate the journey, as well as those alongside you, as competence develops into the fourth stage, proficiency.

Proficient nurses can demonstrate graciousness by helping nurses at earlier stages see the whole picture. You recognize you were once where they are and help minimize their fears and uncertainty. At this point, you have learned how to survive and thrive in your workplace. Don't take that for granted; chances are that more experienced nurses helped you get where you are today, or you were bolstered by an innate sense of right versus wrong and had the strength to blaze your own path in ways that contribute to the greater good, every day.

The fifth stage, expert, is further fortified by your daily gracious presence in your workplace. You are highly experienced, intuitive, and powerful; you have learned so much about clinical skill and diverse cultures. You inform and educate others through storytelling of your very own case studies, sharing what you've observed and benefitted from along the way. You use your power for good.

At the expert stage, you must be nontoxic in your approach to others and step in to neutralize toxicity where you see it. You are a clinical force to be reckoned with. You attract respect and admiration from others, below and above you, without using fear or shame to get what you want. You recognize red flags. Your practiced eye and deft hands move beautifully from one situation to the next as you stay fully aware of your environment, ever-observant and ready for anything. You are a gracious mentor and peer. You stop abuse in its tracks and diffuse any cultural tensions or awkwardness in others. You don't need to take credit for anyone else's ideas; rather, you freely encourage good ideas and best practices from anyone and promote them with goodwill and cheer. You promote others, reward dedication, network to advance the field of nursing, and actively drive a culture of graciousness in your workplace.

Using concrete examples, it is important to assess where you are in Benner's five stages. Seek input from someone well-versed in her five clinical stages of competence for input about your status. It is simply too easy to overestimate your own level of competence, especially if you feel you have a very good handle on the role you play. If in doubt, subtract at least one stage from where you think you are. You will also revisit earlier stages when you change jobs or get promoted, though you will likely pass through them more quickly the next time around. Caution: If you assess yourself at a higher stage than your supervisor's assessment, you run the risk of initiating or at least contributing to power struggles and role ambiguity, and undermining your supervisor's authority. This is a recipe for career suicide, not development or advancement. You can recover from such faux pas or regrettable circumstances, but it will take time, patience, humility, and a concentrated effort with a willing supervisor to turn things around. This type of situation may be what is really spurring you on to find a new job elsewhere.

Assess which stage you are at in terms of clinical competence. How do you demonstrate graciousness? How can you become more gracious in your workplace? How will you overcome barriers or challenges that you perceive to be especially troublesome?

Etiquette

Etiquette is a code of behavior that dictates what is appropriate or can be flexibly applied in a specific situation. Demonstrate etiquette by the way you interact socially and professionally with others, observe certain conventions and proper protocols, and combine the elements of consistency and graciousness with your unique self. Think of ethics as the larger umbrella under which etiquette is the demonstrable activity, depending on the context. Etiquette is the marriage of good manners and common sense. These are the types of things parents try to instill in their children from an early age, the basic dos and don'ts across various contexts, such as while dining, when visiting a friend, and in school. Unlike ethics, which should be applied even when no one is looking, etiquette only happens when at least one other person is involved.

Etiquette in any context makes for a great first impression. It proves you are a cultured individual who knows how to behave across different situations. Good etiquette allows you to earn respect and appreciation from others sooner than you might otherwise. It says something about your personality and values that brings a sense of comfort to those around you, as long as your approach is genuine. For more on this topic, see *The Nurse's Etiquette Advantage* by Kathleen D. Pagana.

Essentially, you want to create a list of professional dos and don'ts based on the contexts within your work life. Adding polish and graciousness to the mix allows you to show the utmost respect toward others. Here is a collection of examples:

Nursing and Workplace Etiquette

- Arrive for your shift a few minutes early so that when your shift begins, you are truly ready and able to start. Leave any personal issues "at the door"; do not bring them to work. Your focus while working is caring for your patients, period. Professional etiquette demands that you be part of an effective team; even if you work in a highly autonomous environment, you must still interact with coworkers with integrity and grace. Don't take unnecessary or unsafe shortcuts. If you are unsure how to do something or, seek help and do everything in your power to retain the information gained so as to apply it the next time around.
- Always introduce yourself to patients, families, and new colleagues. Define the specific role you play, so that everyone can understand how to best work on behalf of the patient. Make a point of learning and remembering people's names, and call them by their preferred name to create and maintain a personal bond in vulnerable situations. Don't give patients and families nicknames that are easier for you to remember than their own names, like "dear," "hon," or "honey," as such endearments can be perceived as belittling or demeaning. Introduce other care professionals who enter a patient's room and ask if they have yet had the opportunity to meet one another. When entering a patient's room, pause briefly to give the patient and family time to acknowledge your presence, invite you in, or give permission for you to enter. Provide information about the frequency and purpose of checking on the patient in order to offer proper care. This gives the patient a much appreciated sense of control.

- If you do not know the answer to a question, state honestly that you don't know. Offer to find out and give them a time by which you will have an answer, or at least alert them that you are still investigating the matter. Hold to your promises. Never be tempted to take a patient's possessions or medication; if you are, seek help immediately. If you observe a patient, visitor, or another health care professional doing something incorrectly or in an unethical or disruptive manner, quietly let them know in just one or two sentences what you observed. Describe the impact it may have, and suggest a resource for them to get help or advice.
- If it is also something you will need to report, simply state that it is a reportable incident and that you will be following the protocol as you were trained to do. After you've made your statement, there is no need to belabor your point, dwell on your concerns, or shame the other person in any way. Step away from the situation. Unless you are the person's direct supervisor, it is not your issue to resolve, and trying to do so would be inappropriate. Do not gossip about it; keep it to yourself. Your confidentiality will be appreciated, sooner or later.

  Likewise, when you observe a patient or colleague doing something well, a brief compliment to acknowledge what you saw (or heard) is a simple yet effective form of etiquette. Your actions help to reinforce the positive behavior, which further creates a culture of graciousness.

Advancement/Promotion Etiquette

When you are promoted, leave it to your supervisor to dictate how and when your promotion will be announced or otherwise made known to others. You may suggest a method once, and then let things unfold as they will, even if it doesn't happen in the way you wanted or expected. Do not gloat or brag to your peers, as they may also have vied for the role. Step up your level of graciousness and help others see that your supervisor made the right choice, and help your supervisor remain comfortable and confident in his or her decision.

Understand your new role and its expectations. If you will be supervising others for the first time, seek guidance and training. Do not assume it will be easy, or that you will simply figure it out as you go. There is both an art and a science to supervising others; you may want to initiate such training from tried and true (and gracious) sources before your new appointment is announced, so you can start strong. Understand and practice the tenets of servant leadership as espoused by Robert K. Greenleaf. "The servant-leader *is* servant first. ... It begins with the natural feeling that one wants to serve, to serve *first*. Then conscious choice brings one to aspire to lead. That person is sharply different from one who is *leader* first; perhaps because of the need to assuage an unusual power drive or to acquire material possessions. ...The leader-first and the servant-first are two extreme types. Between them there are shadings and blends that are part of the infinite variety of human nature" (Greenleaf Center, n.d., para. 2).

Think about how you can apply the concepts of gracious servant leadership within your own role. If someone else gets a promotion or special project to lead that you wanted, acquiesce graciously to the choice made. Do not badmouth or gossip about the others involved or engage in incredulous dismay at the ridiculous outcome. Rise above. Congratulate and assure them that you will continue to work with the new appointee as effectively as ever. It is perfectly all right to grieve the loss of an opportunity; that is a normal reaction. However, it is important to remember that opportunity never knocks only once and your time will come, so persevere while creating opportunity for yourself along the way.

Meeting Etiquette

Come prepared and on time. If you called the meeting, have a clear agenda not only prepared but shared in advanced if possible. Never meet just to meet—don't hold a meeting just because. Everyone appreciates a break from standing meetings now and again. Take a seat at the head of the table, which is generally opposite the doorway so you can see everyone coming in, or sit in front of a whiteboard or projection screen; be sure you can make eye contact with everyone, and address each person directly as needed. Start and end meetings on time so not to abuse people's time; they are busy professionals just like you. Let attendees know your expectations up front by defining the purpose of the meeting. Identify whether they will listen to important content, contribute ideas to a brainstorming session, provide updates to team members, or discuss working procedures. Have an assigned note taker to record meeting minutes, designated in advance, even if you assign a different person each time. For note takers, do not be gender- or age-specific, remain equitable, and set clear expectations in advance as to the quality and timeliness of the final minutes, which should be directed to you first for review before disseminating to others.

Seating protocol may be quite informal or relaxed where you work. If in doubt, consider adopting a more formal stance on the subject. If you are attending a meeting someone else called, come prepared and on time, but do not take a seat at the head of the table. If you are an acknowledged "second in command," sit to the immediate right of the person at the head of the table. If you wish to be highly engaged with the head of the meeting, sit to his or her immediate left if you are well-informed of the rest of the attendees and their role at the table. Those sitting at the end of the table are also highly engaging, though they may take a dissenting opinion on the proceedings or are considered an alternate leader, such as the meeting head's direct supervisor. If unsure, take a seat in the middle and observe everyone for a while until you have a better sense of things. You don't want to get stuck in a seat away from the table because you will either a) not be part of the group dynamics in play, b) have to humbly and visibly admit you were too late to get a seat at the table, or c) appear as though you don't care and don't want to be there. If in a classroom-style meeting, avoid the seats in the back for the same reasons.

Management Etiquette

Above all, set a good, gracious, ethical example. Be available to employees. Take the time to meet one-on-one, even if for just a few minutes each week, to hear how things are going and to offer your insights. Do so even if you feel you are just too busy. Making time for your nurses is a requirement, not a luxury.

Set clear expectations of employees, both as individuals and team players, in ways that support the aims of the organization, so that they can take pride and ownership of the larger good. Be genuine in both your praise and your constructive criticism. Never engage in activities designed to shun or shame. Be equitable when assigning projects but also attend to professional objectives and motivations; connect nurses with projects aligned with individual goals and interests. Provide reasons "why" whenever possible. It may not be possible to divulge reasons why, or it may not be the best place and time to discuss them. If the latter is the case, set a time to meet and discuss the issue when you are at liberty to do so.

Treat your employees not only as you would wish to be treated, but find out what motivates each individual. Periodically provide a small token of your appreciation of their efforts, contributions, and successes with a handwritten thank-you note, their favorite candy bar, or extra one-on-one time when you simply listen to them for a change. Be clear about what you appreciate and why. Remember that the farther you go up the ladder, the more you lose touch with the day-to-day frontline operations of the nursing staff. Things change from the way you did things back then. Though you are moving into the proficient and expert stages of your clinical competency, you no longer have the narrow perspective of a novice or experienced beginner, and they will not be able to absorb your much broader worldview of health care. It is better to pair them with a trusted, competent stage nurse who is still doing lower level clinical routines, day in and day out, than to try and dictate such activities yourself. You have bigger things to do at this point.

Articulate your departmental vision, within the parameters set forth by your own supervisor. Allow your nursing staff to carry out that vision without micromanaging and within ethical and compliance mandates. Manage change with patience and grace, avoid losing your temper, and apologize right away if you do. Remain humble to the ideas of servant leadership, and remember that you do not know everything, so continue to learn, grow, and develop your skills as a leader and nurse.

Company Party Etiquette

Company or office parties are designed to strengthen a sense of community and share accomplishment or celebration. Corporate events are a time to give thanks for what has been achieved and to celebrate the team's diversity and common bonds. While more of a relaxed and social atmosphere, maintain your professionalism. Plan ahead and have clear objectives for going. Do attend and dress in appropriate clothing; don't skip out or be overly casual. Arrive on time as a meal may be served, awards may be presented, a tour may be provided; other activities with specific time frames may be part of the festivities. Don't bring guests unless specifically invited. You are still being observed and evaluated by your peers and superiors. This is a good time for junior employees to seek a mentor. Make a point to network with those you do not know as well. Share funny or interesting stories, but do not gossip. Hearing gossip may be unavoidable, but you have a choice as to whether you participate. Similarly, do not engage in any form of horseplay, pranks, or hazing. Move away from any conversation or activity that makes you uncomfortable by excusing yourself politely or making it pleasantly clear upfront that your objective is to mingle and to slip away as needed. Do not drink or dance excessively. Be a visible part of the festivities, but do not make it all about you. Refrain from loosening inhibitions that may come back to haunt you. Do not insert yourself into a conversation being held by those more senior in position to you, but don't hesitate to introduce or re-introduce yourself to such people who are by themselves. Be prepared to cover topics such as what you most appreciate about the organization, whom you most admire and why, what you love about being a nurse, or a fascinating conference or workshop you recently attended. Reciprocate by asking others what they most appreciate about working there, too. Such topics keep the tone positive yet professional in a relaxed way or can add buoyancy to an already cheerful occasion. If you spot someone who seems painfully shy or is awkwardly standing all alone, take a few moments to speak with them and try to introduce them to others; they might be a new employee or someone who has been intentionally ostracized and feeling quite lost. Don't allow it to continue; step up to the plate and take them under your wing. Last but not least, be sure to personally thank the party's organizers and supervisors by pointing out what makes the party unique, especially fun, or comfortable for all.

First Week on the Job Etiquette

Strive to make the finest first impression possible, even though this is also an ongoing endeavor beyond your first week on the job. Present a polished appearance, a warm smile, and an attitude that screams "ready, willing, and able." Be observant and ask lots of questions, especially regarding expectations of you on the job, protocols to observe, and how to use equipment. Complete all required training sessions within the prescribed time and take them seriously. Arrive as early as needed to familiarize yourself with your surroundings and to be truly ready for the start of each shift. Be resolute about activities and behaviors you will refuse to take part in, condone, or overlook in any way. Recognize that you are a novice, in a new situation, and there is much you do not yet know.

Keep a small journal handy to note names, titles, protocols, and tips for success that you learn along the way. Make a point of learning people's names, and don't hesitate to ask again as needed. It helps that nurses tend to wear nametags and identifiable clothing such as color-coded scrubs. Do not abuse breaks or anyone's trust or graciousness toward you. Say please and thank you frequently. Be pleasant; encourage other nurses to take you under their wing.

Voice questions but not concerns or complaints, as it may be too early to tell unless you encounter something egregious. That said, watch closely for anything that sets off inner alarm bells (hint: sudden feelings of anxiety or shame) and smacks of disrespect or contempt, such as a snide or caustic remark, eye rolling, name calling, finger pointing/blame, and ignoring you. Graciously but firmly nip these behaviors in the bud, whether they come from a coworker or your supervisor. You worked too long and too hard to get to where you are to be brought down by a toxic person or environment.

Steel your nerves and have a prepared plan for such eventualities. No one is exempt from such experiences. Tackle them when they first appear, because they will not go away on their own. At the first instance of bad behavior on their part, tell them what you saw them do or heard them say. Indicate how it impacts you, and request that the person refrain from doing it again. Can you turn that person into an ally? Try. Reiterate that you wish to be successful in your new role, and you can't do so without their help. Ask them if they will be your partner in this so that you can both move forward, positively and in each other's good graces. If they agree and commit to such an outcome, great! Most of the time, you will be pleasantly surprised (as they will have been caught off guard by having their own behavior called out in a quiet, graceful manner). But if they don't agree, and some won't, revisit your own strengths and principles and determine your next move up to and including seeking employment elsewhere. Such a point in time may come early on or down the road; remain vigilant over the long haul. This approach takes practice and personal resolve. It will pay off in both the short and long term, as you will not give away any personal power in the process, building confidence in yourself but respect from others as well. You can do this!

Being Unique

A common misconception among job seekers is that you have to be or act a "certain way" to get hired or promoted. Instead, focus on being yourself—your BEST self—and all that makes you unique and gifted as a nurse.

The five stages of clinical competence can be applied to your interpersonal world in ways that make you unique. To be unique as a person means you are either unusually or uncommonly good; you have rare qualities that shine through no matter where you are. Being unique means not following the norm. Therefore, uniqueness requires a strong sense of self and can be associated with how well you have mastered being true to yourself. You might be an expert nurse but still a novice when it comes to withstanding peer or social pressures on the job, or standing up for yourself, or refusing to be bullied by anyone for any reason. Work from novice to expert in being completely true to yourself; that in itself will showcase YOU in a truly unique light. No one else is completely like you; however, it is easy to lose sight of who you really are and to follow your passions as you define them versus trying to fit in, adopting someone else's perspective, or simply following along.

There are several characteristics that make up a unique individual, and surprisingly you can Google it and find tips at wikihow.com, which have been adapted here. Be true to yourself, as discussed above. Try standing in front of a mirror and taking a good, long look at yourself. If that is an uncomfortable exercise, it is likely you have been overly focused on what society commonly dictates about looks, presence, or personality. The idea here is to identify and remove any "false shells," which includes smiling when you don't feel like it, hiding your feelings, dressing a certain way that appeals to others, or anything else that you feel you "should" be to gain or maintain the approval of others. The unique individual cares not one whit for social conventions. As a unique individual, you live life on your own terms and are not bothered by what anyone else says or does. Instead, you develop your own personal style, pursue your own interests, and cultivate your own way of relating to the world that other people are drawn to simply because they appreciate how genuine you are about being YOU.

Think about the extent you waste time. You have a finite amount of time on this earth, and how you spend it is up to you. If you spend your time as you please in pursuit of pleasurable interests and meaningful activities, it is not possible to waste time doing so. It may be wasted time in someone else's eyes, but not to you as you march to the beat of your own drum each and every day. You know exactly what you love to do, and you will always find time to do it; you're never too busy to do what you love. It becomes your way of life.

You are your own best company. You want to be around people you love or find interesting, but you don't actually need anyone else. You don't need someone else to take care of you or provide direction or serve as your conscience. You don't need to be needed. Anything you do need is derived from within, a healthy sense of self with healthy boundaries. You are never lonely when you are alone. In fact, you love spending time alone. If you feel like and want to spend time with others, you do. Being alone is never about being unwanted, unloved, or unworthy in any way. Yes, it is that simple.

You wear what you are. You dress in ways that make you happiest. You wear the accessories, jewelry, and shoes that mesh perfectly with your personality. Or you don't wear any jewelry at all, because it doesn't reflect who you are. Clothing is not a uniform, prop, disguise, or type of armor. When you don scrubs, it is because you love them, love how they are a simple, natural extension of being a nurse because you love being a nurse and cannot imagine doing anything else in the world to make a living. If you take off your scrubs at the end of your shift to revert back to a different version of you, which version is the real you? Do you store clothes in your closet that you never wear? Get rid of them! The reason you don't wear those items is because they are not for you and you know it. If you must dress professionally to do the job you love, you work within the dress code parameters in ways that are uniquely you. It doesn't matter about designer labels or this season's hottest color. It is about pulling together your own sense of style and living your own signature color, the color of you. You don't look like a typical nurse, parent, grandparent, partner, spouse, etc. You just look like you, and when other people see you, their first impression is that they can't pin you down into any particular category, which is part of what makes you unique.

You are in touch with your emotions and feel them vividly and without reserve. If you feel sad, you fully allow yourself to feel that sadness in the moment. If you feel uncertain or anxious, you sit down and visit with that emotion in order to get to the bottom of it. You are at peace with your emotional self. Conversely, you leave other people's emotions and actions to them. You don't take their feelings on as your own or be influenced by them, or take them personally, or assume it has anything to do with you. You can ask if their emotional state has anything to do with you; if yes, you handle that in your own way, and if not, you don't give the matter further thought. If someone is angry, defensive, or brooding, you simply take time out and leave them to handle it in their own way. This doesn't mean that you won't listen or provide a sympathetic ear or offer advice if they have asked for it. It means that you have very clear and unshakable boundaries and are not unduly affected by anyone else's mood. It also means that you are never one to expect another to mirror or attend to your mood. Your mood is your mood. Their emotional state is their own. Period.

Though you have a clear sense of your own values, morals, personal ethics, and opinions, you don't foist them on others because you know that your attitudes are based on who you are, and your sense of the world might not be right for them. You "live and let live." But as the world changes and new theories and perspectives come to light, you are inquisitive and adaptable. You are willing to try a new idea on for size, to see if it resonates with who you are at your core. You can also decide against them, determine they are not for you. You trust your gut; you work with a strong sense of self and innate wisdom about what it means to be you and only you. You are comfortable with ambiguity, trial and error, making mistakes, and coming to a dead end. No matter what, you enjoy and appreciate the journey.

The last item is easy because it is imperative that a genuine person be fully capable of independent thought. No one else can tell you what to do, how to act, or what to become. No, this does not mean that you are antisocial or a tyrant or an anarchist. It means you are never one to succumb to pressures from society, parents, or peers. You are not embarrassed or apologetic about who you are, where you come from, or where you're headed. You have a clear vision of who you are and where you want to go. People are invited to come along for the ride, or you can go your own way without them and no hard feelings. You are true to yourself in word, deed, and belief and do not stray, unless compelled to try something new for the experience and to discover whether it is something to keep or remember fondly as you walk away from it.

LAND THAT JOB!

Think back to your responses to the first self-coaching exercise of this chapter. How might you apply the concepts of being unique to help you become more consistent? Which examples of how to be unique resonated with you the most?

There are numerous challenges to navigate as a nurse; therefore, it is important to remember that you can control more than you think versus being buffeted around by whatever strong winds prevail in the moment. Through consistency, graciousness, and etiquette, you can show the world how you are unique as a nurse and a leader. This chapter has discussed the many ways you can fine-tune your approach in order to rise above and truly shine in both your current role and the next.

References

Collins, S.D. (2008). *Achieving expertise.* Retrieved from http://www.minoritynurse.com/achieving-expertise

Greenleaf Center for Servant Leadership. (n.d.) *What is servant leadership?* Retrieved from http://www.greenleaf.org/whatissl/

Best Candidate Checklist

___ I have determined how, where, and to what extent I am inconsistent in my job search or sense of professionalism.

___ I have evaluated the strong beliefs I hold about myself as a nurse and their associated behaviors.

___ I have scored myself across several variables to determine my level of positive consistency.

___ I have identified ways to practice graciousness every day and across various settings.

___ I have assessed where and how I can assimilate Benner's five stages of clinical competence when it comes to graciousness.

___ I have developed ways to exemplify etiquette on the job, in my role, and throughout my job search.

___ I have considered the ways in which I am unique and made a list with which to remind myself each day.

___ I have fine-tuned my job search approach through the use of consistency, graciousness, etiquette, and uniqueness.

8

The most important ingredient we put into any relationship is not what we say or what we do, but what we are.

–Stephen Covey

Interviewing: The Floor Is Yours

This chapter explores how to be authentically you while presenting yourself in the best possible light. If you are yourself, the hiring manager will have the best sense of whether or not you'll be a good fit with the existing team. By being yourself, you won't have to worry about showing your true colors once you get the job. If you try to be something you're not in an interview, it shows. The interviewer may not be able to name what it is, but will sense it is there and be put off by it. Read on to discover that interviewing is not a game but one of seeking best mutual fit. In doing so, you'll recognize that if you don't get a particular offer, it is not news to take personally. And when you do get that offer, you'll understand that it wasn't how you played the game, but that you are indeed the best new player for the team.

Being Genuine

Be yourself. By being yourself, you will shine with confidence.

You have read about the need to be "ready, willing, and able." This holds true in screening interviews or in more formal settings with one or more interviewers evaluating your talents and potential contributions to the organization. All of the questions you may be asked in any type of interview can be slotted into one of the three categories. Questions to determine your readiness focus on your educational preparation and the passion you have developed for your work. Willingness is gauged through questions about your limits, deal breakers, or ethics. Ability is explored through questions that ferret out the extent to which you have done similar work, how you have handled comparable situations, and how successfully you've met objectives. One of the ways to be genuine is to answer all questions honestly and with concrete, supporting examples.

You can take several approaches in an interview. As you read through the following categories, consider which approaches you have used and to what extent they were effective. Understand that each has pros and cons; each can work for or against you. As such, careful analysis and reflection are necessary before adopting any of these approaches.

The Pleaser is one who strives to convey desire for the job, ability to do the job, and hopefulness about being selected for the job. Pleasers want to fit in, to be liked, and to be given a chance to prove (yet again) that they can do the job. Pleasers see the interview as a test for which all effort must be made to tip the odds in the interviewee's favor. Interviewers like Pleasers if the role is entry-level or the company wants to be sure the candidate won't come in, take the place by storm, and do things his or her own way regardless of company preferences. Pleasers are also the easiest candidates to interview, and newly minted recruiters and hiring managers tend to hire these types first.

Seasoned employers have learned to dig deeper. Why? The Pleaser tends to lack confidence and comes across as obsequious or over-accommodating. Pleasers may need lot of praise to feel adequate. If the candidate is in serious financial straits or has been engaged in a long job search, desperation may be part of the equation and can show up in overt and covert ways. Ultimately, the Pleaser just wants to be given a chance even if the role is a long-shot. As a result, Pleasers tend to follow the interviewer's lead in an effort to be seen as agreeable, well-socialized, and willing to pitch in however needed. The interviewer may genuinely like the candidate but may also suspect he or she is not ready for the role in question. If Pleasers have an undercurrent of begging, the interviewer may feel sorry for them, but that is unlikely to lead to a job offer.

A pleasing approach can work well if the candidate is fresh out of school or is transitioning from one career path to another and realizes he or she doesn't necessarily have all the qualifications for the job in question. This approach does not work as well for management and leadership roles, because it may be perceived that the candidate will require too much hand-holding or won't be able to hold staff accountable. The Pleaser is likely to accept an offer as-is without negotiation.

LAND THAT JOB!

Have you ever played the pleaser role in an interview situation? How did it turn out? How did your experience shape how you approached additional interviews?

The Consultant interviewee chooses to take a more laid-back approach in a way that relieves the pressure of being in the hot seat. Consultants strive to be engaging and informative by suggesting strategies or solutions to benefit the company and demonstrate expertise, leaving the candidate feeling respected on a peer level with and by the interviewer. The interview is collegial, and the process includes a dialogue between two or more professionals. A good time is had by all, but ultimately the job may go to someone else.

Motivations for this approach can include the need to alleviate the inherent pressure of an interview when the job may be perceived "below" the interviewee's abilities. Consultants also choose this approach, even though they know deep down that being their own boss might be a better solution. Therefore, this tactic is not recommended for the traditional job seeker. However, this approach can work beautifully for those who are applying for freelance roles or are setting up as an independent, private duty nurse. It can also be effective for pursuing high-level positions where the consultative style will be appreciated and valued.

Passive job seekers (those not actively seeking out a new role but still interested in hearing more about opportunities that might exist) should look out for clues when they are engaged in preliminary meetings where their superiors (or other known entities) are feeling them out for a possible promotion. Since you won't always recognize when such discussions are happening, start practicing with your current supervisor and in networking situations to gauge your comfort and to what extent they favorably respond. Favorable responses would include their willingness to engage in the conversation at all or longer than you might have expected; whether they ask you to join or lead a project team during or shortly after the consultative discussion; and if the other person starts to seek you out to discuss strategies or issues as a professional confidante. Put another way, your ears should perk up if such discussions touch on anything that involves you and more responsibility. You must recognize potential upward movement simply from a supervisor's willingness to engage in a long conversation with you about what you like, how you might approach a particular problem, and so on. Companies that take organizational development seriously continually think about succession planning at all levels.

LAND THAT JOB!

Reflect on discussions you have had with your supervisor in the past 6 months. Can you spot any opportunities you might have missed at the time? If desired, schedule a time to speak with your supervisor again to circle back to that conversation and ask about how he or she might envision expanding your role at some point. See where it leads.

The Commander is an interesting candidate. Such a person will toe the company line, do whatever it takes to get the job done, take an aggressive posture as needed, and drive measurable results. In the current metric-driven and outcomes-dependent culture, this can be a successful approach as long as the candidate has the proven track record to back it up, especially for those pursuing roles in sales, start-ups, and middle management.

This approach works well when the candidate can demonstrate progressive, measureable results. While traditionally viewed as a masculine approach, metrics and results are gender-neutral; meaning so long as the metric is met or exceeded, it doesn't matter if who did so is male or female, which should encourage more women to experiment in this area. This candidate makes confident, assumptive statements in ways that will assure recruiters and hiring managers that he or she is indeed the best candidate for the job. It is usually assumed this candidate will negotiate for a higher salary and may be thought less of if he or she doesn't. However, hard-driving candidates can turn off a potential employer if they come across as too arrogant, unrealistic, or likely to create a toxic work environment.

The Buddha candidate has a strong sense of self, with an easy and natural manner that exudes a quiet confidence without arrogance. Buddhas are compassionate and empathetic but won't suffer fools gladly. They dress for success but with their own sense of style that is interesting but never offensive or inappropriate. Buddhas answer questions honestly yet also ask as many as needed to determine if the company is a good fit for them, too, and not just the other way around. These individuals are unhurried yet highly observant and are just as likely to turn an offer down as to accept; they don't take it personally if they are rejected for a job. This approach is easiest to pull off if indeed genuine and for either currently employed/passive job seekers or those who have the means to get by until the right role is found. Buddhas are focused on truth, not understating their talents but never over-inflating them, either. They know who they are, know what contributions they are capable of and passionate about, and have a clear sense of what they want and expect within an employer-employee relationship. While it is not about the money, the individual is not about to sell themself short, either, and will likely negotiate for more time off, professional development resources, and related perks.

LAND THAT JOB!

After reviewing the four main approaches above, which would you consider the best route to take? Do you have an individual approach that takes the best aspects of each? Another approach is to think about any interviewing advice you have ever given to another job seeker and how it relates to the four approaches listed above.

The Larger Picture

As a talented, competent, caring nurse, you can turn off an interviewer by approaching the interview as a test you are terrified to fail. Likewise, over-practicing interview responses can leave you sounding rehearsed and disingenuous. Lack of confidence can rear its ugly head in the form of nervousness, awkwardness, answering too quickly as though the "test" was timed, or babbling like a brook without enough self-awareness to realize it is time to stop and listen.

Be yourself. Realize that no matter what the interviewer's role, you will be engaging in a productive dialogue with another human being who is just trying to do his or her job. Know that you have every reason to expect to be treated with respect and dignity, to be listened to, and to be seen for the talented contributor you truly are. You will be interviewed well so long as you a) follow the general protocols and etiquette of interviewing, b) understand that your responses are gauging not only your fit for them but their fit for you, and c) be your genuine self. If you get the job offer, the ball is in your court to accept, negotiate, or decline. If you don't get the job offer, you can continue to seek out new opportunities without taking the rejection personally.

Traits or attributes that turn off the interviewer include arrogance, negativity, suggesting certain roles are better or lesser than others, punitive management style, martyrdom, lone rangerism, contrarianism, self-centeredness, apathy, condescension, antisocial awkwardness, rabid rule follower, job jumper, hyperactivity, or extreme intensity. These are same traits that drive you nuts when you see them in coworkers. The overriding message you'll silently convey with such traits is, "I'm NOT a team player." Employers give no value to such employees, especially a nurse.

Everyone has challenging or less admirable traits. Know and manage such tendencies and seek supportive cultures to join. Such actions can go a long way if you can find common, mutually supportive roles. For example, if you are naturally bossy yet productive, seek management roles. If you are prone to socializing on the job, look for roles that keep you out of the immediate vicinity of others, such as private-duty care or telephonic case management. If you are lazy or a late starter, focus on part-time roles that start later in the day. If you tend to take things too personally or are overly anxious, seek a calmer environment with a laid-back, positive boss who gives regular feedback. If you think you are smarter than everyone else, write a book as a subject-matter expert in your spare time and have it professionally reviewed, which will either affirm your brilliance or provide a humbling life lesson.

The point is that once hired, the organization has to work with you, and you have to work with the organization. That means you'll need to relax, get along, remain professional, consistently do your best work, own up to your own challenges, and manage your weaknesses to the best of your ability. If there's something you don't know how to do or are not passionate about, say so. If you are trying to interview for a job that just isn't right for you, stop. Instead of trying to be who you are not, focus on who you are and what makes you happy or inspires you to fully contribute. Be you. Be genuine.

It's Not Bragging if It's True

As a caregiver, it may seem offensive to brag. But don't confuse bragging with the act of making your strengths and talents known. In a trauma situation, if you see someone jeopardizing the health and safety of the patient or someone on the team, you will step in swiftly and intervene without hesitation and be recognized for it. You can then relate that experience in an interview setting to show how you stepped up in a critical moment and salvaged a potentially disastrous scenario.

If you serve on a board of directors and are in a position to positively influence decision-makers of any large health care system, you can wield your authority for good and take your talent straight to the bank. If you have a special way to work quickly and effectively with difficult patients, other caregivers have every reason to get out of your way and let you shine.

You earn your educational certificates and degrees, which set the minimum bar for your competency as a nurse. You then gain real-world experience in life-and-death situations, which further pronounces that you are very capable. You continue to refine your talents with professionalism, graciousness, and continuous improvement. You have the metrics to support it all, such as number of patients per shift; number of nurses supervised, trained, or mentored; evidence of zero errors; earned awards for specific achievements; and a number of stellar recommendations.

The trick is to discuss your accomplishments versus your abilities. Abilities are developed along the way and contribute to your accomplishments. However, ability without accomplishment is nothing to brag about. Also, your personal opinion of yourself is not brag-worthy. But anything externally validated through awards and other forms of recognition or public acknowledgement is something truly earned, including the right to share it.

Balance appropriate bragging on both the personal and professional levels. It is not only acceptable but expected that you will spell out your accomplishments on a resume and in an interview. Make true statements, support them with clear examples, and indicate how such claims can be verified or who will vouch for your claims, including references. If your work as a nurse consultant directly led to a 20% spike in sales for a medical device company or a 30% decrease in workers' compensation claims in a mere 6 months, you are indeed a rock star with strong business acumen. Include these achievements on your resume and in an interview, and give examples of public acknowledgement for your efforts. Examples might be a salary increase or bonus, an award, a press release, or a glowing reference. Pull together what is commonly known as a "brag book," which is akin to a portfolio that exhibits or showcases your achievements. However, avoid telling someone more than once or twice about the same accomplishment, unless you are asked or it is brought up. Practice restraint so you do not needlessly overstate or overexaggerate your efforts and outcomes.

There are certain unsupported yet excessively boastful statements that will automatically turn off a recruiter or hiring manager. Here is a list of examples:

- That company couldn't survive without me (delusions of grandeur).
- I made twice that in my last job (first nursing job).
- Nursing school was so easy, I sailed through it with my eyes closed (highly unlikely).
- I have many, many years of experience (only 2 years listed on resume).
- In my spare time, I run a free clinic out of my home (unethical, illegal, improbable).
- I am clearly ready for more responsibility (was fired from last job).
- Everyone thought I should get the promotion (hiring manager didn't).
- I ran circles around my boss; I did his/her job (arrogant, inflated ego).
- I was practically a doctor (overstated role, poor boundaries).

Bragging should be done graciously and serve a specific purpose of supporting a concrete objective. It should serve to illustrate a point, build trust, validate experiences, and support credentials. Bragging should not be engaged in an attempt to elevate yourself above others out of jealousy or to make yourself appear more accomplished than you are (in nursing, that can cause real and serious harm).

Bragging to yourself can be a healthy exercise if used to re-affirm your talents and experience, especially if you tend to humbly downplay your contributions. But be cautious if your inner monologue is regularly talking about how great you are and how everyone else is stupid if they can't see it. Chances are they don't because your self-talk is not publicly supported. This doesn't mean you have to go out there and win every conceivable award; it simply serves to remind you that all you can brag about are things you have actually achieved that are acknowledged, honored, and appreciated by others.

By embracing this mind-set, you can focus your efforts in ways that are more about others than about you. When your supervisor gives you praise, ask if there are ways to formalize it by way of a project or committee assignment. Talk about your career path and ask for an honest assessment about how soon they think you'll be ready for the next level. Volunteer your time as a way to shine in the face of others. Look for avenues of recognition, and follow the criteria to the letter. Ask for recommendations and concrete examples of how they will discuss what they see as your finest accomplishments. No matter what, obtain current, external validation (and beyond your immediate peer group) before you boast.

Ready, Willing, and Able

When interviewing, the floor is yours. You may demonstrate that you are ready, willing, and able to take on the role in question. You will find that in doing so, some things are within your control whereas others are not. You can control what you say and how you say it. You can control your mannerisms, gestures, and nervousness. You can control how much homework or research you do in advance, as well as the extent to which you practice. What you cannot control includes the personality and motivations of the interviewer, which questions will be asked, and the strength of your competition.

But what about the sheer number of questions that might be asked? How in the world do you prepare for a potentially infinite array of inquiries? Just remember this simple truth: Every question asked is designed to determine to what extent you are ready, willing, and able. Look at the following standard and nonstandard interview questions, and see how they fit into the three categories:

Questions to determine your readiness

Tell me about your nursing and/or caregiving experience.

Why did you choose a nursing career?

How do you personally define success?

Why should I hire you?

What are your greatest strengths as a nurse?

What are your weaknesses or limitations as a colleague?

What are the biggest pressures in your present nursing job?

Why are you leaving your present nursing job?

What is the worst thing your nursing supervisor could say about you?

Why should we employ you rather than the other candidates?

Have you ever felt your boss or a physician was wrong or handling something poorly, and how did you handle it?

Questions to determine your willingness

What attributes do you possess that make you a team player on the nursing floor?

What do you know about our company or health care system?

Why are you interested in our company?

Do you have any plans for further education?

What do you see yourself doing 5 years from now?

What kind of salary are you looking for?

Are you willing to relocate? Travel?

What qualities do you feel a successful manager should have?

What motivates you?

What would you do tomorrow if you won the lottery today?

Questions to determine your ability

Describe a situation in which you were successful in your nursing role.

As a nurse, do you most enjoy your work with information, people, or equipment?

Tell me about some of your recent goals and what you did to achieve them.

Have you ever had a conflict with a patient? How did you resolve it?

How long would it take you to make a contribution to our company?

How sensitive are you to criticism, and how have you improved in this area?

How do you define a stressful work environment, and how do you manage stressful situations?

How long or well would you survive if alone on a deserted, tropical island?

The category in which an interview item appears helps you understand the rationale for responding to the item. Review the list above once more as you begin to understand the motivations of each as presented below.

Readiness looks at your level of preparation, how much research you have done, if you are truly up for a new challenge based on how you have progressed in your prior roles, and the attributes you bring to the table that will help you succeed.

Willingness looks at your motivations for taking a new role, what your deal breakers might be, and how committed you might be in the new role or with the company for the long term.

Ability looks at how well you can do something, to what extent you have proven such abilities in the past, how quickly you can accomplish something, and where your faults might lie that would hinder your success.

It is important that you understand the significance of the ready-willing-able trifecta. Please note that there are loads of additional interview questions and tips you can easily find on the Internet or in books in your library. They are all typically comprised of sound advice. This book strives to help you look deeply into the processes and cycles inherent throughout your interview phase.

That said, here are 10 tips to refine and enhance how you apply the three categories for interviewing success:

1. Bring at least five extra copies of your resume. Bring the original or an improved version. Also bring several blank thank-you cards, envelopes, and stamps, but leave them in your car or bag during the interview.
2. Arrive early, within 5 or 8 minutes of the appointed time. You want to give yourself a few minutes to stop and breathe, slow your heart rate, check your composure, get your bearings, and organize yourself for the initial handshake.
3. Let the interviewer take the lead with small talk or other initial activities before the interview gets underway. You may ask if there might be time for a quick tour of the work area before you leave.
4. Upon sitting down, take 15 seconds to organize your immediate space. You may have a pad of paper or small notebook and pen. Provide additional, fresh copies of your resume. Check your posture. You want to be relaxed and comfortable yet professional, without being rigid or tense. Imagine yourself welcoming the interview. Say thank you for the opportunity to interview. Convey that you have been looking forward to this meeting.
5. The opening question in any interview is often some variation of "Tell me about yourself." Practice your professional response in advance. Think of it as giving the 2-minute CliffsNotes version of your resume.
6. Keep all responses brief, under 1 or 2 minutes. Give a concise answer, and then ask the interviewer if he or she would like more detail. Some will and others won't, so be prepared either way.
7. Have at least five questions prepared that you will ask at the end of the interview. Ask about the supervisor's management style; workplace culture; staffing patterns; turnover rates of the nursing staff; and the first negative comments, concerns, or controversies you will hear about if hired. This is your turn to find out what it will be like to work for this organization, so you can gauge the likelihood of success. Never ask about salary, benefits, or opportunities for advancement, however. Such items are premature at this point, and asking will leave the interviewers questioning your motivation for being there. Your last item could be a reminder that you would appreciate a quick tour of the work area before you leave the building.

8. Ask for the business cards of all who take part in the interview. You want to have the names, titles, and addresses available after you leave.
9. As you are saying goodbye and shaking hands one final time, sum up in one sentence that you appreciated their time and wish to leave them with the firm sense that you are ready, willing, and able to take on the new role. Say it with confidence and radiate a warm smile.
10. As soon as you are clear of the building, hand write thank-you notes to each person who interviewed you (as well as to the recruiter who set up the appointment, if applicable). Reiterate your understanding of something that was clearly important to them during the interview. Remind them again that you are ready, willing, and able to take on the new role with a passion. Find a mailbox on your way home.

Negotiating Offers

By knowing your strengths and talents and learning what those are really worth—a lot—you will find yourself in a stronger position to negotiate a higher salary and better benefits.

Remember, job postings have changed greatly in scope. They have become much more informative, illuminating the organization's mission and culture. It is simply not enough anymore to hire a nurse solely upon basic qualifications. Though they are an essential minimum to ascertain at the outset, hospitals and health care systems want to hire nurses who are going to be a great fit with interdisciplinary teams, patients, doctors, and administrators. They want nurses who are not only knowledgeable but also professional, adaptable, and collaborative—nurses who will truly contribute to the greater good or the higher purpose. Being able to demonstrate that about yourself, in no uncertain terms, will go a long way toward your negotiating power.

How do you demonstrate all this? Simply, by putting in place and truly living what earlier chapters have illuminated. Never complain about your workplace or colleagues on Facebook or other social media sites. Curb your negativity when you're in the elevator at work or dropping by a different department. Understand that health care professionals in acute care have a different way of approaching situations than those in chronic or long-term care. Don't complain to anyone and everyone who will listen about how short-staffed your unit is or suggest the hospital doesn't take patient care seriously. Never pilfer medications or supplies or act in any way that would be unethical or illegal. Imagine that such behaviors cause a dark, interpersonal cloud to form around you. The more you engage in such behaviors, the darker and stormier it gets. It won't be long before that cloud is clear for all to see and seek to avoid.

In other words, before you can even get to the offer stage, you have to have been awarded the initial offer. In order to get the job offer, you have to have demonstrated that you are ready, willing, and able to do the job well and with a consistently positive and highly professional demeanor. While you are establishing your credentials and credibility with the prospective employers, which may well include your current employer if you are angling for a promotion, you need to understand that your time to negotiate has not yet come to pass. That is right; you can derail your job search success by trying to negotiate too soon. Premature negotiation can turn off interviewers and make it appear that it is all about you. It is not all about you until you have an explicit offer. That is when it is your turn to negotiate.

Negotiation involves the give and take or dialogue to arrive at a mutually satisfactory outcome or plan of action. Inherent to negotiation is that both sides are vying for the greater advantage. Both sides have something at stake, something to lose. Both sides want a favorable outcome; everyone wants to win. It often results in a compromise with neither side getting everything they wanted. It is to be an ethical process with neither side acting in bad faith.

How do you view negotiation? Depending upon your feelings about it, you will approach the process in different ways. Do you see resources as finite with only so much to go around? If so, you may feel more anxious about the negotiation process or be more likely to take the outcome personally and negatively, possibly feeling cheated if you don't get everything you wanted. You might see negotiation as a sort of zero-sum game in which your gain or loss is balanced out by their gain or loss with a net sum of zero, whereby the only way to win is if everyone gains or loses the same amount.

Do you see negotiation as more integrative or collaborative? In this case, you have more trust in the process and the other parties. This approach involves creative problem-solving and making concessions as both sides are understood and valued. Human resources may take an advocate's approach to negotiation by determining early on what each side needs at a minimum and serving as a neutral party to craft a favorable outcome. Ultimately, you need to be willing to enter into any negotiation as a partner versus an adversary. (This can be a challenge for anyone socialized to view negotiation as a negative or naturally adversarial process.)

You also need to have a good understanding of your role within the negotiation process. In his 2006 book *Bargaining for Advantage*, G.R. Shell identifies five styles of negotiation. Your style may be: accommodating, avoiding, collaborating, competing, or compromising. The accommodating, collaborating, and compromising styles all require a modicum of trust and natural goodwill between parties. If you are distrustful throughout the process, you will be unable to take on such roles. Accommodators may give ground too soon, which may be the case if you want the job no matter what and don't wish to lose out altogether. Avoiders find the very idea of negotiation distasteful, and they tend to accept whatever is offered. Sometimes, avoiders hide behind a veil of tact and diplomacy but simply talk in circles without any actual negotiation strategies in play.

Compromisers also may agree to terms too soon as a way to keep any perceived conflict to a minimum in their desire to end the negotiation process quickly. Competing roles aim to win, to dominate. For some, winning is the most important element—and this selfish style makes it difficult to collaborate with others for the best arrangement for all. Competitive negotiation places little to no value on the relationship between the parties, which is not helpful when a long-term employer-employee working relationship is expected to follow the outcome of the negotiation. But the collaborative negotiator looks at the process with an appreciation for the complexities at hand and is comfortable taking time to look at what every possibility entails in order to come up with the best solution for all parties. This approach is best, yet only works if both parties are collaborative. Imagine for a few moments what a negotiating process might look like between a collaborator and an avoider, or between a compromising role and a competing role. As you may quickly realize, it is important to glean the likely type of negotiator you will be interacting with before moving into the actual process.

LAND THAT JOB!

Which of the five styles best reflects your approach? Have you used different approaches at different times? How has your approach evolved over time? How would you like to strengthen your approach to negotiation?

In any negotiation, you need to know two things: a) everything you might possibly want in ranked order and b) your deal breakers. Here is a quick list of items that job seekers and advancers typically consider:

- Type of supervisor you want to work for
- Salary, amount of money needed for you to make the leap
- Hiring bonus
- Tuition assistance or reimbursement for additional education and certification
- Paid dues to join or maintain professional organization membership
- Union versus non-union environment
- Amount of autonomy and/or decision-making power
- Types of benefits including vision and dental, flex spending, employee discounts, stock options
- Relocation funds and/or transportation or parking stipends
- Corporate credit card, especially if you will need to travel or purchase work items
- Amount of and/or types of projects or special assignments to lead or be part of
- Vacation time, paid or unpaid sabbaticals, time off for missionary or off-site humanitarian/volunteer work, and/or additional weeks before actual start date

Once you receive a job offer, which includes a salary amount and list of standard benefits, the first thing to do is let them know how much you appreciate their offer. The second thing to tell them is that they have given you much to think about, and so you'd like 24 hours to consider their offer. You then want to write down and fully define your ranked needs and deal breakers. This allows you to plan your counteroffer, which may require additional research on your part to better understand your monetary market value.

Additional considerations include the amount of time the position has been open. The longer it has been open, the harder they have had to work to find a solid candidate, and the more leverage you have when negotiating. If you want them to help pay for your next degree, find out how much that next degree will cost (tuition, fees, and books). Figure out how much it will cost you to get to work, park, and dress for success. Are they a publicly traded company? Look them up online and check out not only their stock price over the past year, but read about the financial health of the company and how they rank among their competitors. If financially strong, they are in a better position to honor your counteroffer. If they are financially struggling, you may want to consider other places to work.

To counteroffer, prepare a list of the two things you want most, along with two or three things you would like but can live without. Then, within 24 hours of the offer, call or e-mail your counteroffer. If you plan to call, prepare by rehearsing how you will respond to hesitation, reluctance, or an outright "no." After each item on your list, allow a bit of time for the human resources staff member to write it down and consider it. If they seem readily amenable or if they ask "Anything else," give them the next item on your list.

They will likely need to time to think it over and consult with others in the company. Let them. Let any uncomfortable silences be your friend. They may use silence as a mild intimidation tactic. Let them. Don't rush to fill the silence; that's where many negotiations are blown on the candidate side. If this seems too stressful as an approach, send the list via e-mail with a gracious "thank you again," and indicate that you would love to work for the company if the following conditions can be met. That shows you are willing to compromise. They will then write or call you after they have come up with responses or counters of their own. When they do, know your deal breakers. Use your "want but don't need" items as "throwaways" to get the items that are dearly important to you.

Once an agreement is reached that both sides can live with, obtain a finalized offer in writing. In other words, tell them that as soon as you receive an updated offer letter with the new items included, you will officially and happily accept. Thank them profusely for their time and let them know how much their willingness to hear you out and consider your counter means to you as a new employee. Don't give any ultimatums unless you are truly willing to walk away from it all without regrets. And don't be afraid to do just that if it is the right thing to do.

Beyond offers, there is an art to negotiating shift differentials including overtime, time and a half, and holiday pay. Many nurses have learned how to make more money by cleverly choosing shifts without taking an extra tax hit.

This approach deserves a consultation with your accountant. There is a caution, too. Focusing solely on fine-tuning your paycheck can leave you less likely to advance through professional development opportunities. There is growth beyond mere monetary means, and you are strongly encouraged to look at the full range of pros and cons when negotiating your shift schedule. Also, as you negotiate, you are setting the tone for how you will work with the organization into the future. When done collaboratively, negotiation establishes a sense of mutual understanding and respect that carries into opportunities going forward. Don't hesitate to negotiate; rather, model how you'd like to be able to continue negotiating changes over time.

Negotiating opportunities happen more often than you might think. Whenever your company asks you to "do more," consider it carefully. Make sure you understand what is being asked and the expected duration of your commitment. Try to set a deadline or at least a point at which you will determine whether you want to continue. Ask about tools and resources available to foster your success. Remind them that this new request goes beyond what you were hired to do, and while you are happy to pitch in and help out, you are concerned that this new task will compromise the healthy work/life balance you have achieved and maintained. Tell them you don't want to do anything to jeopardize your current success, and, therefore, you'd like to take a day to think and get back to them with any questions or concerns you might have. If it turns out that you are fully expected to "just do it" with no questions asked and no compromise, perks, or pay differential, decide if it is worth an ultimatum, saying no and letting the chips fall where they may. Or decide if you can adopt a positive outlook and a "why not?" attitude, and see how it goes. Your inner alarm bells may go off warning you that it's time to start shopping for a new supervisor or company.

The point here is that you spend an inordinate amount of time in your life working. Chances are you spend anywhere from 1500-2400 hours on the job out of a total 8765 hours per year. That is roughly 20-25% of your time within your adult working life. You can look at it as a significant chunk of time that is not to be squandered on supervisors and work environments that don't deserve you. You can also decide that after another 25% of time is spent sleeping, the full 50% remaining is all yours to spend as you please and that your work environment is just a small part. Consider, however, that your work life and salary can directly and significantly impact the quality of all other time spent. In that light, your ability to earn what you need to while being joyful and passionate about what you do is not something to take lightly.

LAND THAT JOB!

Do your own calculations. How many hours per year do you spend working? How do those work hours contrast with sleeping and free/personal time? Can you anticipate future points in time at work where you might get another chance to negotiate?

This chapter closes with a reminder to be good to you. Expect others to be good to you. You deserve the right to have an open, collaborative discussion about your starting point within an organization and to set the tone for negotiations down the road. Don't let a natural fear of negotiation hold you back or foster later resentment. Face your fear, do your homework, know your deal breakers, and proceed with confidence while letting pauses in the conversation work in your favor. You can do this!

Reference

Shell, G.R. (2006). *Bargaining for advanatage: Negotiation strategies for reasonable people.* New York, NY: Penguin.

Best Candidate Checklist

___ I have explored which approaches I have taken in interviews in the past and assessed their effectiveness.

___ I have realized that being my best, true self in any interview situation is the finest approach.

___ I have articulated my accomplishments in addition to my abilities.

___ I have eliminated any overestimates of my abilities and talents and brought them into a realistic and accurate framework.

___ I have listed all the ways I can demonstrate that I am ready, willing, and able in an interview situation.

___ I have practiced my best responses to common interview questions.

___ I have created an "interview toolkit" for myself based on all the tips and suggested approaches discussed in this chapter.

___ I have determined concrete ways to stretch beyond my normal comfort zone in negotiations.

___ I have faced my fears, done my homework, know my deal breakers, and am prepared to negotiate with confidence.

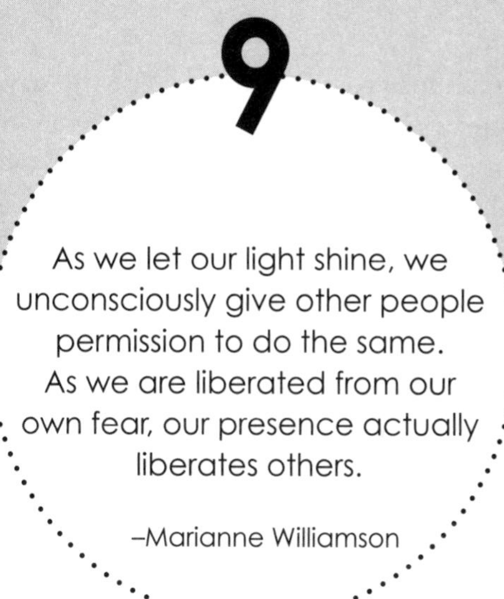

9
As we let our light shine, we unconsciously give other people permission to do the same. As we are liberated from our own fear, our presence actually liberates others.
–Marianne Williamson

Be the Best Nurse Candidate Ever

The economy continues to swing back and forth like a pendulum between recession and growth, between austerity and prosperity, as we move between bearish and bullish financial markets. Though you cannot change the direction of the pendulum swing, you can understand where it is now and where it's headed. You can arm yourself with knowledge around best steps to take and ways to either protect yourself or take advantage of the situation, because the pendulum swing directly impacts employment and hiring practices.

You have likely heard the phrase that it is "easier to find a job when you already have a job." Reasons are three-fold: Your current income keeps you from feeling desperate to find something/anything else, you can be more selective and only accept offers that are truly in your best interest, and you are more desirable as a candidate. Yes, more desirable by other employers. Many employers consider their prime (or only) candidate pool to be comprised of those who are already working in their field. It is believed that the skill sets of those workers are more current, and it is assumed that those who are unemployed will have more problems or emotional baggage. It is harsh, but true.

Similar to what you see in the housing market, when economic growth is strong and unemployment rates are low, it is a job seeker's market, as recruiters have to work hard to get anyone they can find. Full-time roles with benefits are the norm. This is needed to be able to lure professionals away from jobs they already have. It is a good time to advance up the career ladder and take on new roles and challenges. However, when times are tighter and unemployment is higher, it becomes an employer's market, and one by-product is that recruiters tend to narrow their focus to those who are currently employed, deepening the stigma around unemployment.

When job searching in an employer's market, be patient, work every job lead thoroughly, network at every opportunity, and do your best to hold on to the job you have, as even online applications and postings will say or strongly imply something along the lines of "only those currently employed need apply." When the market begins to recover, employers start hiring again, and you have remained employed, they will see you in a more favorable light as you survived layoffs, rose through the ranks in hard times, and/or have learned how to navigate a very lean culture and staffing landscape. Now that you have a basic sense of how the market impacts not only employment but employer perceptions, take a look at specific ways to leverage opportunities that arise every day.

You Were Interviewed Twice This Week Already

As a nurse, you may not realize that you are being interviewed all the time. Chances are you have been evaluated and assessed for something more than twice this week already. Recognize the cues that this is happening. This section goes beyond reputation management, challenging you to recognize and promote opportunities in everyday situations.

There are a number of informal, passive, off-the-record interview events, including:

your midyear and end-of-year performance evaluations

periodic performance assessments

any presentations you make to a group

anytime you step up and volunteer to help out

when you serve as a trainer or mentor

when you handle an awkward situation or stand up to a bully with professionalism and grace

at a company event

anytime you represent your organization in the public eye

the way you speak about your company off-hours or away from the nursing floor

whenever you tell a supervisor what he or she needs to hear versus wants to hear (briefly and diplomatically, of course)

the way you describe your job and workplace to others

when others read your nametag

when you alert a supervisor to a process gap or new safety concern and present a solution

when you are asked to join a meeting you were not previously part of

anytime you are asked to take on additional duties or pilot a new project, introduced to those higher up the chain of command, asked for your opinion about something, and more.

Anytime that these types of scenarios transpire, you must recognize them in the moment and be prepared to capitalize upon them. You should already be dressed for the part, so by paying close attention to your grooming and dressing habits each day, you'll already have this item covered. Routine, cyclical items such as performance appraisals should not catch you off guard, so plan for them in advance. When goals are set at the beginning of the year, get a written copy and keep them handy. Every few weeks, jot down ways you have met or exceeded the goals in question so when discussions are held about your progress, you are ready with concrete examples and enviable metrics to show for it.

Since you are the consummate nursing professional already, you naturally watch what you say and do in regard to your profession and workplace. So, there's no need to worry about an ugly or short-sighted posting that you authored coming to light through social media channels. You can and do routinely seek out where and how information is shared about new projects, opportunities to volunteer, and new employees that you can introduce yourself to. You also may take part in a formal mentoring partnership; attend employer-sponsored workshops, trainings, and events; and take advantage of tuition assistance or reimbursement programs that will further advance your expertise and career. You continue to pay attention to how you come across to others and are self-aware enough to know your strengths and limitations and how to leverage or manage each, respectively.

LAND THAT JOB!

What passive forms of evaluation in the content above best describe your circumstances? Identify those that represent missed opportunities you could take advantage of in the future. Practice raising your awareness of these opportunities and engaging in them with a more professional approach.

Swimming Successfully in the Recruiters' Pool

Recruiters, especially third-party recruiters, strive to build a primary healthy candidate pool that they look to whenever they are charged with filling a position. It is important to know how to rocket to the top of their list and stay on their radar.

Recruiter contacts need to be regularly developed and strengthened just like any other type of professional within your network. How many recruiters should you get to know? Ideally, all of them, as their very way of living depends upon how well and frequently they can fulfill client needs. In most cases, recruiters' clients are health care systems, insurance companies, and so forth. Start by reaching out and interviewing them well before you send your resume. Get to know them first; hear their spiel and philosophy; understand the types of clients they serve and how frequently they are expected to fill orders (open job requisitions); and whether they work only open orders or if they also build employer candidate pipelines and conduct confidential searches. Find out what level of nursing professionals are targeted and where the recruiter likes to look, which job boards are used, if recruiting takes place through the nursing schools, and how community-based job fairs are leveraged. Just like with any profession, the recruiting industry has its share of good and bad apples. Taking a few minutes up front to interview recruiters before revealing anything about yourself helps you to discern how they should rank within your professional network. You don't want to weed yourself out of the candidate pool because you said your wants and needs first, and the recruiter automatically assumed he or she doesn't have any clients that need you.

Start with the recruiter in the "hot seat." Have your questions ready and realize you won't get much more than 5 minutes of his or her time. The recruiter will talk to you for as long as it takes to decide (accurately or otherwise) whether you can help meet or exceed recruitment goals. This exercise also helps you learn what type of recruiter they are. For example, they might work directly for one particular company, act as an on-site contract recruiter, or work as a third-party recruiter who serves the interests of many employers. They might even be a job seeker agent who works for you for a fee. Fee-based job seeker agents come and go; their availability is largely dictated by the demand for such services and sufficient volume within a moderate employment market. In other words, such services spring up or scale back depending upon the recruiters' likelihood of success in finding you a job that is high-paying enough to cover the time it takes on their end to develop viable leads for you.

Figure out who the "cream of the recruiting crop" is based on how closely their role aligns with your wants and needs. Then, based on your research, customize a resume that leverages your new knowledge. Send the recruiter two versions of your resume, a long and comprehensive version as well as a shorter, one-page version. Use pdf format for each and indicate that you want to know what edits are needed before presenting your credentials to any particular client. Also understand that no matter what your resume looks like, the recruiter will want to make edits based on knowledge of the employer preferences and biases around resume content, layout, and length.

Most of the recruiters you meet work for company clients, not directly for you. You cannot place any demands on them. Doing so will simply turn them off and blind them to your talents. The recruiter will ask you for your preferences and whether you can relocate. But understand that he or she is not asking you such questions to be able to find what you are looking for. Rather, the recruiter is gauging to what extent you are flexible. Don't lie but do know your deal breakers; convey them sooner rather than waste anyone's time.

After you identify recruiters of interest, establish contact and ask questions. Keep a list handy with their names, contact information, and responses to your questions, so you can follow up with ease, pick up where you left off, and stay organized. One of the items to learn from each is how often you should follow up and make contact again. This could range from once per week to once per month; whatever it is, honor it. You might set aside an hour or two each week simply to review your list of contacts and the notes you have collected so far, reach out to follow up, and identify new potential contacts to add to the cycle as you go.

When following up with recruiters, let them know you are checking in as promised, find out which positions they are currently sourcing candidates for, learn whether there already are strong candidates for the positions in question and what would help make you a stronger candidate (within reason, of course). No matter what the outcome, genuinely thank them. Let them know if you might be able to refer another candidate for something you are not qualified to fill, and tell them you'll check back in another week or so. You may need to follow this cycle many, many times before the recruiter thinks of you first for an available position. Candidates ahead of you on the list have likely been following up for some time.

Continue to seek out and get to know new recruiters. You can conduct an online search, ask other nurses whom they recommend, visit job fairs and career open houses, talk to the career center staff at your nursing school, check with professional nursing organizations, query professional networking sites, and more.

LAND THAT JOB!

How many recruiters are you in contact with on a weekly basis? Consider tripling that number, and plan your action steps accordingly.

Optimism or Law of Attraction

The law of attraction has been around for more than 100 years. Though its veracity is debated, there are many who believe that by visualizing what you want, you are more likely to receive it. At the very least, a popularized perspective calling for a positive outlook has emerged. Plus, it can make any goal more personally meaningful and fun to pursue. Healthy optimism, coupled with methodical follow-through, is necessary in any job search.

Attraction is bi-directional; you either want to attract something to you or you are more likely to be attracted to one thing more than another. Different people will attribute successful and positive attraction to various causes: good looks and/or force of personality, being in the right place at the right time, dogged perseverance, having the right connections or at least a ripe sense of entitlement, or being just plain lucky. It may be a combination of things. You want to attract what you believe you deserve. Believe this: You deserve to work within a respectful setting with people who recognize your hard work and professional talents and will compensate you fairly. That may be your reality; it may not be. Only you can determine that. Keep in mind that two people can hold the same type of role in the same place with the same supervisor and have different perceptions of how well they are treated and how many opportunities are available to them. The differences can be associated with the extent to which they each attract what they perceive they are getting.

So, how do you attract the things and people you want versus those you don't? The mother of positive thinking, Louise Hay, would tell you that it starts with positive and specific statements about what you want in life, combined with an implied or explicit "I will" pronouncement to the world at large. The premise is that by stating what you want, you "advertise" for it and so get it. Conversely, if you make negative statements or say what you do want plus an "I can't," you'll receive what you "advertised" for—nothing. In this way, positivity is transformative. Happy, positive people attract other happy, positive people or at least those who want to be even if they haven't quite figured out how. Robert Merton, author of *Social Theory and Social Structure* (1968) promoted the concept of self-fulfilling prophecy by which believing or stating something to be true actually brings it about.

You may have also heard the phrase "like begets like." We attract those most like ourselves in terms of gender, race, and socioeconomic status. But the law of attraction takes it a step further to say that you attract whom and what you want to attract by being whom and what you want to attract more of. So, if you are an energetic, engaging, and well-respected professional in the nursing profession, you will attract others like you. By contrast, if your conscious or subconscious statement to the world is that you are a gossipy bully with a contrarian attitude who lives to bring others down around you as a way to feel better inside, that is precisely the type of people you will attract. Whether you are a firm believer or think it's all spiritual fluff, consider who you have been attracting up until now, how well you attract those you need as allies in your job search, and to what extent these concepts may influence your ability to network comfortably and successfully.

When you apply healthy optimism to your job search and career development, you shine with greater confidence, and others take notice and are drawn to your wonderfully infectious attitude. It is up to you to make the most of this enduring phenomenon; it is something you can control.

LAND THAT JOB!

What are the qualities or people you want to attract (e.g., respect, recruiters)? How does that mesh with or differ from who you currently attract, in either a personal or professional sense? If positive congruence is evident, great! If not, what would you like to do about it? How might you put the power of positivity to work for your professional benefit?

Visibility Plus

The idea of "visibility plus" comes out of two camps: safety tools and professional networking. Both of these ideas can serve your job search; the parallels may be quite obvious to you. The use of safety tools helps to minimize risk, which is something you want to do in your job search or overall career. You don't want to do anything that will get you fired or put you in a position to make good on an ultimatum to quit your job. Much like a rock climber, you don't want to fall after having worked so hard to get up as high as you can. Having the right tools helps you make it safely to the top and protects you in those scarier moments along the way.

Think about the tools you have (or should have) at your disposal to help make your job search or career development "climb" more successful. Your tools may be degrees held, professional networking contacts, willingness to grow outside your comfort zone, ability to show grace under pressure, ability to prioritize and communicate and keep things in perspective, not sweating the small stuff, employing tact and reserve, or staying calm in a crisis. It might be the ability to recognize "loose rock" such as gossip, negativity, and unsafe conditions and use the best tools to get you to safer strongholds as quickly as possible.

Similarly, visibility plus refers to business development, which is how you create or find opportunities to generate revenue for a business. Business development is a process by which you undertake a set of tasks, aided with tools and applications, to drive growth and revenue. Your career is your business; treat it as such. Think of your paycheck as how you pay yourself as CEO of your professional life. See job leads in a business development light and view all the activities of job searching, such as browsing for ideal postings, submitting online applications, and participating in networking events, as the very essence of business development as you build public or private awareness of your company's (your) offerings to prospective employers (the marketplace). This also means that you need to put your "sales" hat on and "market" your wares to a "targeted audience" that you have identified through the appropriate market research to determine your best niche and effectively "price" your services accordingly.

In this regard, you can start to see how the concept of branding becomes important and why you should develop a set of statements around your "company's" mission, vision, and values. Here's a tutorial on these basic business tenets:

Mission

Your mission is what you actively do. You are a nurse; you are presently engaged in the art and science of nursing in a particular specialty and setting, such as acute, chronic, long-term, or end-of-life care. Take a few minutes and create a mission statement that spells out in one sentence what it is that you do best, here and now.

Vision

Your vision is where you are headed, a description of what that vision looks like. Vision statements often start with phrases such as, "To become …, to grow …, to provide for all time …, to leave a lasting legacy …," coupled with a specific, desirable goal that has not yet been achieved. For example, you knew you wanted to become a nurse, so you went to nursing school and fulfilled your vision. Continue to develop your vision for your professional future. It could be anything you want to achieve: "to specialize in pediatrics," "to launch a nonprofit organization to support nurse leaders," or "to be recognized as the Florence Nightingale of my time."

Values

Your values are the fundamental ethics and beliefs that guide your actions as you carry out your mission and strive to realize your vision.

Job Search Activity

Use the following activity to jot down ideas you can use to craft mission, vision, and values statements.

Mission: Fill in the boxes with words that describe or are associated with what you do best as a nurse, every day.

Vision: Fill in the boxes with words that describe or are associated with what you are passionate and motivated to achieve at some point.

Values: Fill in the boxes with words that describe or are associated with your beliefs and ethics.

Use the next lines to experiment with possible mission statements until you craft a great one you can use for the next few years.

____

____

____

____

____

____

____

____

Use the next several lines to experiment with possible vision statements until you have articulated a clear and important stretch goal, or other specific professional objective that will take some time and won't be easy. In other words, how can you stretch yourself and your thinking to accomplish more than you might accomplish naturally?

____

____

____

____

____

____

____

____

Last but not least, use the next lines to develop a series of values statements; then choose the best three or four to call your own as you grow professionally.

____

____

____

____

____

____

____

____

The health care organization you work for now and those you have worked for in the past all have a mission, vision, and guiding values. It is from this overarching trio that strategic operating plans are built, accompanied by specific action plans and predetermined milestones for success. Organizational language leads to the development of job titles and descriptions, along with a bulleted list of priorities or expectations and required and desired qualifications for each role.

Your own professional mission, vision, and value statements can be readily communicated wherever you go. Think back to the chapter on interviewing. During any interview, you convey the best and most pertinent things about you and how you will be an asset to the team to support continued organizational growth. You express this with your customized resume and cover letter. You talk about it in networking opportunities, and you showcase it in your current role every day.

LAND THAT JOB!

In what ways has your thinking changed since you started reading this book? What alterations and improvements have you made in your professional life? What evidence have you seen to attest to these changes, including positive comments from others?

You have now come full circle. Reflect on all that you have learned in this book. By taking everything you have learned, combined with your greater understanding of how the self and the larger world interact, along with a clearer perspective of how much you really do influence and control versus what you cannot, you are able to present yourself to anyone in the most professional, positive, and congruent way. Since goals are not achieved overnight, you recognize that not only is patience required, but consistency as well. Persevere, as you leave your professional mark wherever you go, every day. Job search and career development are not periodic or episodic, but rather ever-evolving ways of being with cyclical activities that you can continuously improve upon. Think about it!

Your career is your business. Your job search plan is a strategic, operational treatise that guides your way as you develop your own professional business career, live your mission, journey to your vision, and embrace your values every step of the way. Use all these tools, all the proven business development techniques, and the power of positive thinking to be the best nurse candidate ever.

Best Candidate Checklist

- ___ I have assessed how the current economy impacts my job search and have adapted my strategy accordingly.
- ___ I have begun to recognize the ways I am being regularly assessed and interviewed in very informal, understated ways.
- ___ I have reached out to and interviewed recruiters after developing an action plan that will enhance my job search success.
- ___ I have attracted positive attention as I work my plan and continue positive self-affirmations.
- ___ I have rejected the attitudes and behaviors around me that are negative and hurting my chances for job search success.
- ___ I have become more visible in positive and professional ways.
- ___ I have drafted my own personal mission, vision, and values statements.

Success is a state of mind.
If you want success, start thinking
of yourself as a success.

–Dr. Joyce Brothers

Effectively Marketing the Nurse in You

Now that you are thinking of yourself in business terms, here are ways to take that premise and run with it. This chapter takes tried-and-true small-business tactics for marketing, promotion, and sales and helps you to see tangible parallels that you can apply to your job search. No matter how you go forward at this point, the biggest resource you need to invest in your self-marketing plan is time. An hour per day gets you started, and it can be grouped into an initial 5- or 6-hour stretch on your day off with shorter, weekly follow-up points from then on. The second biggest resource you need is courage. It takes a bit of bravery to "put yourself out there," which in many cases starts out as bravado or a "fake it 'til you make it" attitude to help you through the initial foray. Remember reading about expanding your comfort zone in the first two chapters? The third biggest resource you need is creativity. allowing you to articulate your ideas so that others can visualize and appreciate what you are trying to accomplish. Time, courage, and creativity—three things you can draw upon and leverage at any point throughout your career.

Basic Marketing and Promotional Approaches

Marketing and promotion are used by every business to build awareness and appreciation for products and services in order to turn a profit, fueling further growth regardless of the competitive landscape. Sounds like job search and career development, doesn't it? Think about the ways that businesses market products and services to you, and get ready to follow the example. Here are five ideas that can work wonders with your budgeted time, a bit of courage, and a healthy dose of creativity.

E-mail blast

The first step in pulling off an e-mail blast is to pull together a list of recipients and their e-mail addresses. Think about whom you want your audience to be. If you are targeting different groups, tweak your e-mail blast message accordingly. In other words, don't force one message to do the work of three. You may want to target a) your friends, family, and acquaintances, b) recruiters, and c) hiring managers and other health care professionals within your nursing specialty.

Document the names and e-mail addresses in a spreadsheet or database such as a free customer relationship management (CRM) application. For best results, separate first names from last names into individual cells. Each e-mail address should be in its own cell or field, as well. There is no minimum number, so don't fret if you only have 20 or so names and addresses within a particular recipient category. This is an exercise that builds over time. Because you send your message out over the course of many months, you'll add to your recipients. You may, however, have a maximum number that your e-mail program allows you to send. Do a quick online search using the terms "send e-mail rate limit," plus your e-mail application name, to find your maximum per-day limit.

You may also choose to use a free service or invest in a low-cost e-mail blast application. The nice thing about such services and applications is they often provide templates to help you create a great-looking blast.

After you have developed your list of names and e-mails, craft your message. Specify your message to appeal to one segment of your target populations. For example, suppose your list of contacts includes nursing recruiters, charge nurses, directors of nursing, nursing faculty, and your nursing/health care peers. Each of these subgroups merits a unique message. To your peer group, your message might revolve around what a great team player you are and how you'd like to help them capitalize on any employee referral bonuses that may be available where they work. To recruiters, your message is about how you can help them meet or exceed their staffing goals with your credentials, tremendous capacity to care for others while working well with the care team, and willingness to work hard-to-fill shifts. You would have a similar message for charge nurses and directors of nursing, but with added elements around your understanding of the business aspects of health care and the need for cost-containment and effectiveness measures that relate to nursing outcomes. Other ways to split up your target market include the type of care facility, geographical area, supplemental roles such as adjunct nursing faculty positions, and more. If willing and able to relocate (which can greatly expand your opportunities), make sure to note that in your message.

LAND THAT JOB!

What is your comfort level with the suggested approach discussed above? Whom do you want to target first, and what would you like your main point or objective to be when you reach out to them?

Reflect on what approaches are right for your situation. Keep your messages short, simple, and to the point. Make sure there are no grammatical errors or typos anywhere. Your name and contact information should be clear. If you have a relevant and current website, direct them to it. Or simply provide your e-mail address and phone number in case they request your resume, proof of credentials, and references.

Yes, your message will encounter someone's spam filter and wind up in the junk folder. The software you choose may have a feature that allows you to track how well your message is received in terms of whether it is opened, quickly deleted, or bounced back as undeliverable. The point is that you will have gotten your message out there. As an additional and necessary step, call recipients a few days later to let them know you sent an e-mail and that you're interested in speaking with them further about current and foreseeable opportunities within their organization.

Direct Mail Postcards

Using much the same approach as the e-mail blast, you can create inexpensive postcards that can be printed in different quantities. Visit local or online printers such as Vistaprint or Moo for details. Once printed, simply affix a prepared mailing label with each person's name and address. This can be a novel way to get their attention, and there's no chance it will go "unopened."

Cold Calling

Just about every small business employs cold calling at some point to develop new business leads. You can, too! And it's easy once you establish a game plan. Just like e-mail blasts and postcards, you define your target audience and make sure you have valid phone numbers. If you do not have their direct line, have the main phone number handy. Start by organizing the information you have and add room to insert the information you'll learn as you make your calls. For example, in an Excel spreadsheet, make a list of the names and numbers you wish to call. Leave enough space to the right of each entry to note the date/time you called, whether you made contact or left a message, whom you spoke to (or whose voicemail you reached), and what they are able to share with you once contact is made. After you have your list ready, focus your attention on your "script." Create a script or "spiel" that is short, simple, and straightforward. When calling a list of directors of nursing (DONs), you might try something along these lines:

> *Hello, my name is ___________, and I am an RN with 3 years of experience who is looking for new nursing opportunities. I've been aware of (name of company) for several years and appreciate its good reputation in the community. So, I'm reaching out to learn about current or foreseeable hiring needs you may have and how I can quickly and easily fill those needs. What types of nursing openings do you foresee in the near future? What types of credentials are you looking for in those roles? (Or, if you reach their voicemail, finish in this way instead.) You may reach me at (your phone number) to*

learn more about my credentials, at which point I'd also be happy to forward my resume to you. Thanks and have a great day!

Notice how the message can be quickly and easily adapted whether you speak with a person or need to leave a voicemail. If the idea of cold-calling gives you the willies, yet you see the benefit of doing so, call early in the morning before they are likely to be in the office and leave a voicemail message. Most voicemail systems play oldest messages first, so yours may easily be the last one they hear right as they are about to jump into their day. Good timing!

What is your comfort level with the suggested approach discussed above? Whom do you want to target first, and what would you like your main point or objective to be when you reach out to them?

Create a Video Introduction or Video Resume

There are several free online services that allow you to create a 1-minute introduction in video format. Once complete, you receive a specific URL address that you can then embed in e-mail, showcase on your LinkedIn profile, or add to your existing resume at the very end as a way to invite them to learn more about you. The only equipment needed is a video camera, a microphone, and video software. Newer laptop computers have these features already built in and ready to use. For older machines, you can purchase a small inexpensive camera that sits atop your computer monitor, a headset that plugs in to a microphone slot or USB port, and compatible software available on the Internet or from your local store. These items can be purchased for less than $50.

A short video lets viewers get an immediate sense of your personality and presence. You must smile warmly, introduce yourself, and state your intentions. Give a brief summary of your credentials and work history, follow up with the top three personality traits that make you a joy to work with, and close with what you love about nursing. Lastly, state that you'd like to connect and continue the conversation in person at their earliest convenience. You can provide your contact information then, too, or provide it through supplemental means, such as within the body of the e-mail you send them with the video URL link. This method is helpful for recruiters and hiring managers who work remotely; for work-at-home positions such as telephonic case management and related consulting roles; or online, adjunct teaching jobs.

What is your comfort level with the suggested approach discussed above? Whom do you want to target first, and what would you like your main point or objective to be when you reach out to them?

Business Cards

Whenever you are out and about and meet someone new, the conversation could easily touch on your desire to find new opportunities as a nurse. You want to encourage follow-up at every turn, so it is very helpful to have a personal card to leave with them. You can model yours after any number of cards you have seen across every industry. These cards are roughly 2" by 3.5" and contain your name, certification acronyms earned, and contact information, along with the marketing tagline you may be using on your resume or a line that simply states, "Seeking new opportunities in nursing." You can have them professionally printed or make your own with free templates and a good printer connected to your computer. For best results, you can also create your own, save it to a flash drive, and take it to a local copy center as a low-cost but professional-looking compromise for producing your business cards. If you make your own, do a quick online review of best practices when designing a business card and have a few other people look it over to make sure they look crisp, professional, and contain no errors (this happens surprisingly often when nondesign professionals create their own cards, so do your due diligence in this area). Once printed, give these cards out like candy! You may give someone well-connected in health care a bunch and ask him or her to mention you favorably and give your cards to anyone connected to hiring decisions in the nursing field. Yes, get other health care professionals to help you get your cards out there!

LAND THAT JOB!

What is your comfort level with the suggested approach discussed above? Whom do you want to target first, and what would you like your main point or objective to be when you reach out to them?

Maximizing Your Marketing

Putting yourself out there can be relatively easy and free/low-cost, and the benefits far outweigh any initial discomfort you may experience. Once you have your recipients determined and message crafted using any of these modes of marketing and promotion, turn your attention toward how you can maximize what you have to work with in terms of education, experience, attitude, and giving back.

Education

Make the most of your nurse education and certifications, especially if these are stronger than your actual nursing experience. This is the case for new nursing graduates; your education always outweighs your experience. Do remember that working in medical and caregiving environments while you are in school is an excellent way to deepen your understanding of medical terminology, basic medical procedures, charting and documentation, working in a team environment, and practicing professionalism. Working part-time while in school and in a related role is part of the education you can capitalize on after you graduate.

Essential certifications can include Basic Life Support (BLS), Advanced Cardiovascular Life Support (ACLS), Pediatric Advanced Life Support (PALS), Neonatal Resuscitation Program (NRP), IV Therapy, and more. Certifications help demonstrate your commitment to a particular line of work that further raises your level of preparedness for the job.

When your nursing education is the most relevant part of your resume, play it to the hilt. List it just below your professional profile. Indicate which specific degree(s) you earned, the name and location of the school, graduation date, and GPA. Highlight specific courses that you took and excelled in that align well with the type of role you desire. For example, if you want to work as a medical-surgical nurse, highlight those types of courses. You should also highlight special projects you completed during your studies, such as a significant research paper, mock clinical exercises, field trips or service learning you participated in, guest lectures you attended, student memberships in nursing societies and organizations, and any leadership roles you held in school groups or clubs. Demonstrate how you immersed yourself in the art and science of becoming a nurse. Then just below the education section of your resume, list clinical rotations and preceptorships. Go back and review Chapter 3 for more details, as needed.

After you have thoroughly discussed your educational endeavors toward becoming a nurse, list your work experience. This is where you highlight any medical or caregiving environments you have worked in along the way, whether paid or volunteer. If you are reading this book while still in school, you must stretch your comfort zone to land a part-time job that is as close as possible to nursing and in the type of setting you wish to work in upon graduation. Seek out roles as a certified nursing assistant and keep that job for as long as you can while in school (start early, stay on board throughout). You might work at just one location, travel locally through an agency, or serve on a float pool. Think ahead about how you can leverage experience that is supplementing your nursing education to your greatest benefit. Such jobs put you face to face with those who can hire you outright once you graduate, provide an excellent reference for you, introduce you to other decision makers, and more.

Experience

Make the most of your nursing experience, especially when it is stronger than your educational background. Nurses must continue their education as they go. A minimum annual requirement makes nursing one of the few fields where it can be difficult to create a serious gap between one's years of experience and formal credentials. In other words, you don't really run the risk of your experience outpacing your education or vice versa unless you have taken time out of the workforce to raise a family. If that is the case, do your best to keep credentials current on your own until you are ready to return to nursing. This is a bigger concern in other career fields, so you can count your blessings on this front. Whenever you inwardly groan at the thought of getting another certification or taking a class for continuing education credit, be glad that it's required to remain a nurse. But, suppose that up until now you have done the bare minimum. You may strongly (and rightly) suspect that the competition has more education and credentials to highlight than you do.

Take heart! The first thing to do is investigate which certifications you can earn quickly as a way to bolster your credentials. Then, and until you have additional certification or CEUs to showcase, talk up your experience! You will want to truly capture the impact you have had as a nurse; highlight the toughest challenges you have encountered, and help your audience to visualize you in action and succeeding no matter what the environment. Ensure your resume and cover letter are keyword-rich to attract the attention of resume-scanning and automated applicant tracking software. Use numbers/metrics to show how many patients you care for per shift, the kinds of equipment you can expertly use, types of presenting patients you care for, the committees you have served on, improvements you recommended and helped to implement, junior nurses you have mentored and trained, how you've emerged as a go-to resource, and your ability to pick up extra shifts. But what if you are reading this with a sinking heart as you realize you haven't done any of these things? Take control; take action. Start doing these things immediately. If you are currently unemployed, find a local organization with which you can volunteer your nursing skills. Challenge yourself to step as far outside your comfort zone as needed to make results happen sooner than later; time is of the essence.

Attitude

A great attitude goes a long way, can be the tiebreaker between you and your strongest competition, and helps you make the most of your strengths. There are dozens of benefits to be derived from having a great attitude, and realizing these benefits helps make your great attitude sustainable over time. No one is an overnight success. The greatest nurse role models you have ever met have taken time and attention to craft their talent to what appears so effortless to the casual observer.

Think about it! A great attitude fuels itself and makes anything worth doing seem that much more possible. It drives inspiration, motivation, and creativity. It helps you see possibilities and opportunities where others might only see obstacles and overwhelming challenges. Happiness and stress relief are further fueled with a great outlook and consistent optimism. It helps you to become more influential; others are far more likely to listen to and take the advice of people who shine in how they speak and present themselves. There's a natural level of respect and appreciation that is more readily shown to those who are optimistic problem solvers who don't shy away from a challenge, and who put themselves out there to accomplish great things. It makes people want to be around you, and your attitude will inspire theirs. It helps you to enjoy your work more even as you seek new opportunities elsewhere. In fact, when you respectfully submit your resignation, a great attitude that you've had all along can inspire your current supervisor to offer you a raise or other perks to keep you on board rather than lose you.

You can showcase a great attitude in your resume and cover letter by providing examples. Instead of simply stating that you have "excellent communication skills," rev it up by stating that you "demonstrate excellent communication skills through a combination of a great attitude, professional tact, and appropriate humor to keep things running smoothly on the nursing floor." Instead of simply saying you train and mentor nurses, indicate how you "champion new nurses on the team to help them start strong and become a contributing team member." As discussed in Chapter 4, focus on impact and outcomes of your action in terms that hiring managers will appreciate and covet.

As a nurse, you already know the benefits of a great attitude when it comes to duration of illness, coping skills, and recovery time. Take a page out of your own nursing book and apply this tremendously effective approach for your own long-term benefit.

Giving Back

By its definition, giving is doing. It is an active, conscious, and intentional activity that contributes directly or indirectly to the greater good. When applied to your job search and career development, you strengthen others' perceptions of you as a nurse professional. Optimize your visibility and present yourself as the best nurse candidate ever for your next role.

Think back to all this book has discussed about networking. If you are still struggling to expand your comfort zone in this area, focus your attention squarely on reaching out to help others with no thought to ancillary benefits you might receive in return. Trust that such benefits will happen naturally. Volunteer your time and talents. Organize an event for a special cause. Help a colleague find information to gain his or her next certification. Pull together other nurses you know who are job searching and get together for coffee to share main themes from this book as a way to help one another. Give everyone you see your most dazzling smile even if you are not feeling quite that positive in the moment; in other words, do it for them. Help out a fellow single parent and offer to take all the kids to the playground for an hour. While you are there, talk to other parents and look for ways to offer a piece of helpful pediatric advice, or to look on the bright side with them, or to celebrate their own great attitude. Bring a dessert item to the employee lounge with a note to all to enjoy a sweet treat while they enjoy their day, and add a big smiley face to it. Heck, make smiley face cupcakes!

LAND THAT JOB!

Of the suggested activities, which ones can you make happen? Which ones are sustainable for you over time versus a one-time or occasional activity?

In other words, look each day for ways to commit random acts of kindness. That is the simplest and most sustainable way to "give back" and let ancillary benefits run their course. That said, whenever people ask if they can do something in return for you or repay your kindness in any way, step up and articulate your job search goal and ask them to help you reach that goal anyway they can. Being humble is a beautiful thing, but there's not as much glory in being a completely selfless martyr. It can lead to disillusionment and grudges. Don't put yourself in such a predicament; spend your time and energy wisely, and monitor the arrival and frequency of those naturally occurring benefits. If good things don't come to fruition as often or as quickly as you desire, step up your game, strengthen your approach, and be bolder about articulating your needs while continuing to commit random acts of kindness along the way.

Whether you are more likely to channel Donald Trump, Don King, or Mother Teresa in your pursuit of a new job, find your comfort zone first, and then challenge yourself to expand that zone to meet and even exceed your goals. You can do this!

___ I have developed effective outreach approaches such as e-mail blasts or similar marketing tools.

___ I have created and printed business cards that are ready for use.

___ I have maximized how to market myself across my education, experience, and attitude.

___ I have found concrete ways to give back.

> Lead yourself, lead your superiors, lead your peers, and free your people to do the same.
>
> –Dee Hock

The Nursing Culture and Impacts Upon the Job Search

You came into contact with the nursing culture the first time you met a nurse or visited a hospital or clinic. You noticed the uniform and made a split-second judgment about the nurse's professional demeanor. Over the years, your view of nursing broadened and refined itself until you decided to become a nurse, too. You likely had to work harder to get into nursing school than your peers choosing other professions; just to get into nursing school can be very competitive. You realized quickly that the workload would be heavy, and you may have questioned your ability to do what it takes to be trained as a competent nurse. You learned about the qualities and temperament needed. And you did it; you became a nurse! But your work was not done by any means. New nurses quickly learn the confusing challenges of putting all that training into actual day-to-day practice. The nursing culture can be perplexing and downright scary as you learn the ropes and become not just skilled but savvy in navigating the landscape.

LAND THAT JOB!

How might you define the culture of nursing? How do you and fellow nurses come together in your workplace and make nursing what it is? How do you recognize each other by role and rank? How do you work together to make the practice of nursing one of care and excellence? How does the practice of outcomes-based care impact the culture of nursing as it continues to evolve?

Defining the Nursing Culture

What is the culture of nursing? What does it look and feel like? Culture is strongly associated with values as held by the majority of members within a certain organizational grouping. In nursing, it can depend on how you want to approach it whether by rituals, gender, or power (Suominen, Kovasin, & Ketola, 1997). While culture in of itself is not good, bad, or otherwise, both those within and outside of the nursing profession may make value judgments about various aspects. In the positive realm, it is how nursing professionals come together to champion daily acts of heroism. When you chose to become a nurse, you likely did so for reasons around personally meaningful work and to contribute to the greater good, effect positive change in the health care industry, and enjoy solid job prospects. If all goes well, you do enjoy such benefits of a nursing career. These are common threads among people who choose to become nurses, a field still dominated by women.

At some point, you may find yourself struggling to keep those ideals alive in the face of difficult doctors; bullying peers; demanding supervisors; fragile patients who get in their own way; shift differential politics; overly personal rants in social media that make all nurses look bad; negative media glare on various aspects of the profession, including unions; staffing cuts; bureaucratic imperatives that seem to change every week; and the daily fear of making a fatal mistake, which can lead to a host of unhealthy coping mechanisms. Part of the nursing culture is how nurses cope as a group with such day-to-day challenges.

In the face of all that, it is no wonder that so many nurses struggle to care for themselves regarding weight, blood pressure, regular bathroom use, exercise, smoking and alcohol, and the time to meditate and think creatively to maintain or increase mental and emotional fortitude.

There are negative cultural themes afoot in many nurses' minds. From a more cynical or jaded perspective, it may seem that nursing school focuses on developing clinical competency in terms of best practices, general procedures, and medical terminology within a culture that strongly suggests that nursing is the only occupation of real value, and that there is no higher honor or form of responsibility to the human race. Emphasis is on academic rigor, getting excellent grades, following directions, and passing board exams. Then, there may be a surprisingly maddening and tedious job search that takes far longer than you bargained for, to land a part-time nursing job in an environment you had ruled out for yourself. Once on the job, suddenly the high grade point average, the paper your degree is printed on, and the all-important competency checklists moldering in a folder somewhere don't amount to a hill of beans compared to the need to improve patient satisfaction scores in the face of a host of environmental and emotional challenges. Add to that the pressure that results when one doctor managing the acute aspects of a patient's care doesn't agree with another doctor managing the more chronic aspects of that same patient's care, leaving the nurse in the middle to make it all work to the patient's benefit.

Take heart! Culture evolves based on the needs of its members. Each of the issues listed above and more have been brought to light and examined in terms of costs and benefits. Those findings have been used to continually shape what are considered to be "best practices" in nursing schools and across different health care settings. Cultural change does not happen overnight. Cultural change can be driven from different directions, such as from the bottom up in grassroots efforts to better conditions by those on the nursing floor or from the top down as administrators look at how cost, quality of care, and other factors are impacted by the current nursing culture.

Nursing schools espouse characteristics of care, excellence, and empowerment, yet students can find the actual nursing school experience itself to be bureaucratic, subjective, and punitive as they are prepared for the "real world" of health care. Actual work experience can feel like a chore-driven race within which essential communication with others is never adequate. New nurses are not encouraged to make mistakes or learn as they go, but rather to sink or swim on their own in an environment where mistakes can be fatal. Therefore, the environment shapes the culture. Cultural attributes of a successful nurse become less about care and empathy and more about resilience and exceptional time management, which can make the concept of patient-centered care a difficult pill to swallow.

As mentioned earlier in this book, bullying has been an all-too-common problem. There has been increased scrutiny over recent years about nurse bullying and phrases abound, such as "nurses eating their young," which is the practice of experienced nurses teaching new nurses a "lesson" by forcing them to sink or swim, undermining their chances of early success as a "weed out" mechanism, and more. For all the stereotypically positive attributes of nurses, including compassion, patience, and selfless giving, fellow nurses can often expect far less ideal treatment for themselves. There is an earnest push to eradicate such poor treatment and bolster the ideals of nursing culture to apply to all, but such efforts are at various stages across the US and international health care systems.

There is also the mixed message out there that expects you to be Florence Nightingale or Nancy Nurse day in and day out as though such bureaucratic and interpersonal realities don't exist except in your own head, and if that is true, then you must not be cut out for nursing. That may lead you to feeling that it would be best to give up and find another line of work. Alas, the grass is not greener on the other side of the proverbial fence, whether you job search within the nursing field or outside of it.

In other fields, you will also find staffing cuts, bureaucratic logjams, scrutiny in the media, whiners and complainers, abusive bosses, processes that don't mesh with policies, lack of adequate funding, and legislative games as much as you might see a host of positive aspects. Within the field, you must realize that every environment is different. Each organization is going to be farther along than (or behind) others in positive and negative aspects, including the need to clean up its act when it comes to bullying, regardless of where it comes from.

Policies and protocols in every environment differ. Each represents the "language" of the workplace, and moving from one employer to another means relearning the language. In the face of all just discussed, it is not uncommon for a nurse to work in one place for several years, decide he or she can and will do better elsewhere, change jobs, and last a few months in the new environment, only to end up going back where he or she had been before. What was necessary to escape as soon as possible becomes a familiar beacon of belonging. Sometimes you need to take a break from a place to recognize not only its benefits, but the role you play in being a force for good. There are a number of questions you can ask of nurses who work elsewhere, in networking and interviewing situations about or at the hospital or clinic in question, including: What is the onboarding or orientation length and purpose? How strong and active is the nurse mentoring program? What safeguards have been established to prevent nurse bullying? How are new nurses assisted in developing confidence on the job? Asking such questions helps you to determine if a new employer is mindful of the dangers and has taken adequate, preventive measures.

It is imperative that you keep yourself healthy on all levels—physical, emotional, mental—to fully reap the benefits of all the positive aspects of the nursing culture. You really do get the chance to help others and do good things every day. Find the joy in all the little successes along the way. There is an inherent respect for nurses by those who are not in the health care arena, as you are seen as something of a medical expert. Successful nurses tend to have a real talent for balancing kindness with toughness and using both as needed. People who know you are a nurse will sometimes ask personal health care questions. Having healthy professional and personal boundaries can set the stage for responding to an individual's questions while not compromising integrity or putting oneself in a difficult situation for giving such advice.

There are many different settings in which you can apply your trade, from smaller or larger nonprofit to public, corporate, or international environs. In other words, there are dozens of ways and places to BE a nurse. That means that your view of your profession, positive or negative, is entirely up to you. If you find yourself complaining each day or at least in the presence of daily complainers, it is up to YOU to make things different. Therefore, if you are feeling drained, fried, washed out, and overly cynical about your role or workplace, give yourself a time out, reflect on your strengths and goals, and create a new action plan.

LAND THAT JOB!

In your opinion, what are the attributes of a successful nurse where you work? Are those attributes ideal, or do they seem largely reactionary to a larger, bureaucratic system? Do you believe you can be successful in your current environment? Why or why not? What changes on your part might help you to be more successful in that environment? Or what type of environment might be better suited to your attributes as a nurse?

Fit In

You know that it is important to fit in. The trick is fitting in with the right people, the people who are positive and uplifting and can bolster your career choices. Common traits among nurses that you want to capitalize upon include caring and kind natures, a desire to help along with the ability to empathize, mental and emotional resilience, and the need to make everything better. Look for those nurses, get to know them better, and strive to fit in with the healthy nursing crowd.

Don't worry so much if who you find is a brand-new nurse fresh out of college or someone who has seen it all over the past 20 years; chances are it will be a blend of each and everyone in between. Think about who is better to work with: someone cocky and sure they know it all or the nurse who, no matter how experienced, humbly believes there is always more to learn. There is absolutely no point in contributing to negativity, surrounding yourself with it, crumbling in the face of it, or even listening to it. If you find yourself mired in it, it is up to you and you alone to get yourself out of it. This isn't high school anymore; cliques need not apply. Harsh but true—your relationship with negativity says a lot about your mental and emotional fortitude; your ability to live up to your own great expectations as a nurse; your ability to problem-solve effectively in the face of day-to-day challenges, to adapt to changing priorities; and above all, your work ethic.

Fitting in is not about following the proverbial herd or acting as a yea-sayer all the time. Rather, fitting in pushes you to assimilate into a desired culture and bring your own passion, ideas, and sense of identity to the playing field. Fitting in means joining those with desired traits and outlook; it behooves you to push toward the positive few versus the surliest bunch to tackle a changing reality that will take you in or spit you out based on your attitude and presentation. No one has ever succeeded in the long run to "return things to the way they were" as a righteous endeavor. Change is a constant. It is driven by too many factors in play all at once to think that stubbornly holding out on one or even a few principles will magically change the outcome. In other words, negativity never wins in the long term, so how long do you plan to fight a losing battle? Instead, dig deep, pull yourself up by your strengths, and forge ahead into the unknown, which is where opportunity and legacy come home to roost.

Ultimately, you'll end up either staying with your current health care company and making the needed changes within yourself or making the leap to a new landing pad and making the most of a different scene. Even if you know in your heart that the best choice for you is to move on, practice fitting in wherever you are currently earning a paycheck. Do not go down in flames, don't burn bridges on the way out, and don't make life miserable for anyone else. You are better than that, and, frankly, other people deserve more than that from you, as well.

To help you determine whether to stay or go, create a list of likely (though never guaranteed) benefits and outcomes:

Benefits of Staying Put	Benefits of Jumping Ship

Fitting in means being a part of a readily identifiable group of nurses in which members recognize their own along with others' universal traits, such as emotional maturity, sound judgment, kindness toward all, strengthening those who are fragile, communicating as a way to seek understanding, recognizing the work is never truly done, paying it forward, quick thinking, enduring spirit, genuineness, and positivity. Think about the nurses you know who routinely display such traits and assess how well, closely, and willingly you work with them.

LAND THAT JOB!

How often do you seek nurses in the group described in the previous paragraph versus avoiding them and why? Would your supervisor put those nurses in the same group or see them in the same way as you do? Why or why not?

It is also important to understand how you "fit in" with the best job seekers out there. Do you regularly run into each other at networking events and workshops? Do you seem to be progressing at a similar rate in terms of job search duration and level of activity? Are you at your competitive best, and can you "run with" the job seekers who have a clear plan, leverage all resources and supports, and have a realistic timetable and a consistently great attitude and outlook for success?

Stand Out

Given the various day-to-day and environmental challenges of the nursing profession, you still have the opportunity to stand out and be recognized for all you do. In the face of an often hectic and chaotic health care arena, learn to serve as your own public relations agent. Perhaps you can recall watching the movie "Yes Man" with Jim Carrey. He was chronically negative, complained bitterly about his lot in life, and was generally apathetic to life being any different. Then he was challenged to say yes! at every opportunity where he previously would have said no, and that's where the movie takes off. If you think you've got it bad, see how heroes and heroines not only survive but thrive in the face of challenges in movies including "The Devil Wears Prada," "Erin Brockovich," "Julie & Julia," "Working Girl," "Baby Boom," "The Pursuit of Happyness," and more (list compliments of SugarSavvy.com in a May 25, 2012, article). Want to see movies and shows about nurses in different environments and contexts? Check out "The 15 Best Movies About Nursing" compliments of Nurseblogger (2011), including "The Bag of Knees," "Florence Nightingale," and "13 Weeks."

Though your life is not a movie, cinematic examples do serve to showcase alternative ways of being along the journey of discovering your genuine self. So, go ahead and add your name to that next sign-up sheet. Be the first to raise your hand and volunteer. Be the first one to smile at everyone you encounter in the hallway or elevator. Be the first to arrive at a routine meeting. Find someone each day to give a bit of public praise. Suggest an outrageous idea. Give each of your colleagues a note to say what you most appreciate about working with them. Tell your boss you are in the midst of a great day. Tell cranky patients you know they are doing the best they can in the face of things, and you're rooting for them, and more.

LAND THAT JOB!

Which movies come to mind for you that could serve as inspiration during your job search? The writers for *Scrubs: The Nurse's Guide to Good Living* recommend several in a July 30, 2010, blog post, including "Wit," "Precious," "The English Patient," "Magnolia," "Eastern Promises," and "Steel Magnolias." Conduct a quick online search for inspirational books for nurses, and make a list of five to delve into on your next day off.

Make a list of 10 creative ways you can stand out for just 30 seconds, any given day of the week.

I can shine for just 30 seconds by:

____

____

____

____

____

____

____

____

____

____

You are the life you create. You are the force that you allow to evolve. You are the one who will make the most of various opportunities or allow them to pass by. Specifically, you are the one who will willingly and consistently make time, buckle down, be patient, consider unorthodox options, be brave, take a stand, be positive, make a change, follow thorough, speak up, take the lead, and so much more.

In fact, such is the case that you can now come up with a concrete way to do each of these things as it pertains to your job search. Fill in the following lines.

I can:

Make time for my job search by

____

Buckle down in my job search by

____

Be patient with my job search by

____

Consider new/other options such as

____

Be brave in my job search by

____

Take a stand in my job search by

____

Stay positive in my job search by

____

Make needed changes such as

____

Follow through in my job search by

____

Speak up about my job search to

____

Take the lead in my job search by

____

Enjoy my job search journey by

____

Feel free to continue this list in your own way. Then, hang it up somewhere prominently visible and live it! In essence, stand out and shine with your own job search.

Change can be hard for anyone, whether the changes are positive or negative. It is important that you routinely explore the facets of both, learn effective ways to manage through common types of change, and realize that only through change does the magic of career success happen. The key emphasis here is on managing change. Face it, change is going to happen and keep happening, whether you like it or not. So don't focus on the liking it part; instead, focus on the strengths you'll develop further by not only surviving but thriving in the face of change. Your change in attitude will build resiliency and make success seem possible again. You'll also become a more agile thinker and doer throughout your nursing career. You need to learn to manage change not just well, but VERY well. Otherwise, change will manage you, and deep down few people really want to be managed at all.

The fact is that it is up to you whether you will view a change as positive or negative. This doesn't mean you shouldn't grieve as appropriate; many unforeseen and unfortunate changes are permanent or longer term than you think you can handle. If you view change as an event, you can get stuck on what you perceive as the negative consequences or outcomes of that event. That can easily happen if the "change event" is a job loss, a serious injury or illness, or the death of a loved one. It is more proactive to view change as an ongoing process, and you must manage it effectively on personal and professional levels.

Change may have its precipitating events, but change itself is a process with a lifecycle. It can be proactively managed at each stage. The stages of change, or transtheoretical, model of change, credited to James O. Prochaska (1994), stipulates six stages of change used across psychotherapy for dealing with issues such as terminal illness, corporate management, and weight loss. In this case, it can also be used for job search strategies.

The stages for job search strategies are pre-contemplation, contemplation, preparation, action, and maintenance.

Pre-contemplation is referred to as the "not ready" stage, where a person is not aware of the need to change or dismisses such needs as unimportant, even if it relates to behavior that negatively affects self or others. For example, suppose you are not happy with your current employment. If you are reacting negatively to issues at work, complaining about how bad it is to anyone who will listen, but you have not made a decision to start job searching yet to find someplace better for you, you could be in the pre-contemplation stage.

The contemplation stage begins when you realize the negativity you are generating is unhealthy (perhaps because others have told you as much), and you start to question the pros and cons of initiating a job search.

The preparation stage is launched when you are ready to start making small changes. It could be demonstrated by reading this book, creating an action plan, or browsing online job postings.

The action stage is where the rubber meets the road, and the small changes made in the preparation stage become a new way of thinking and looking at the world around you. It's the stage where you go to all of the networking events you may have ferreted out or send resumes for specific job openings that you have discovered. This could also be the stage where you take steps to be more positive and proactive about your current work situation, so that it is more bearable for as long as you still work there.

Lastly, the maintenance stage consists of the steps you take to prevent yourself from relapsing into previous negative behaviors. It includes ongoing actions to continue as part of a job search until the right opportunity materializes. The model includes a sixth stage called termination. This is the point at which you are no longer tempted by or sucked into negativity. This stage is challenging to achieve, especially if you assume or believe that you must continue in the maintenance stage indefinitely or risk unwanted relapse, which might require "recycling" back through all the stages. Look at it this way: The maintenance phase calls you to remain positive and resilient in the face of adversity and an ever-evolving and changing work environment.

The stages need not be discrete (and often aren't), nor would you likely spend the same amount of time and energy in each phase. However, the model is helpful in terms of personal feedback. Think about the phrases you use with others when discussing your job search; chances are the language you use will help you determine where you are in the change process.

LAND THAT JOB!

Based on the five stages of change, are you more in the contemplation, action, or maintenance phase? How long have you been at this stage, and/or what small steps might create momentum to achieve the next stage? If you are not in the maintenance stage (which can be long-term), how might you push yourself out of your comfort zone and move toward it?

Job searching can be viewed as either an event or a process. If viewed as an event, you are only in job search mode for as long as it takes to land a new role or give up if you haven't found success within a predetermined period of time. However, by viewing job searching, or more specifically career development, as a process that never really ends until you retire, you remove the episodic "pain," creating a state of being in which you indefinitely keep your eye out for opportunities, become a natural networker, routinely sign up for workshops and training opportunities, and obtain new certifications as a matter of career health. By living the career development process over the long term, sustaining and beneficial behaviors become instilled and radically alter your approach to "work" itself. In other words, you're never not job searching. You never take your eye off the ball. You refuse to become complacent or just "go through the motions" on the job. You truly become the CEO and managing partner of You, Inc.

Have you been viewing job search as an event or a process? Reflect on times that you have treated job search as a process. How can such activities become more sustainable for you?

Networking for Long-Term Benefit

At various points, you will find a new opportunity to pursue and do so successfully. After you have landed your next role or achieved that promotion, keep up your momentum. Continue networking for long-term benefit. Remember, you are indeed the CEO and managing partner of You, Inc. This is not the time to sit back on your laurels, as now you have a stronger and more vigorous reputation to maintain.

Put yourself on a "maintenance program" and understand the long-term benefits of doing so. Accomplishing a set of goals doesn't happen without a plan, and it certainly doesn't happen without effort. Much like any long-term investment, you can apply the concept of dollar-cost averaging to your job search and career development. Dollar cost averaging is the method by which you invest the same amount of money at regular intervals to ultimately earn more than you put in, over time. For example, you can put $100 per paycheck into a retirement fund. Each pay period, another $100 is invested, no matter what. The only thing that changes is how much the share price of what you're investing in fluctuates. If the stock or fund is trading at $10 per share one month, your investment will purchase 10 shares. The next month, the share price might be only $9 per share, which means you will get more than 10 shares that month. Or the share price might be $15 per share, in which case you will purchase fewer shares that month, but all shares previously purchased for less than $15 per share are all now worth significantly more than what you originally paid. This concept can be used with any form of currency.

How can you apply this concept to your job search? One type of currency, a finite resource, is time. You have probably heard the phrase "time is money." How much time can you invest in your job search and overall career development each day, week, or month? This is where it becomes clear that the more you put in can vastly influence either how much you get out of it or how long you may need to invest to reach your desired goal.

In the retirement fund example, your time horizon can dictate whether $100 per paycheck will be enough (if you start this in your early 20s) or if you'll need to invest $1,000 per paycheck (if you start building your nest egg later in life). Your time horizon to land your next role can be longer if you are currently employed and your income exceeds your expenses. However, if you are unemployed without adequate supports or savings or if your income is not meeting your expenses, you need your situation to change much sooner than later.

Applying the principles of dollar cost averaging to your job search can help you enormously. For example, say you make it a point to invest 10 hours per month in your job search and career development, and you spend those hours doing some combination of networking, applying for nursing jobs of interest, volunteering, and continuing your education. Then, if you are suddenly downsized out of a job, you will already have a robust network, current online profiles with many prospective employers and recruiters, people who will readily serve as a reference for you, and current certifications. Think about how dollar cost averaging throughout your career can also serve as your rainy day fund should your job suddenly go away. In this case, your investment is also a form of insurance. Everyone buys insurance "in case," but not everyone ends up needing to file a claim. Unlike insurance money that you don't get back if you don't use it, networking and other activities that are done regularly can pay big dividends in terms of how your career advances, how you move up the ranks, and how you earn an ever-increasing salary along the way.

As you can see, there is serious long-term benefit in developing your career all along. Every time you choose not to go to that certain networking event, not apply for that particular job, or not pursue that next certification when opportunity knocks, you are putting your investment (your career development) at risk. By investing just 10 hours per month, you can avoid having to spend 50 hours per month when it really counts, and you have to make up for lost time, fast.

LAND THAT JOB!

How much time will you invest each month to further your career? Are you in a position that requires you to invest more time per month? How much? What long-term benefits can you readily imagine being able to take advantage of by making this routine investment in You, Inc?

Conclusion

Look at how much ground you have covered! You have immersed yourself in the process of understanding how your career development has been shaped by time and context and how those in turn influence your job search approach. You've learned effective strategies and are able to apply them to your job search. Chances are you can readily think of at least a dozen people who put off what they need to do; just because a person knows what to do doesn't mean he or she actually does it. Don't allow yourself to fall into that trap when it comes to your livelihood and professional identity.

At this point, knowing what to do needs to be paired with tips and tools to remain focused and motivated. Throughout this book, you have uncovered and reflected upon your strengths and weaknesses. The trick now is to use your strengths to propel you forward while managing your weaknesses, so they don't derail you along the way.

Here is one last assessment to identify what will help you reach your goals. Respond to each of the following 50 statements by making a checkmark under either TRUE or FALSE. Be brutally honest with yourself in each case. To respond to a statement as TRUE, the entire statement must be consistently true.

	Statement	TRUE	FALSE
1.	I feel positive about and truly enjoy my job search activities.	❒	❒
2.	I am clear about which job search activities to pursue and why.	❒	❒
3.	I understand which activities and behaviors were hindering my progress.	❒	❒
4.	I recognize the core differences between HR and recruiting.	❒	❒
5.	Online applications are just one small piece of my job search plan.	❒	❒
6.	When companies are silent, it means I haven't captured their attention.	❒	❒
7.	Wherever I go, there I am (all my strengths and all my weaknesses).	❒	❒
8.	My internal self-talk is positive, encouraging, and geared for success.	❒	❒
9.	I know how my skills fit into the current marketplace.	❒	❒
10.	My previous job search assumptions have been evaluated for accuracy.	❒	❒
11.	I am comfortable reaching out to company insiders I don't already know.	❒	❒
12.	I approach networking opportunities with confidence.	❒	❒
13.	Submitting my resume and cover letter is a follow-up activity, not a first point of contact.	❒	❒
14.	I understand the anatomy of a successful resume.	❒	❒
15.	In strengthening my resume, I have added substance and eliminated fluff.	❒	❒
16.	I am able to make quick, easy, and effective customizations to my resume.	❒	❒

	Statement	TRUE	FALSE
17.	I know how to "speak the language" of my intended audience.	❐	❐
18.	My cover letters command attention.	❐	❐
19.	I have thoroughly critiqued my resume as a quality assurance exercise.	❐	❐
20.	I have confronted any negativity and successfully turned it around.	❐	❐
21.	I know how to stay positive and achieve balance throughout my job search.	❐	❐
22.	I am ready, willing, and able to do what's needed to land my next role.	❐	❐
23.	I have mapped out my time horizon for both short- and long-term goals.	❐	❐
24.	I am doing my job search, not dreaming about it.	❐	❐
25.	I have strategized constructively, have a solid plan, and am carrying it out.	❐	❐
26.	My calendar is robust enough to keep my search on time and on track.	❐	❐
27.	I have clearly identified manageable milestones to meet in my search.	❐	❐
28.	I am consistent in my job search in ways that matter.	❐	❐
29.	I am gracious throughout my job search in how I interact with others.	❐	❐
30.	I have identified ways in which I am unique in my career.	❐	❐
31.	I demonstrate proper etiquette throughout my job search.	❐	❐
32.	I am my genuine self in interviews.	❐	❐
33.	If what I say is true, I'm not bragging about my accomplishments.	❐	❐
34.	I know exactly how to negotiate my next job offer with confidence.	❐	❐

Statement	TRUE	FALSE
35. My performance as a nurse was evaluated at least twice last week.	❒	❒
36. I am already swimming successfully in the nursing recruiter pool.	❒	❒
37. I consistently appreciate the need for optimism throughout my job search.	❒	❒
38. I have become positively visible to others during my job search.	❒	❒
39. My education is well-leveraged on my resume.	❒	❒
40. My experience is well-leveraged on my resume.	❒	❒
41. I have seen how my attitude can make all the difference in my job search.	❒	❒
42. I am currently giving back or volunteering in some way to enhance my search.	❒	❒
43. I understand the nursing culture and its impact on my job search.	❒	❒
44. I have already found ways to stand out on the job, and they are working.	❒	❒
45. I'm comfortable with where I am at within the five stages of change.	❒	❒
46. I'm already applying dollar cost averaging principles in my job search.	❒	❒
47. I'm already seeing the benefits of investing time each month in my job search.	❒	❒
48. My friends and family have noticed a fundamental difference in how I job search.	❒	❒
49. My own confidence in my job search has noticeably increased.	❒	❒
50. I have recently landed a new position or promotion.	❒	❒

Now, count up the number of TRUE responses and give yourself two points for every TRUE statement. Change that number into a percentage. For example, if you scored only 26 points out of 100 possible points, that is equivalent to only 26%, which can stand significant improvement. All items directly correspond with topics discussed throughout the book, in order. As needed, go back to various chapters within the book and revisit any areas in which your response is FALSE. The only way to score a high percentage is not only to read and understand each area but to apply it consistently. Therefore, it will take time and effort to be able to earn a high score on this last assessment. You are strongly encouraged to go back through the book, again and again, applying new approaches as you go and taking the necessary time to practice them until you are truly comfortable with each. This may take weeks or several months. No matter how long it takes, appreciate that this is a wonderfully meaningful and satisfaction-earning investment in You, Inc. You can do this!

Last note: Do you already have success to share? Please visit Lisa Mauri Thomas on LinkedIn to share your latest job search success, no matter how small or big the milestone! Also, find ways to share your positive and confident self with other nurses who are in the midst of a life-changing job search, just like you.

References

Nurseblogger. (2011, July 6). *The 15 best movies about nursing.* Retrieved from http://onlinebsn.org/2011/the-15-best-movies-about-nursing/

Prochaska, J. O. (1994). *Changing for good: The revolutionary program that explains the six stages of change and teaches you how to free yourself from bad habits.* New York: W. Morrow.

Suominen, T., Kovasin, M., & Ketola, O. (1997). Nursing culture—some viewpoints. *Journal of Advanced Nursing, 25*(1), 186-190.

Best Candidate Checklist

___ I have defined the culture of nursing I experience and assessed how well I fit in.

___ I have come to terms with the realities of nursing while still embracing the powerful and positive ideals that launched my career.

___ I have determined how I can help shape the nursing culture over time.

___ I have assessed whether or not bullying exists in my workplace and know what to do about it.

___ I have evaluated both the costs and benefits of staying put versus moving on.

___ I have made a list of ways I can actively stand out as a nurse and pledge to honor such ideals.

___ I have determined concrete ways that I can stand out in my job search.

___ I have developed an understanding of the five stages of change, plus I can see where I am and what it will take to get to the next stage.

___ I have identified ways to apply dollar-cost averaging principles to my long-term networking objectives.

___ I have assessed to what extent my job search efforts have noticeably improved since I started reading this book.

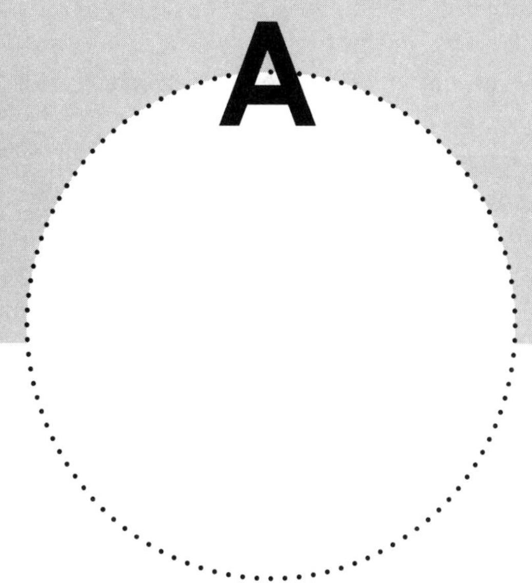

Nurse Resume Critique Checklist

Directions: With resume in hand, conduct a line-by-line evaluation of the entire document using the criteria listed below AFTER you have compared your resume side-by-side with an actual posting. Comparison to the posting allows you to focus on content. The checklist provides additional polish.

Contact Information Section

- Personal contact information must contain your name, designation, e-mail, and phone; mailing address is optional. This assists a prospective employer in making contact with you. Note: Your name should be listed above all other items, in a slightly larger font (16 point or less), and in bold.

- If two sets of contact information are listed, they are labeled as temporary vs. permanent and/or have effective dates listed for each to show the time frames when one address is no longer valid and the other one begins. Note: Two addresses are best viewed with one contact area formatted to the far left and the other formatted to the far right. This formatting technique is preferred for someone relocating or about to graduate from college, where a move is anticipated in the near future. If only one set of contact information is being used, it is NOT labeled as permanent or temporary and does NOT have effective dates listed.
- A single contact item may be formatted in any number of ways. The primary cautions include: not too cramped in terms of spacing, 10-12 point font, formatted to the far left or the far right, centered below the person's name, or centered at the very bottom of a single page resume. Do not use graphics for any documents you intend to submit electronically or upload into an online application system, as those systems may not "read" your information well, making your materials difficult to store and retrieve later. For these same reasons, do not place your name and contact information within the "header" of your Word document or within inserted tables, text boxes, or columns.

Objective or Profile

- Objective statements can be made if desired, but they are typically only used in entry-level situations and must specifically indicate the job title within a specific field. More can be said in the form of a professional profile, but it must still directly support the specific job title pursued. Use a title bar if desired: job title pursued and two keywords.
- Objective statements should NOT include any mention of seeking a challenging or rewarding position, opportunities for advancement, or using my education and experience or any other vague generalities. Such items do not belong within an objective statement and only serve to cloud the intent or create a generic/vague sense of purpose.
- A professional profile should be used for advanced positions and should reflect what you ultimately bring to the table in terms of skills and abilities that are directly relevant for desired positions. A new

nursing graduate may also use a professional profile, though it may be more focused upon common attributes needed in nursing positions rather than hard experience.

- Additional customizable keywords and/or key phrases should appear just below your profile. These will appear "bulleted" but instead of creating actual bullets, which is a formatted style, insert dashes or other text-based, nonformatted symbols. Use your tab key to create columns versus using actual column formatting tools. Try not to use your space bar, only the tab key.

Education Section

- The education section should come BEFORE the employment section on all nursing resumes, unless you have many years of in-field and directly relevant experience. At that point, education can be stated simply and sparsely after the work history section.
- Highlight either the name of the school OR the name of the degree earned as the primary element of this section. This can be accomplished by listing one of the items first, or by using a bold font style. Bolding the degree first is preferred, leaving where you went to school unbolded, unless you attended a very prestigious nursing school. After the name of the school is listed, indicate the location of the school (city, state). Write out or abbreviate using standard post office abbreviation (two capital letters, no punctuation applied), depending on space available. List consistently across education and experience entries. Do not abbreviate a city name. Note: Do NOT include a street address, zip code, or phone number for any reason, as this constitutes reference information, which does not belong on a resume.
- List the actual or expected graduation date: i.e., June 6, 2013. Do not list an abbreviated date (unless formatting truly leaves no other option). Do not refer to graduation date by quarter/semester (Spring) or month only (June). List an actual date, even if graduation is well into the future. Avoid words such as "graduating" or "will graduate," as it can be easy to overlook the need to update the verb tense when you do graduate. There is no reason to list dates of attendance (September 2010-June 2012).

- For nursing students and very recent graduates, list additional information in a bulleted format, such as GPA; professional nursing organizations of which you are a student member; and licensure, certificates, or awards earned that support your goal. List major projects or research papers completed that specifically highlight skills needed to support the job title being pursued. List general education coursework that ties in specifically with requirements listed in a job posting. For instance, does the posting indicate a need for you to be a team player, possess excellent communication skills, and be proficient with computers? Then list courses completed in communications, diversity, computers, etc.
- If more than one school was attended, the same basic format should apply to the second entry, though the information provided might be quite brief. Always list current or most recent school FIRST, then list earlier schools in reverse chronological order (working backward in time). Do not give the impression that you graduated from a school when that is not the case. Instead, indicate number of credits completed and in which discipline.
- Do NOT list high school information unless a) you are still in high school while taking college-level courses, b) you attended high school in a different geographical area and you wish to return to that area for employment, or c) your accomplishments in high school support your objective or are directly relevant to the job title or type of position you seek (i.e., your high school specifically prepared you for a nursing career). Once you graduate from high school and none of the above reasons is accurate anymore, drop the high school entry from your resume. This will free up space to discuss more valuable, relevant information in other sections.

Employment/Experience Section

- List current or most recent job held FIRST, and then list previous jobs held in reverse chronological order.
- Highlight either the name of the company OR the job title you hold/held as the primary element of this section. This can be accomplished by listing one of the items first, and by using a bold font style for that first item. It is preferred that you bold your job title unless you worked

most recently in a highly acclaimed medical center. You must then consistently format all entries that follow.

- After the name of the company is listed, also indicate the location (city, state). Write out or abbreviate using standard post office abbreviation depending on space available. Do not abbreviate a city name. Note: Do NOT include a supervisor's name, company street address, zip code, or phone number for any reason, as this constitutes reference information, which does not belong on a resume.
- Always list dates of employment for each position held, even if more than one position was held in one company (due to transfer, promotion, etc.). Dates should be formatted consistently with other dates. If the dates are not indicative of a long, stable work history, or if only one job has ever been held, place dates toward the far right side of the entry. If you want to highlight strong dates of employment without obvious gaps in your work history, you may place dates toward the left of your entry. Items to the left are more visually apparent than items to the right.
- Use a bulleted format to list highly relevant skills to a prospective employer. Preferable formula to use: action word + detail + impact. Use the specific qualifications and applicable job duties listed in the posting, and use the same "language" in your resume to show that you are a great fit for that position. Simply listing mundane job tasks of the past does not serve the goal and purpose of your resume in any way. A prospective employer wants to know what you can bring to the table, to the team, that will make the health care system more productive, profitable, and service-oriented. Look online for additional company information including mission statement, vision, and values, and incorporate this information into your list of talents and abilities to show how you are an excellent fit.
- All bulleted items should begin with action verbs that accurately describe at a glance what you can do or what your strengths are. Strong, assertive action verbs include care, provide, communicate, handle, coordinate, respond, manage, supervise, plan, and schedule. There are many more action verbs to choose from than one person could ever use. Use different verbs as much as possible, so the bulleted points do not appear redundant.

- The sentence structure of any bulleted action statement should include an invisible, implied "I" at the beginning, form a complete sentence, and end with a period. The idea is that so long as the "I" is implied, the sentence is grammatically correct. Test each bulleted statement under the experience section by mentally inserting an "I" at the beginning as you read it back to yourself. Examples:
    - "I" Communicate effectively to resolve customer concerns within 2 hours. (Good)
    - "I" Responsible for monthly cost-budget analysis. (Poor—doesn't read correctly if you start with "I")
- Quantify your talents and expertise wherever possible. Demonstrate what you can do by indicating amount, frequency, level, etc. Instead of indicating you have supervised others, clarify that you have supervised 3 entry-level employees. Use numeric characters such as 3 instead of writing out the word three, as numeric characters will be more readily visible to the prospective employer. They visually pop off the page and command attention. Numbers written out as words tend to blend in with other text; make them more visible.
- Use present-tense verbs for current jobs and past-tense verbs for previous jobs. Be sure that verb tenses are consistently applied in each employment entry.

End of Resume

- Do not state "References provided upon request." Such an approach is inadequate. It is better to emphasize that your transcripts, an annotated reference page, a professional profile URL, a portfolio URL, or other work samples can be provided. You may link directly to URLs on your resume, or specify that such items will be provided during an interview.

Final Tips

- Choose font styles and sizes wisely. Do not use more than two highly complementary styles. If an area is highlighted in bold, do not also underline or italicize it. Use bold type sparingly. It is most effective when highlighting the bare specifics you wish to leap off the page and into a prospective employer's brain. For instance, you might apply bold type to your name, the job title you are seeking, your degree, and each job title held—especially if highly relevant to the job you are applying for. If you do need additional pages, clearly indicate at bottom of each the page number out of how many total pages. Your name should also be clearly listed on subsequent pages. Too often, subsequent pages get separated or lost if not clearly identified.
- Be certain that all category headings are consistently formatted: Professional Profile, Education, and Nursing Experience. You may choose to omit headings altogether. No heading is needed for the contact information or the reference area. Category headings should be left-justified or centered and be of the same font style and not bolded. Category headings take up space, so experiment with whether they appear best suited immediately to the left, to the left and just above the first line of that category's entry, centered above the contents of each category, or left off entirely.
- Visually inspect the way the bullets line up in each category. Bullets within the education category must all line up together. Bullets within the employment category must all line up together from entry to entry. However, bullets in education do not have to line up with bullets in employment. Consistency is important within each section, not necessarily across the entire page.
- Proofread, proofread, proofread! All your efforts can fly out the window if your resume contains spelling, grammar, and punctuation errors. These include errors in capitalization of proper nouns and abbreviations, misspelling your name (it happens), and related items. Be sure to proof for words that sound the same but are spelled differently and have very different meanings. For example, if you used to stock shelves in a store, don't misspell your former job title of Stocker as Stalker.

Note for New Nurses

- List clinical rotations and preceptorships below education, yet before non-nursing/health care work experience.

Note for Published Nurses

- List your publications after work experience and in proper APA format.

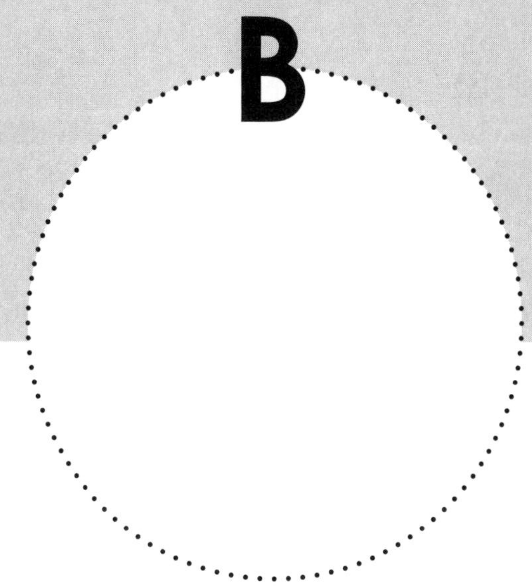

Interview Resources

Read through the following tips a day or two before preparing for an interview.

What to Wear

While you would wear scrubs on the nursing floor, an interview is a formal, professional meeting. Wear meeting attire such as a suit (preferable) or at the very least, dress slacks and a dress shirt or blouse with a jacket and dress shoes.

What to Bring

- Crisp, clean, and updated copies of your resume. It's better to have too many copies than not enough. Be prepared with 5-10 full sets of copies.
- Proof of credentials—diploma earned, nursing school transcripts, certificates earned (prepare copies; you keep originals), and references.
- List of prepared questions to ask at the end and brief talking points to reference throughout.

25 Sample Questions You Should Be Prepared to Answer

1. Why did you decide to become a nurse (or choose this specialty)?
2. Do you work better independently or as part of a team? Describe.
3. What do you find most challenging or difficult about being a nurse? How do you motivate yourself to get through such difficulties?
4. What do you find to be most rewarding about being a nurse? Which aspects of nursing do you find most satisfying/enjoyable and why?
5. Give examples of how you have provided patient-centered care. Explain your understanding of outcomes-based care.
6. Describe a time when a physician gave an order that you believed was incorrect. How did you handle it?
7. Describe a time when you were unsure of the best protocol to follow. How did you handle it?
8. Describe a time when you had a conflict or disagreement with your supervisor. How did you handle it? What was the outcome?
9. How do you handle patients who complain or become abusive?
10. How have you handled coworkers, physicians, or others you work with who become rude or demanding?

11. What types of situations do you find stressful on the nursing floor? How do you manage those stressors?
12. Have you ever worked in [this] type of environment before or with [these] kinds of patients? What made you successful?
13. How do you stay current within the nursing field? What publications do you read? What research findings interest you?
14. Are you currently affiliated with any professional nursing organizations? How has membership benefitted you?
15. How would you handle it if you had to stay late on your shift, unexpectedly and with little or no notice?
16. How many times in the past year have you been late for your nursing shift? How many shifts did you miss and why?
17. What environment or dynamics help you to be your best as a nurse? What are your qualities or attributes that make you a great nurse?
18. How would your nursing coworkers describe you? How would your nursing supervisor describe you?
19. Why do you want this job? Why do you want to work for this organization? What do you know about this organization?
20. Describe a time you worked on a special project. What was your contribution? What were successful outcomes?
21. Describe a time you have trained or mentored new nurses or nurses who were new to your organization.
22. What do you see yourself doing in 5 years?
23. How do you feel your background has prepared you for this role?
24. If offered this role, how soon could you start?
25. Is there any reason why we should not hire you for this role?

15 Sample Questions to Ask Your Interviewer

1. What is the nurse-to-patient ratio?
2. How often does the company hire nurses? What is the turnover rate of the nursing staff?
3. Who does this position report to? (Ask to meet the supervisor if you haven't already.)
4. What is the management style of the company? Of the supervisor?
5. What do other nurses love about working here? What concerns, if any, have they raised recently?
6. Do you have a mentoring program for nurses new to the organization?
7. Can you describe the orientation process?
8. In your opinion, what makes this organization a great place to work for?
9. How is patient satisfaction measured here, and what were the most recent findings? Initiatives for improvements?
10. How are nurses kept informed about new initiatives, projects, and events happening within the organization?
11. What would you say are the top two to three qualities of the most successful nurses currently working here?
12. If hired for this role, how would I be evaluated for performance, and how often throughout the year?
13. Are there any other questions I can answer for you about my qualifications or my desire to join your organization?
14. What is the next stage of the interview process for this position?
15. How soon do you expect to make a hiring decision? Or, how soon would you like the new person to start working?

What Not to Do

- Don't be late for any reason. Arrive 5-10 minutes early. If you arrive earlier than that, do not check in until 5-10 minutes before your scheduled interview time. Any earlier might send the message that you do not respect your interviewer's or HR contact's time.
- Don't smoke or put on perfume/cologne before the interview. No strong smells of any kind.
- Don't dominate the conversation, and don't ramble. Answer each question within 1-2 minutes. Try to be succinct and stay on topic. This is much easier when you are prepared.
- Don't risk having your cell phone interrupt the interview. Turn it off! Also, if you are in a waiting area, it's better to read a magazine the company has set out than to pass the time on Facebook or Twitter. It sends the wrong message to the staff that you cannot disconnect from your mobile device, and it can also derail you from your preparations if someone makes you nervous.
- Don't lie about anything. It's not bragging if it's true, so no need to exaggerate the details.
- Don't ask any questions about salary, advancement, time off, or anything that will cause them to doubt your commitment to the role in question.
- Don't come unprepared. Bringing what you need and planning your time accordingly will increase your confidence.

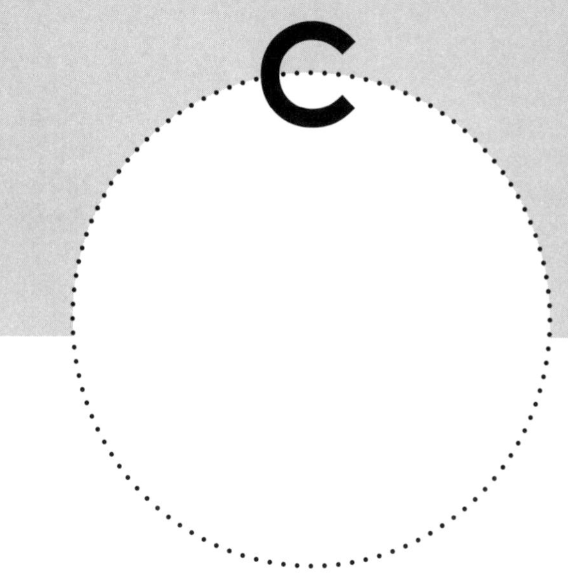

Sample Job Search Calendars

Additional sample calendars provide ideas and strategies you may consider depending upon the variables of your own circumstances. Use elements of any calendar to best suit your job search needs and strategies.

Sample calendar: single, currently employed nurse in a hectic, overnight ER setting who is launching a job search. The first day reflects the pre-job search schedule.

Sunday	Monday	Tuesday	Wednesday	Thursday	Friday	Saturday
Commute	Commute/ reflect	Sleep 7-8 hours	Get up/ exercise	Get up/ exercise	Commute/ reflect	Commute/ reflect
Sleep 7-8 hours	Sleep 7-8 hours	Get up/ exercise	Personal care/ eat	Personal care/ eat	Sleep 7-8 hours	Sleep 7-8 hours
Get up/ exercise	Get up/exercise	Personal care/ eat	Make list of all known professional contacts and determine whom to reach out to as a direct or indirect strategic ally	Locate 10+ companies to target, roles to pursue; conduct a salary survey	Get up/ exercise	Get up/ exercise
Personal care/ eat	Personal care/ eat	Create a LinkedIn profile or use similar site; explore the sites, join groups, invite new connections	Create annotated reference list	Have dinner	Personal care/eat	Personal care/ eat
Watch TV	Make a job search plan	Laundry	Dinner/TV/ movie	Commute/ reflect	Identify 20+ hiring managers and recruiters to invite into your LinkedIn network	Craft new master/base resume and cover letter templates for quick customizing later.
Have dinner date	Request different shift at work if feasible	House/yard work, decide to hire a service, call to set it up	Sleep 7-8 hours	Work 7p-7a	Have dinner	Have dinner
Commute	Have dinner	Dinner/TV/ movie		Jot down notes when able at work	Commute/ reflect	Commute/ reflect
Work 7p-7a	Commute/ reflect	Sleep 5+ hours		Sleep 7-8 hours	Work 7p-7a	Work 7p-7a
"Happy Hour"	Work 7p-7a				Jot down notes when able at work	Jot down notes when able at work
	"Happy Hour"					

Sunday	Monday	Tuesday	Wednesday	Thursday	Friday	Saturday
Commute/ listen to inspirational or informative CDs	Commute/listen to inspirational or informative CDs	Sleep 7-8 hours	Get up/ exercise	Commute/ listen to inspirational or informative CDs	Commute/ listen to inspirational or informative CDs	Commute/ listen to inspirational or informative CDs
Sleep 7-8 hours	Sleep 7-8 hours	Get up/ exercise	Personal care/ eat	Sleep 7-8 hours	Sleep 7-8 hours	Sleep 7-8 hours
Get up/ exercise	Get up/exercise	Personal care/ eat	Follow up with everyone who accepted your invite and start a dialogue	Get up/ exercise	Get up/ exercise	Get up/ exercise
Personal care/ eat	Personal care/ eat	Explore LinkedIn or other professional networking site more, add to your contacts, participate in forums, answer questions, post your master resume, apply for 5 jobs	Apply for 3 jobs	Personal care/ eat	Personal care/eat	Personal care/ eat
Outreach and request 20+ informational interviews, apply for 2 jobs	Outreach and request 20+ informational interviews, apply for 2 jobs	Dinner/TV/ movie	Locate upcoming local events to attend	Conduct informational interviews, apply for 2 jobs	Conduct informational interviews, apply for 2 jobs	Outreach and request 20+ informational interviews, apply for 2 jobs
Have dinner	Have dinner		Update your notes/stay organized	Have dinner	Have dinner	Have dinner
Commute/ listen to inspirational or informative CDs	Commute/listen to inspirational or informative CDs		Dinner/TV/ movie	Commute/ listen to inspirational or informative CDs	Commute/ listen to inspirational or informative CDs	Commute/ listen to inspirational or informative CDs
Work 7p-7a	Work 7p-7a		Sleep 7+ hours	Work 7p-7a	Work 7p-7a	Work 7p-7a
Network at work	Network at work			Networking breakfast	Networking breakfast	Network at work

Sunday	Monday	Tuesday	Wednesday	Thursday	Friday	Saturday
Commute/ listen to inspirational or informative CDs	Commute/listen to inspirational or informative CDs	Sleep 7-8 hours	Get up/ exercise	Get up/ exercise	Commute/ listen to inspirational or informative CDs	Commute/ listen to inspirational or informative CDs
Sleep 7-8 hours	Sleep 7-8 hours	Get up/ exercise	Personal care/ eat	Personal care/ eat	Sleep 7-8 hours	Sleep 7-8 hours
Get up/ exercise	Get up/exercise	Personal care/ eat	Follow up with everyone who accepted your invite and start a dialogue	Attend networking events and go to interviews, or apply for 3 jobs	Get up/ exercise	Get up/ exercise
Personal care/ eat	Personal care/ eat	Explore LinkedIn or other professional networking site more, add to your contacts, participate in forums, answer questions, post your master resume, apply for 5 jobs	Apply for 3 jobs	Have dinner	Personal care/eat	Personal care/ eat
Attend networking events, outreach for interviews, or apply for 3 jobs	Attend networking events and go to interviews, or apply for 3 jobs	Dinner/TV/ movie	Locate upcoming local events to attend	Commute/ listen to inspirational or informative CDs	Attend networking events and go to interviews, or apply for 3 jobs	Attend networking events, outreach for interviews, or apply for 3 jobs
Have dinner	Have dinner		Update your notes/stay organized	Work 7p-7a	Have dinner	Have dinner
Commute/ listen to inspirational or informative CDs	Commute/listen to inspirational or informative CDs		Dinner/TV/ movie	Networking breakfast	Commute/ listen to inspirational or informative CDs	Commute/ listen to inspirational or informative CDs
Work 7p-7a	Work 7p-7a		Sleep 7+ hours	Sleep 7+ hours	Work 7p-7a	Work 7p-7a
Network at work	Networking breakfast				Networking breakfast	Network at work

Repeat the previous weeks for the next month, adjust as needed, and evaluate your efforts along the way.

This calendar is for a married, currently employed nurse educator with two part-time jobs and a variable work schedule and no days off who wants to develop her network while exploring possible semiretirement options over the next year. The first two days shown reflect the pre-job search schedule.

Sunday	Monday	Tuesday	Wednesday	Thursday	Friday	Saturday
Get up/have coffee/lounge about for an hour	Get up/have coffee/lounge about for an hour	Get up/have coffee/reflect	Get up/reflect	Get up/reflect	Get up/reflect	Get up/reflect
Personal care/eat	Personal care/eat	Personal care/eat	Personal care/eat	Personal care/eat	Personal care/eat	Personal care/eat
Teach online course from home, then grade student work for 2 hours	Commute	Commute/reflect	Commute/reflect	Teach online course from home, then grade student work for 2 hours	Identify all local networking events, sign up	Set up LinkedIn profile, explore the site, and join 30 groups
Lunch	Work at hospital for 8 hours, lunch with friends	Work at hospital for 8 hours, lunch with friends	Work at hospital for 8 hours, lunch with friends	Lunch	Lunch	Lunch
Volunteer or do various errands/house/yard work	Commute	Commute/listen to inspirational or informative CDs	Commute/listen to inspirational or informative CDs	Volunteer or do house/yard work	Delegate house/yard work	Delegate house/yard work
Dinner w/spouse	Dinner w/spouse	Dinner w/spouse	Dinner w/spouse	Dinner w/spouse	Dinner w/spouse	Dinner w/spouse
3 hours of TV	3 hours of TV	Create a networking plan	Make a list of all professional nursing and health care contacts	Identify all local networking events, sign up	Teach course on college campus	Teach online course from home, then grade student work for 2 hours
Sleep 7 hours	Sleep 7 hours	Sleep 7 hours	Sleep 7 hours	Sleep 7 hours	Sleep 7 hours	Sleep 7 hours

Sunday	Monday	Tuesday	Wednesday	Thursday	Friday	Saturday
Get up/ exercise while listening to inspirational CDs	Get up/ exercise	Get up/ exercise	Get up/exercise	Get up/ exercise while listening to inspirational CDs	Get up/ exercise while listening to inspirational CDs	Get up/ exercise while listening to inspirational CDs
Personal care/eat	Personal care/ eat	Personal care/ eat	Personal care/ eat	Personal care/ eat	Personal care/ eat	Personal care/eat
Teach online course from home, then do all grading from work submitted for past several days for 5 hours, with lunch break in between	Commute/ reflect	Commute/ reflect	Commute/ reflect	Teach online course from home, no grading	Attend networking events or build new professional contacts in LinkedIn	Lunch
Dinner w/ spouse	Work at hospital for 8 hours, network at work	Work at hospital for 8 hours, network at work	Work at hospital for 8 hours, network at work	Lunch	Lunch	Follow up with everyone who accepted your invite and start a dialogue, request informational interviews
1 hr TV/ reading	Commute/ listen to inspirational or informative CDs	Commute/ listen to inspirational or informative CDs	Commute/listen to inspirational or informative CDs	Dinner w/ spouse	Dinner w/ spouse	Dinner w/ spouse
Sleep 7 hours	Dinner w/ spouse	Dinner w/ spouse	Dinner w/ spouse	Attend networking events or build new professional contacts in LinkedIn	Teach course on college campus, no grading	Teach online course from home, no grading
	Identify companies of interest and roles desired, conduct salary survey	Reach out to all existing networking contacts, start a dialogue, get involved, gain membership, post to forums	Reach out to all existing networking contacts, start a dialogue, get involved, gain membership, post to forums	1 hr reading	1 hr reading	1 hr reading
	Sleep 7 hours	Sleep 7 hours	Sleep 7 hours	Sleep 7 hours	Sleep 7 hours	Sleep 7 hours

Sunday	Monday	Tuesday	Wednesday	Thursday	Friday	Saturday
Get up/exercise while listening to inspirational CDs	Get up/exercise	Get up/exercise	Get up/exercise	Get up/exercise while listening to inspirational CDs	Get up/exercise while listening to inspirational CDs	Get up/exercise while listening to inspirational CDs
Personal care/eat	Personal care/eat	Personal care/eat	Personal care/eat	Personal care/eat	Personal care/eat	Personal care/eat
Teach online course from home, then do all grading from work submitted for past several days for 5 hours, with lunch break in between	Commute/reflect	Commute/reflect	Commute/reflect	Teach online course from home, no grading	Attend networking events, build new professional contacts in LinkedIn, or facilitate interviews	Follow up with everyone who accepted your invites and start a dialogue, request informational interviews
Dinner w/ spouse	Work at hospital for 8 hours, network at work	Work at hospital for 8 hours, network at work	Work at hospital for 8 hours, network at work	Lunch	Lunch	Dinner w/ spouse
1 hr TV/ reading	Commute/listen to inspirational or informative CDs	Commute/listen to inspirational or informative CDs	Commute/listen to inspirational or informative CDs	Dinner w/ spouse	Dinner w/ spouse	Teach online course from home, no grading
Sleep 7 hours	Dinner w/ spouse	Dinner w/ spouse	Dinner w/ spouse	Attend networking events or build new professional contacts in LinkedIn or facilitate interviews	Teach course on college campus, no grading	1 hr reading
	Attend networking events or take a refresher certification course	Reach out to all existing networking contacts, start a dialogue, actively participate, post to forums, volunteer to plan new events	Reach out and request opportunities to job shadow or visit contacts from new facilities/campuses, start a dialogue, look for new contacts, post to forums	1 hr reading	1 hr reading	Sleep 7 hours
	Sleep 7 hours	Sleep 7 hours	Sleep 7 hours	Sleep 7 hours	Sleep 7 hours	

Repeat the previous weeks for the next month, adjust as needed, and evaluate your efforts along the way.

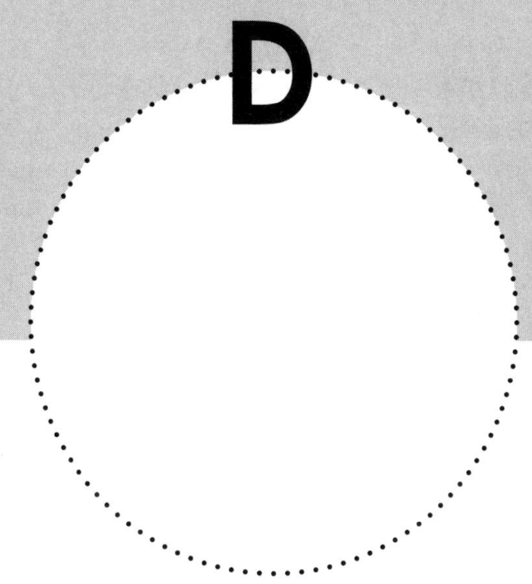

Tools That Work for You

Networking within health care has never been easier. Use of social media tools has increased sharply in recent years (AMN Healthcare, 2011). Simply Google "top social networking sites for nurses," "professional networking sites for nurses," or "networking events for nurses in [your city or state]" to return dozens of leads to explore further. You can easily set aside a whole day to do so and be thoroughly engaged and invigorated along the way. Just be sure to find an effective way to organize all that you learn, so you can follow up in a timely manner. You can also set up a calendar reminder to reoccur once per month to delve into new sites and latest information. The next sections explore three examples of results of the exact search terms listed above.

Top Social Networking Sites for Nurses

AllNurses.com has more than a half million members and more than 50 nursing specialties. There are discussion forums and jobs for all skill levels. The site shows how many visitors are on the site when you are and, at search time, more than 5,000 readers were online.

NurseConnect.com boasts more than 25,000 members at search time. This site is specifically designed to connect nurses to one another for job search, career development, and mentorship opportunities.

NurseTogether.com is a friendly, highly active and approachable site geared to professional discussion on a wide range of nursing topics. It features the EasyFIND job board, online chat events, and continuing education resources.

Professional Networking Sites for Nurses

LinkedIn.com has a robust and highly active membership that grows exponentially by the day and features more than 160 million members at search time. The site allows you to find professionals by name, title, company, geographical area, and industry, as well as connect with them in mutually beneficial ways. A people search for "nurse" yielded more than 636,000 professionals at search time, a list that can be narrowed further by specialty or location. A people search for "nurse recruiter" yielded more than 6,000 names. A search for hospital and health care organizations in the United States yielded more than 2,000 hits. All search results provide profiles and links to more information. A search for nursing jobs yielded more than 1,200 returns of current, active, open positions, as well as information on who posted each one. LinkedIn has become the primary go-to resource of recruiters in many industries, including health care, because of its ease of use and navigation. The site offers both a free, basic membership as well as premium membership services based on your needs.

Facebook.com makes the list here for three reasons, even though it is actually a social networking site versus a professional one. First, there are more than 800 million users, and roughly 75% of those users are over the age of 26. This means that whomever you are looking for, the chances of their having a Facebook account are strong. Secondly, by starting with friends you already know, you can tap into their friends' networks through introductions, and let's face it, everybody knows a nurse or someone who works in health care. Yes, everybody. Third, the first two reasons mentioned have not gone unnoticed by recruiters and health care marketing professionals. Companies now have active profiles, and the Marketplace area features jobs. A cautionary note: When using Facebook for job search and career development, you are urged to maintain a mature and professional image at all times. You can be personable and share ideas, but you must exercise excellent writing skills and professional judgment. Horror stories abound of how an utter lack of tact or professionalism has cost someone a great opportunity or got them reprimanded or fired by their employer.

MeetUp.com is a site with more than 2,000 groups, nearly 10 million members, and 90 million topics at search time. The site is designed to make it easy for anyone to organize or attend group meetings around personal or professional interests. A search for "health," "job search," or "career development" meet-up groups yielded at least 10 offerings across a sampling of different metropolitan areas in the US and Canada. If you don't find a group to join, consider starting one and invite all your nurse friends!

Reference

AMN Healthcare. (2011). *Use of social media and mobile by healthcare professionals: 2011 survey results.* Retrieved from http://www.amnhealthcare.com/uploadedFiles/AMNHealthcare/Industry-Research/Surveys/final.pdf

Index

A

ability, 112–114
  interviews, 173
accomplishments *versus* abilities, 169
achievability of goals, 102–103
ACLS (Advanced Cardiovascular Life Support) certification, 203
action words in resume, 78–79
advancement lifestyle *versus* job searches, 13–15
advancements, etiquette, 152–153
allies, 6–7
annotated reference page of resume, 82
appearance, 142
  uniqueness and, 159
applications
  legal documents, 62
  online, 17–19, 61–62
assessments, job search activities, 21–23
assumptions
  about job searches, quiz, 2–3
  keywords and, 52–53
attitude, 205–206

B

bad experiences in the past, 11–12
behavior
  consistency in, 138–141
  defensiveness, 144
  ethical, 144–145
  etiquette, 150–151
    advancement/promotion, 152–153
    company party, 155–156
    first week on the job, 156–157
    management, 154–155
    meetings, 153–154
    nursing, 151–152
    workplace, 151–152
  fairness, 144–145
  graciousness, 145–150
  inner voice, 141
  instincts, 141
  interviews, being genuine, 164–167
  pressure, handling, 142–143
  priorities and, 140
  taking things personally, 144
  time management skills, 143
  uniqueness and, 157–160
being oneself, 157–160
beliefs about job searches, quiz, 2–3
  results, 3–13
blaming others, 96–98
blocks to moving forward, 94–95
  internal negativity, 95–96
  self-hatred, 95
BLS (Basic Life Support) certification, 203
bragging in interviews, 169–171
Buddha type in interviews, 167
budgeting time, 143
bullying in nursing culture, 212
business cards, 202

C

calendar exercise for goal setting, 130–135
career development
  ignoring need for, 98
  presentation
    current job, 114–116
    job search, 116–117
  SMART goals, 107–109
certifications
  ACLS (Advanced Cardiovascular Life Support), 203
  BLS (Basic Life Support), 203
  NRP (Neonatal Resuscitation Program), 203
  PALS (Pediatric Advanced Life Support), 203
  resume, 74
change, reactions to (exercise), 34–35
Clifton StrengthsFinder assessment, 31
clinical nursing experience on resume, 75–80
clinical rotations, resume, 74–75
Code of Conduct for Nurses, 144–145
Code of Ethics for Nurses, 144–145
cold calling, 200–201
comfort zone, expanding, 27
Commander type in interviews, 166
company insiders, networking and, 54–55
company party etiquette, 155–156
confidence
  building, networking and, 55–59
  in interviews, 167
connections, 6–7
conscious awareness, 28–31
consistency in behaviors, 138–141
Consultant type in interviews, 165–166
contact information on resume, 69–70
counteroffers, 179
courteousness, 145–146

cover letters, 89–92
  necessity, 9
critique of resume, 89
culture of nursing
  bullying, 212
  fitting in, 214–216
  negative themes, 211
  overview, 210–213
  standing out, 216–221
customizable skills area of resume, 72–73

D

defensiveness, 144
degrees earned, 203
details of resume, 78–79
direct mail postcards, 200

E

ease of finding a job, 3–4
economy and job market, 184
Edberg, Henrik, 148
education
  ACLS (Advanced Cardiovascular Life Support) certification, 203
  BLS (Basic Life Support) certification, 203
  degrees earned, 203
  NRP (Neonatal Resuscitation Program) certification, 203
  PALS (Pediatric Advanced Life Support) certification, 203
  resume, 74
e-mail blast, 198–200
emotional self, uniqueness and, 159
employed *versus* unemployed candidates, 183–184
employer's market, 184
ethical behavior, 144–145
  unique self and, 159
etiquette, 150–151
  advancement/promotion, 152–153
  company party, 155–156
  first week on the job, 156–157
  management, 154–155
  meetings, 153–154
  nursing, 151–152
  workplace, 151–152
experience, 204–205
  bad, 11–12
  competition and, 68
  growth phase, 68–69
  networking and, 68
  resume, 68
    clinical nursing, 75–80
    non-nursing, 80
  specialization, 76
  students and, 68
  volunteer work, 76

F

failures/mistakes, learning from, 96–97
fairness, 144–145
focal point for search, 44–45
follow-ups
  networking activities and, 62–67
  recruiters, 188

G

generic resumes, 18
  many openings, 5–6
goals
  micro goals, 101–105, 126–130
  setting
    achievability, 102–103

calendar exercise, 130–135
maintenance goals, 105
measurables, 102
relevance, 104
specifics, 101–102
timeliness, 104–105
time allowance, 120–125
Golden Rule, 146
graciousness, 145–150
growth phase of experience, 68–69

H

handling pressure, 142–143
honors and awards on resume, 81
HR (human resources), *versus* recruiting, 15–16

I

impact statements in resume, 79–80
inconsistency in behavior, 139–140
inner voice, 141
inner monologue. *See* self-talk
insiders, networking and, 54–55
instincts, 141
internal negativity, 95–96
interviews
ability, 171–173
accomplishments *versus* abilities, 169
attitude types
Buddha, 167
Commanders, 166
Consultants, 165–166
Pleasers, 164–165
attributes, turn-off traits, 168
being genuine, 164–167
boastful statements, 170
bragging in, 169–171
confidence, 167
keywords, 51–52
off-the-record events, 184–185
readiness, 171–173
tips, 174–175
willingness, 171–173

J

job fairs, 10–11
job market
employer's market, 184
job seeker's market, 184
job postings, keywords, 49–50
job searches
versus advancement lifestyle, 13–15
myths *versus* truths, 13–20
SMART goals, 105–109
job seeker's market, 184

K

keywords, 45
assumptions and, 52–53
interviews, 51–52
job postings, 49–50
networking and, 45–47
professional development opportunities, 47–48
resumes, 51

L

language style of resume, 85
law of attraction, 189–190
legal documents, applications, 62
letters, cover letters, necessity, 9

LinkedIn, 63–64
  link to from resume, 81–82
long-term benefits of networking, 221–223

M

macro goals, micro goals and, 101-105, 126–129
maintenance goals, 105
management, etiquette, 154–155
market
  confidence building and, 55–59
  skills fit, 44–45
marketing and promotion
  business cards, 202
  cold calling, 200–201
  direct mail postcards, 200
  e-mail blast, 198–200
  video introduction/resume, 201–202
measureables in goal setting, 102
medical directors, networking and, 58
meetings, etiquette, 153–154
micro goals, 101–105, 126–130
mission statement, 191, 192
mistakes/failures, learning from, 96–97
motivation, 94–95
  external, 95
  internal, 94
  internal negativity, 95–96
  self-doubt, 95–96
  self-hatred, 95
moving forward, planning, 100–109

N

negativity, 94–95
  internal, 95–96
negotiations, 175–181
networking, 6–7
  company insiders, 54–55
  company party, 155
  confidence building and, 55–59
  events, 59
  examples, 65–66
  experience strengthening and, 68
  follow-up, 62–67
  keywords and, 45–47
  LinkedIn, 63–64
  long-term benefits, 221–223
  medical directors and, 58
  nurse recruiters and, 57
  nursing supervisors and, 57
  professionalism, 66
  public health directors and, 58
  recruiters and, 186–187
  resumes and, 62
  volunteering and, 58
non-nursing experience, 80
NRP (Neonatal Resuscitation Program) certification, 203
nurse recruiters, networking and, 57
NurseTogether.com, 81
nursing culture
  bullying, 212
  fitting in, 214–216
  negative themes, 211
  overview, 210–213
  standing out, 216–221
nursing etiquette, 151–152
nursing school *versus* practice, 211–212
nursing supervisors, networking and, 57

O

offense taking, 144
offers, negotiating, 175–181

off-the-record interview events, 184–185
online applications, 17–19, 61–62
optimism, 189–190
organizations, professional development, 47–48

P

PALS (Pediatric Advanced Life Support) certification, 203
past jobs
  bad experiences, 11–12
  mistakes/failures, learning from, 96–97
personality, 157–160
physical appearance, 142
  uniqueness and, 159
Platinum Rule, 146
Pleaser type in interviews, 164–165
positivity, 94–95
  law of attraction and, 189
PositivityBlog (Edberg), 148
postcard mailing, 200
preceptorships, resume, 75
presentation
  current job, 114–116
  job search, 116–117
pressure, handling, 142–143
priorities, behaviors and, 140
professional development
  keywords, 47–48
  organizations, 47–48
professional keywords, 45
professional profile section of resume, 71–72
professionalism, networking, 66
promotions, etiquette, 152–153
public health directors, networking and, 58
publications authored, 81
purposeful use of strengths, 40–42

Q

quality *versus* quantity, 20
questions, self-talk, 26

R

reactions to change, 34–35
readiness, 109–110
  interview and, 171–173
recruiters
  following up, 188
  networking and, 186–187
recruiting, *versus* HR (human resources), 15–16
references in resume, 81–83
relevance of goal setting, 104
resources, unemployment, 99
resumes
  ability, demonstrating, 113–114
  action words, 78
  annotated reference page, 82
  certifications, 74
  clinical rotations, 74–75
  contact information, 69–70
  critiques, 89
  customizing for position, 85–88
  details, 78–79
  education, 74
    certifications, 203
    degrees earned, 203
  example, 84
  experience, 68, 204–205
    clinical nursing, 75–80
    non-nursing, 80
  generic, 18
    many openings, 5–6
  honors and awards, 81
  impact statements, 79–80
  keywords, 51
  language style, 85

links to profiles, 81–82
name, 69–70
networking and, 62
preceptorships, 75
professional profile, 71–72
publications authored, 81
readiness, demonstrating, 110
references, 81–83
sections, 67
skills area, 72–73
specialization, 76
students, 68
templates, 7–8
title bar, 70
video, 201–202
volunteer work, 76, 80
willingness, demonstrating, 110–112
work history, 75–80

S

sample resume, 84
self-assessment
assumptions, 2–13
beliefs, 2–13
Clifton StrengthsFinder, 31
self-awareness
conscious awareness, 28–31
responsibility, 36–37
self-talk and, 26–28
strengths and weaknesses, 31–35
self-doubt, 95–96
unemployment, 99–100
self-fulfilling prophecy, 189
self-hatred, 95
self-talk
external motivators, 95
internal motivators, 94
positivity, 189
questions, 26
responsibility, 36–37
self-awareness and, 26–28
strengths and weaknesses, 31–35
skills
market fit, 44–45
resume, 72–73
SMART (specific, measurable, achievable, relevant, timely), 101–104
SMART goals, 105–106
career development, 107–109
job searching, 106–107
specialization on resume, 76
specifics of goal setting, 101–102
starting point for search, 100–101
strengths and weaknesses, 31–35
celebrating strengths, 38–40
purposeful use of strengths, 40–42
students
experience and, 68
resumes, 68
supervisors, etiquette, 152

T

taking things personally, 144
templates for resumes, 7–8
time allowed for goals, 120–125
time management skills, 143
time to find a job, 4
timeliness in goal setting, 104–105
title bar of resume, 70
trusting your gut, 141

U

unemployed *versus* employed candidates, 183–184
unemployment, resources, 99
uniqueness, 157–160

V

values, 192
  job search activity, 193
video introduction/resume, 201–202
visibility plus, 190–195
vision statement, 191–192
volunteering, 58, 206–207
  resume and, 76, 80

W–X–Y–Z

weaknesses, 31–35
  celebrating strengths, 38–40
willingness, 110–112
  interview and, 173
work history on resume, 75–80
workplace etiquette, 151–152